BATMAN
THE LAST ANGEL

W R I T E R
ERIC LUSTBADER

P E N C I L L E R
LEE MODER

I N K E R
SCOTT HANNA

C O L O R I S T
LOVERN KINDZIERSKI

L E T T E R E R
TODD KLEIN

B A T M A N   C R E A T E D   B Y
BOB KANE

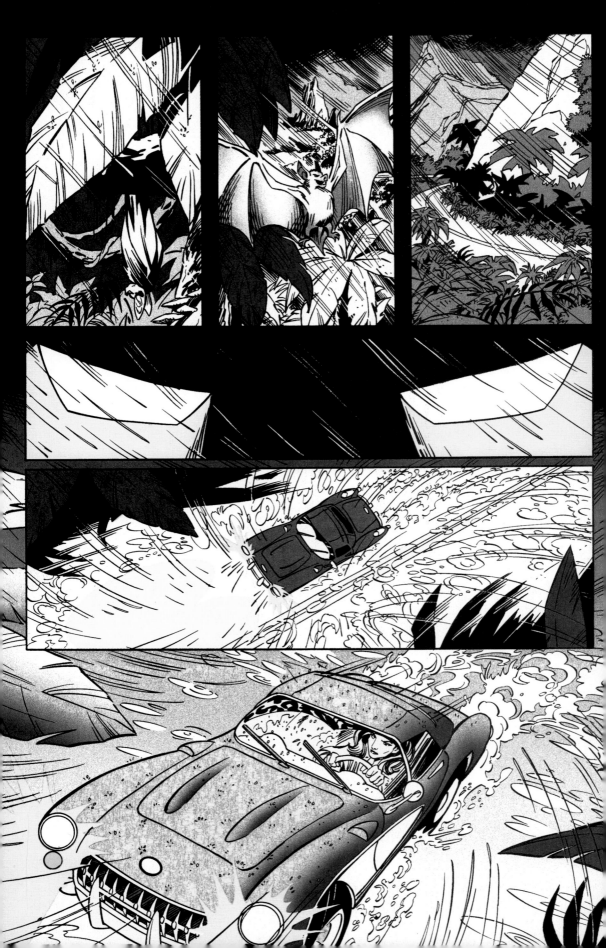

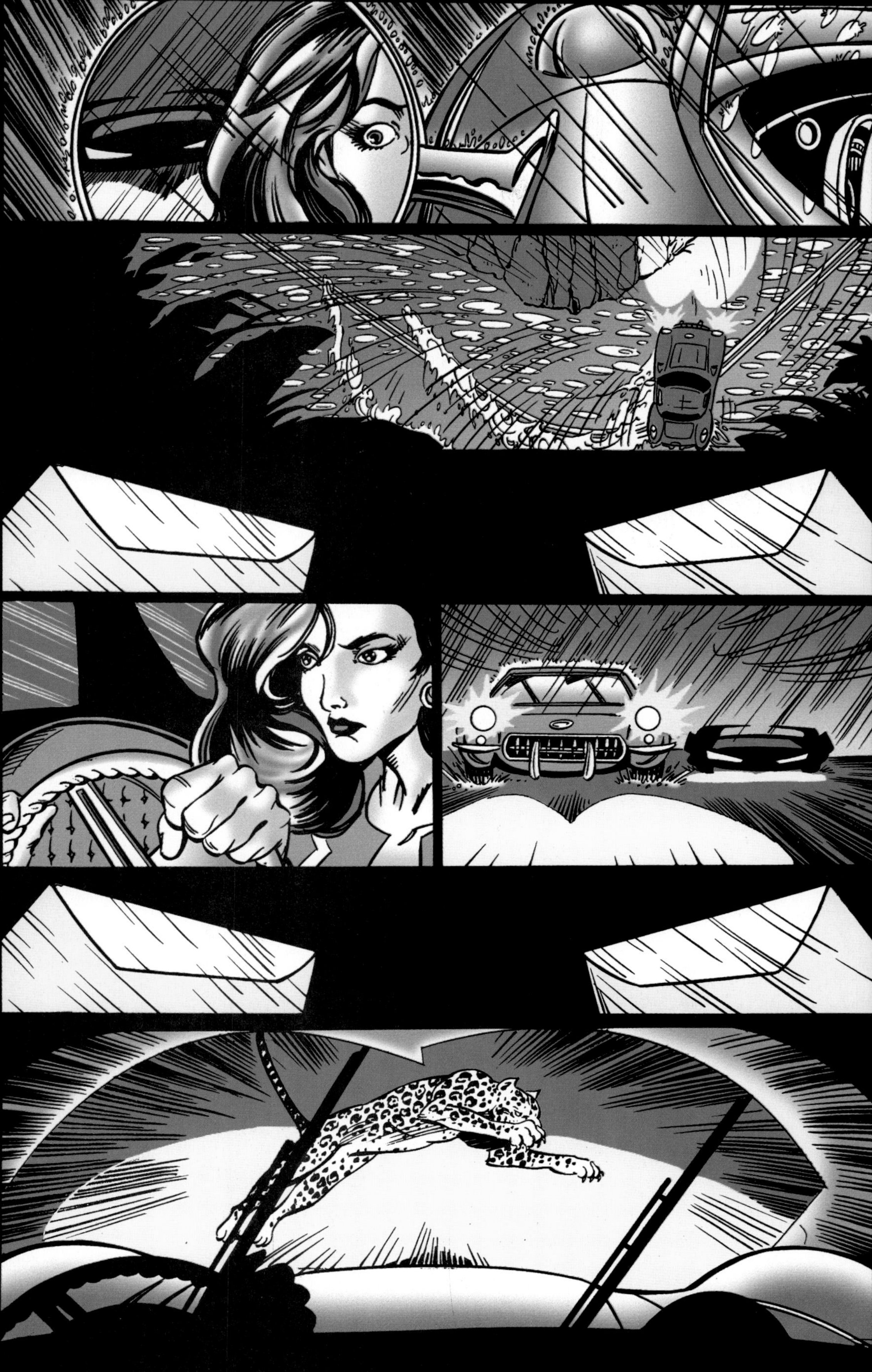

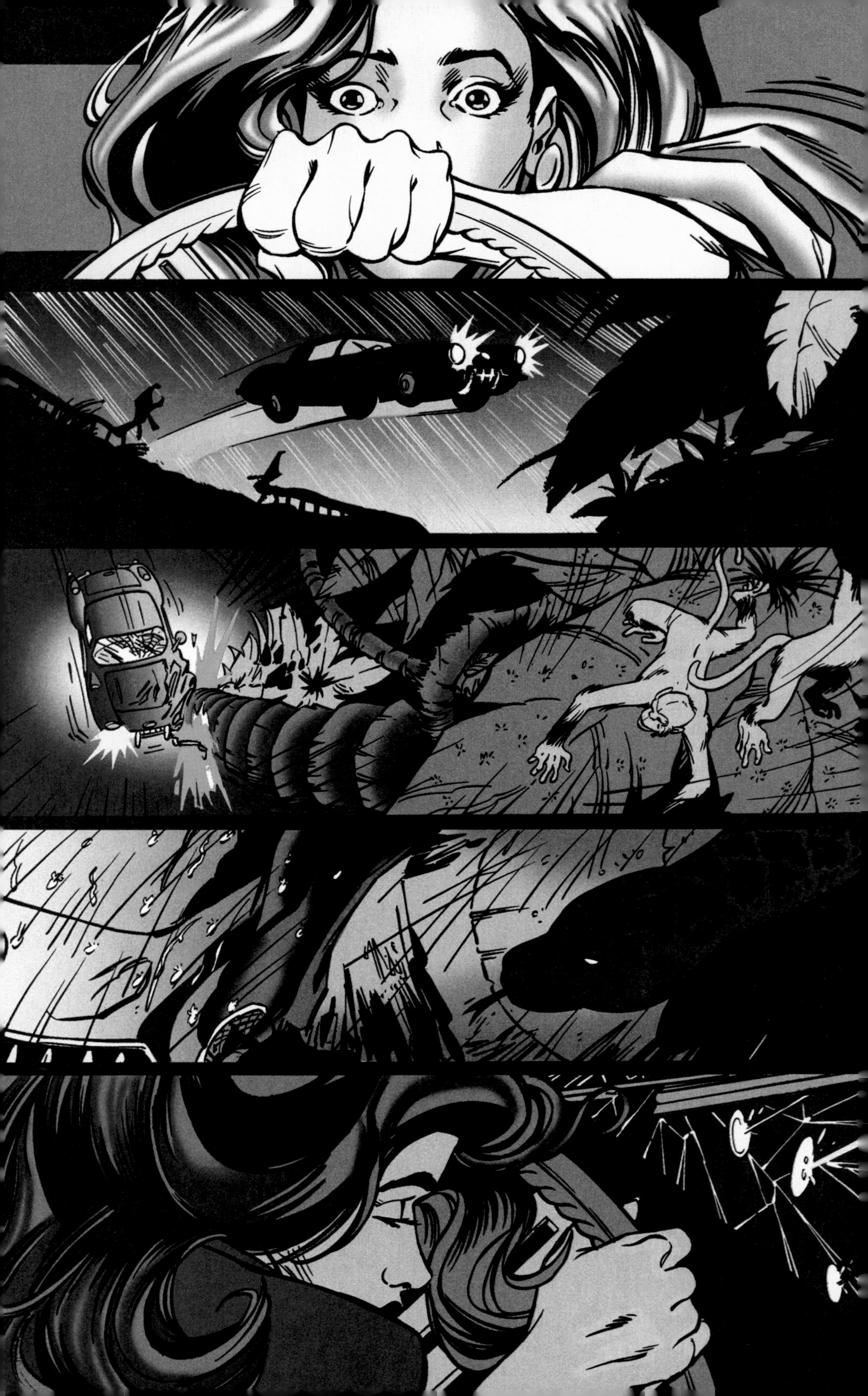

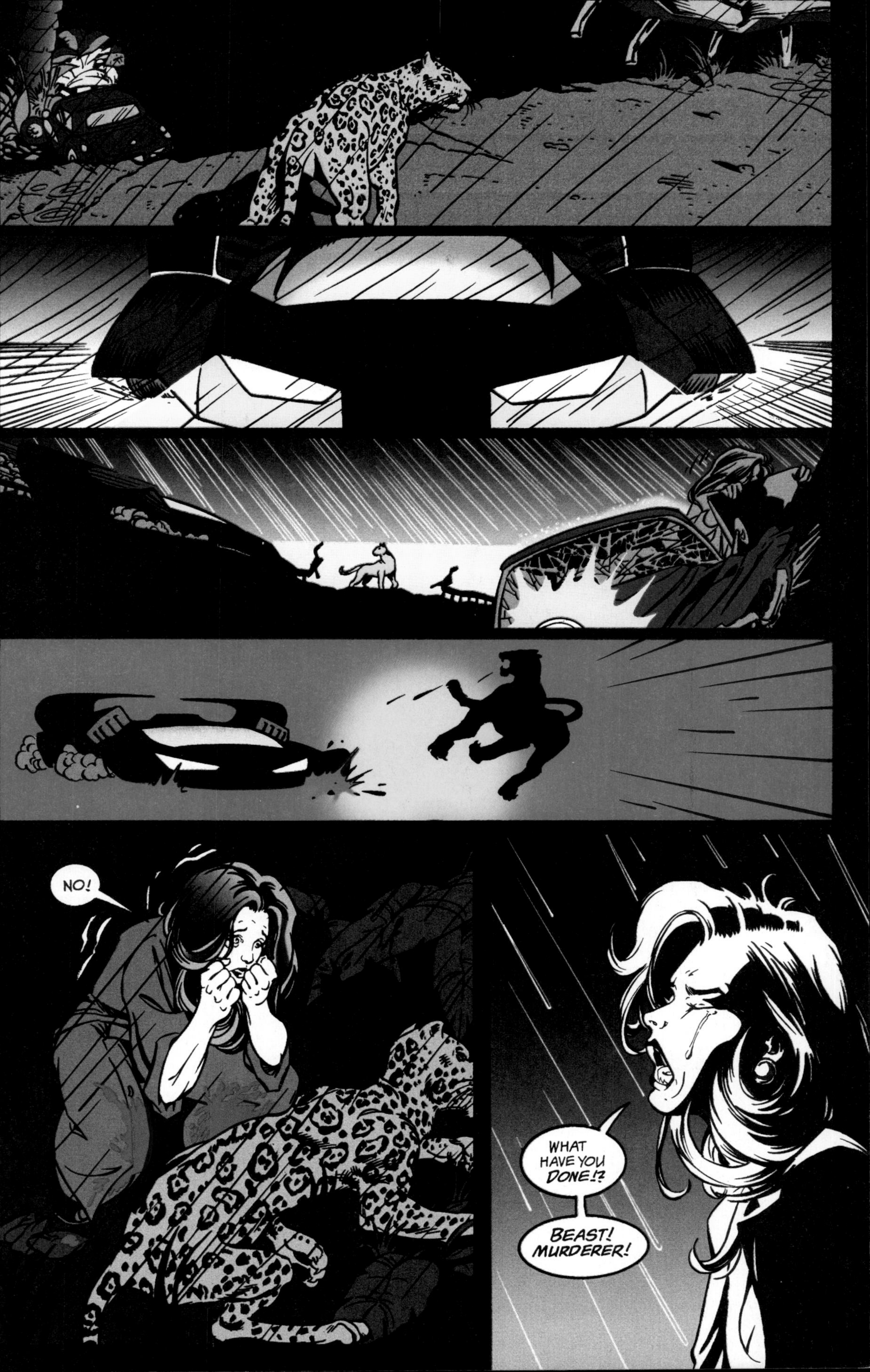
NO!
WHAT HAVE YOU DONE!?
BEAST! MURDERER!

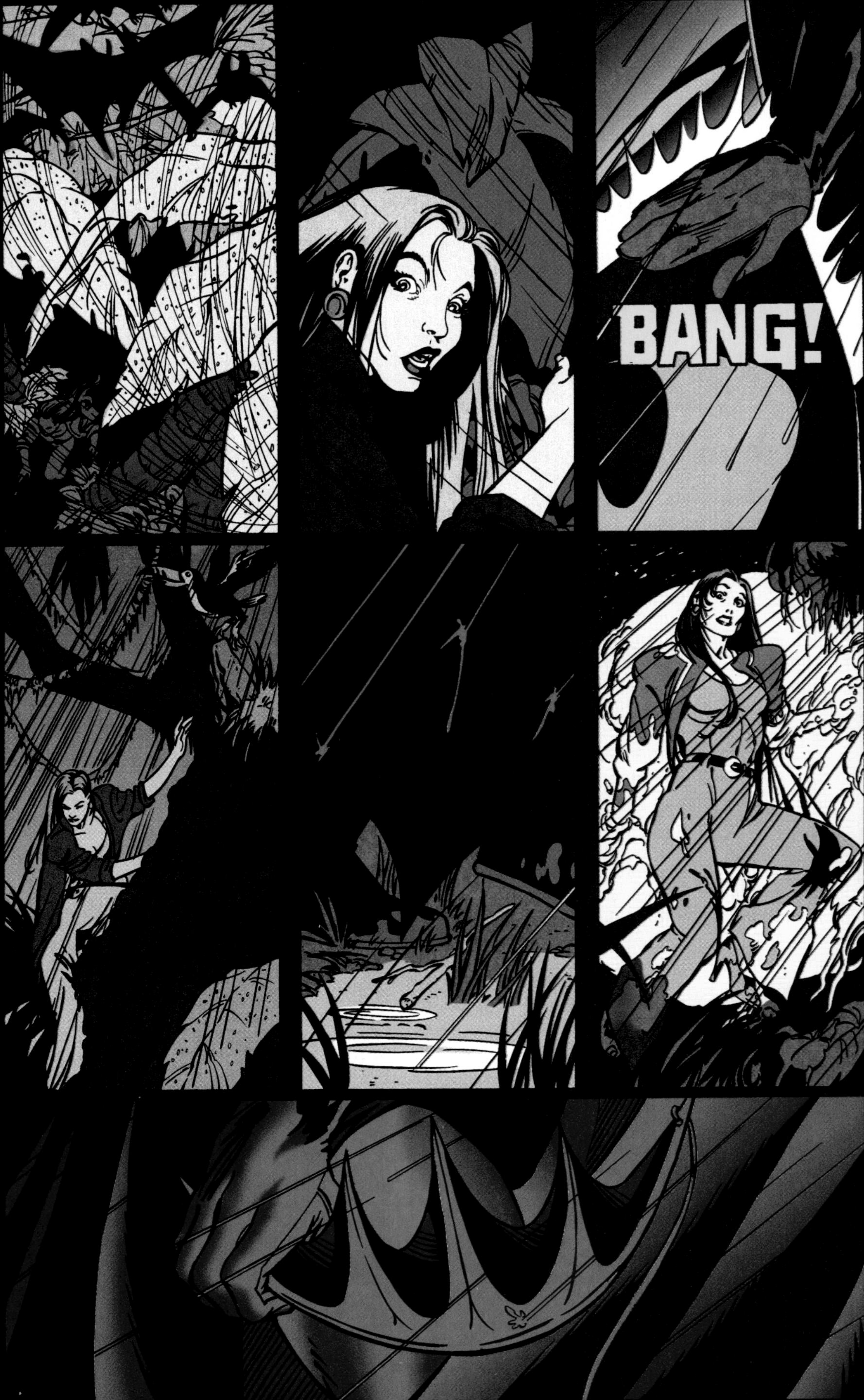
BANG!

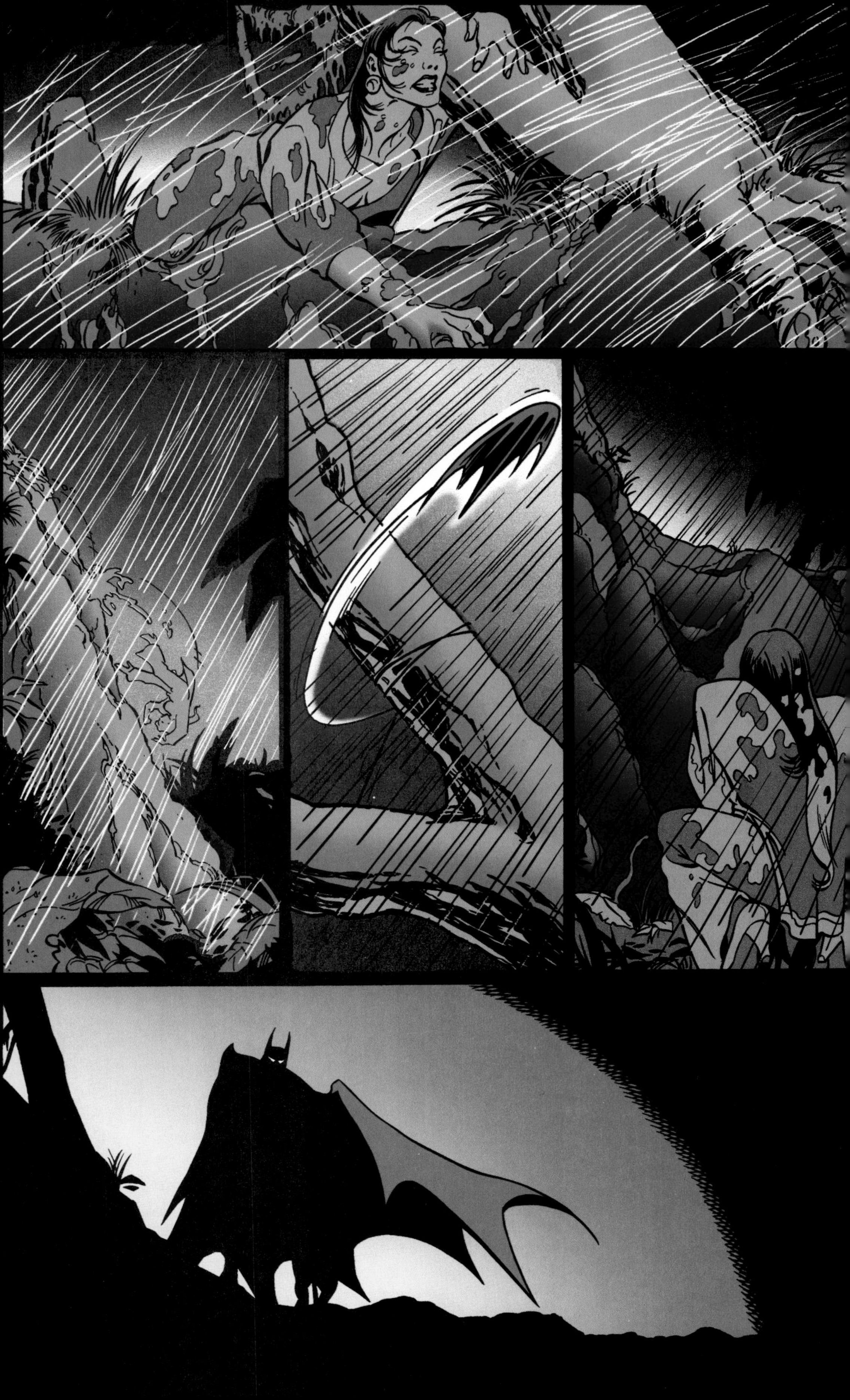

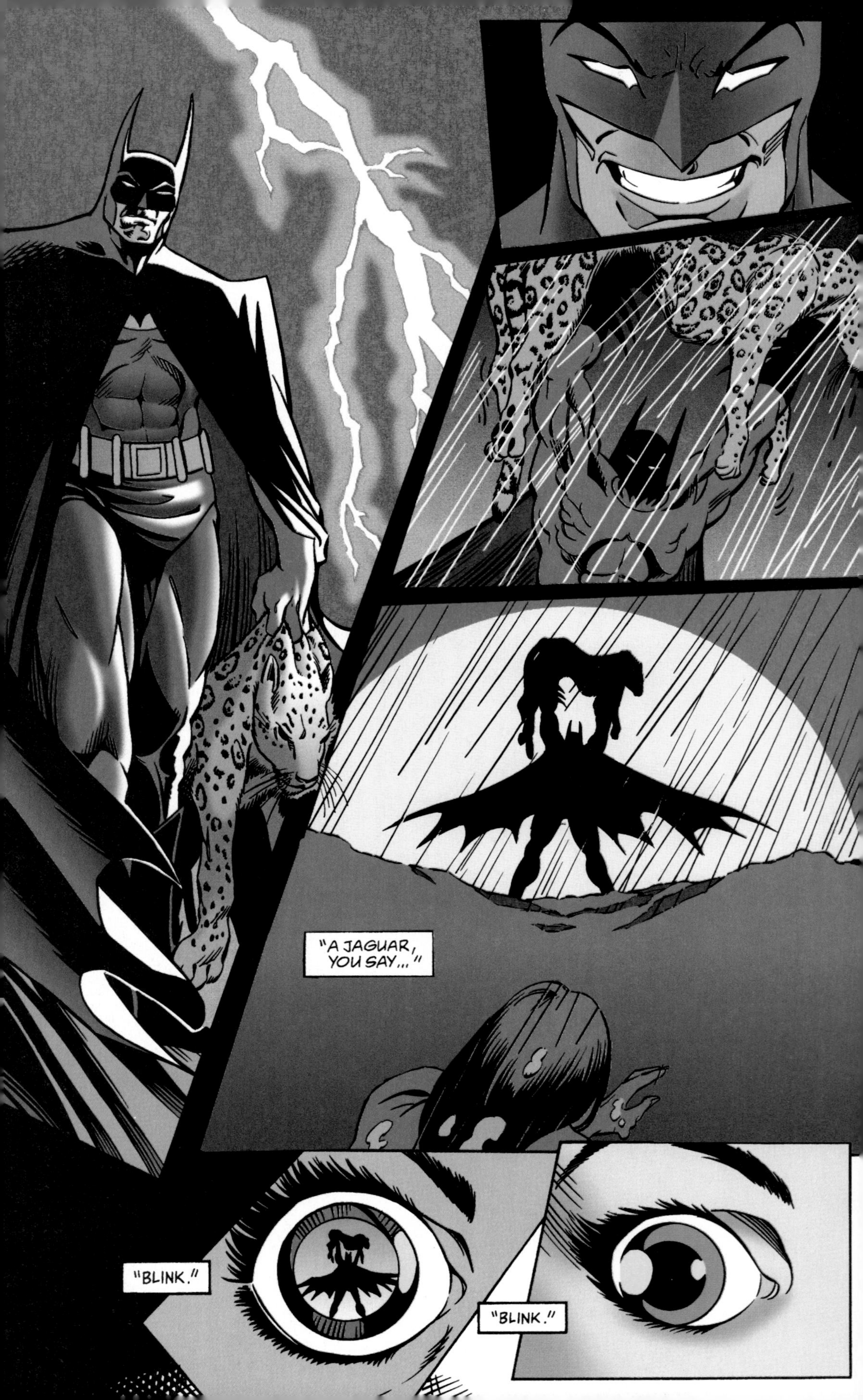
"A JAGUAR, YOU SAY..."
"BLINK."
"BLINK."

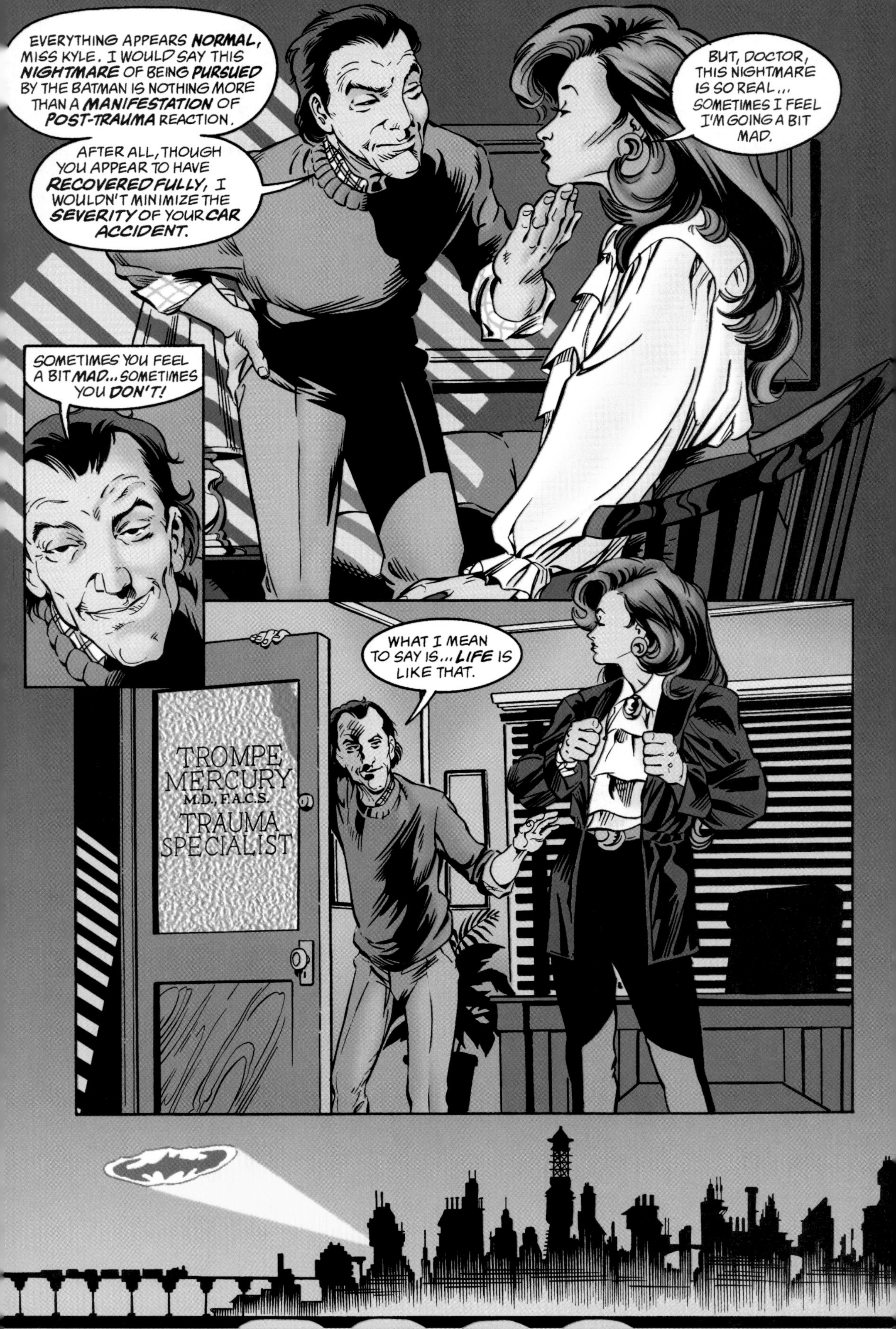
EVERYTHING APPEARS NORMAL, MISS KYLE. I WOULD SAY THIS NIGHTMARE OF BEING PURSUED BY THE BATMAN IS NOTHING MORE THAN A MANIFESTATION OF POST-TRAUMA REACTION.
AFTER ALL, THOUGH YOU APPEAR TO HAVE RECOVERED FULLY, I WOULDN'T MINIMIZE THE SEVERITY OF YOUR CAR ACCIDENT.
BUT, DOCTOR, THIS NIGHTMARE IS SO REAL... SOMETIMES I FEEL I'M GOING A BIT MAD.
SOMETIMES YOU FEEL A BIT MAD... SOMETIMES YOU DON'T!
WHAT I MEAN TO SAY IS... LIFE IS LIKE THAT.
TROMPE MERCURY
M.D., F.A.C.S.
TRAUMA SPECIALIST

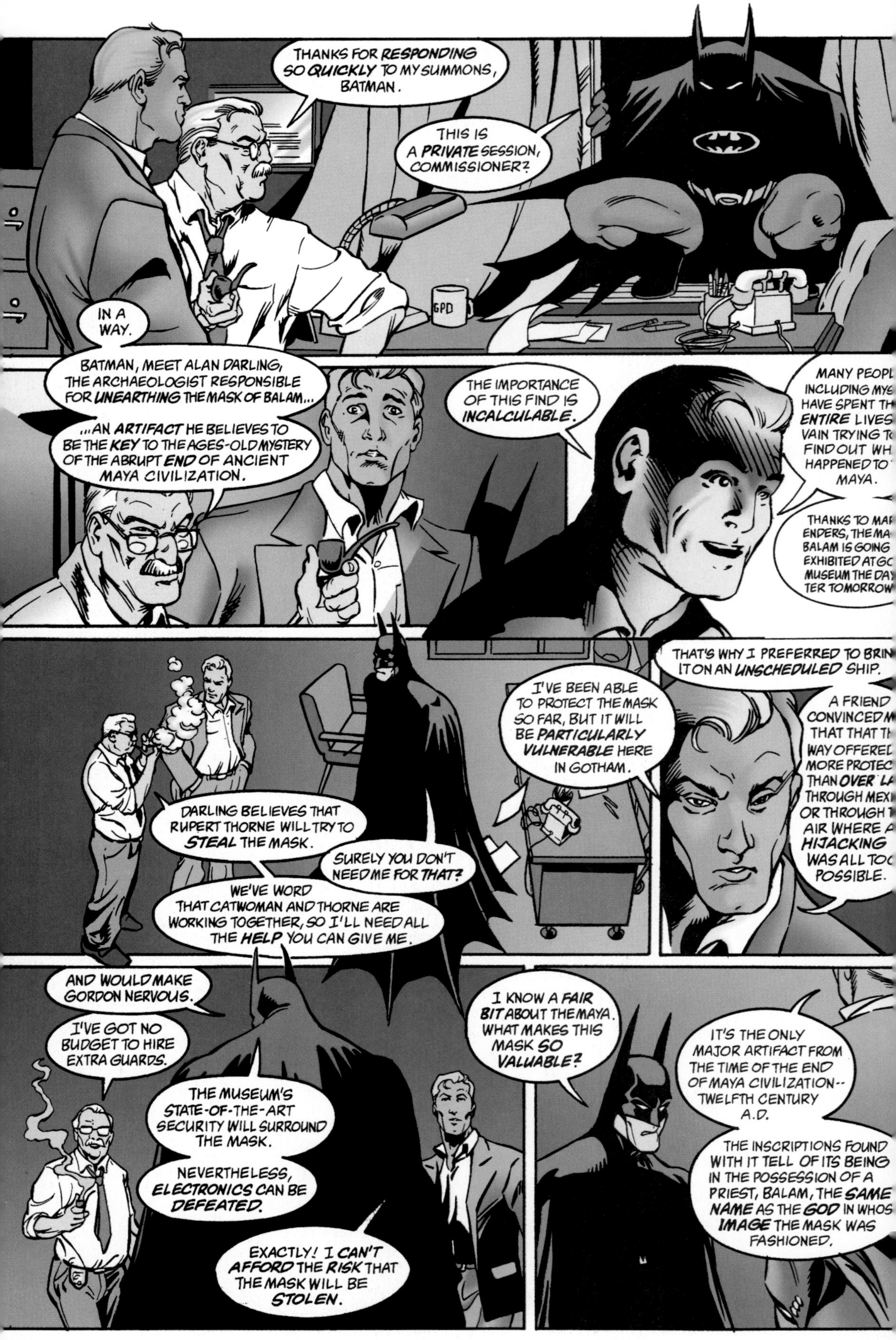
THANKS FOR RESPONDING SO QUICKLY TO MY SUMMONS, BATMAN.
THIS IS A PRIVATE SESSION, COMMISSIONER?
IN A WAY.
BATMAN, MEET ALAN DARLING, THE ARCHAEOLOGIST RESPONSIBLE FOR UNEARTHING THE MASK OF BALAM...
...AN ARTIFACT HE BELIEVES TO BE THE KEY TO THE AGES-OLD MYSTERY OF THE ABRUPT END OF ANCIENT MAYA CIVILIZATION.
THE IMPORTANCE OF THIS FIND IS INCALCULABLE.
MANY PEOPL INCLUDING MYS HAVE SPENT TH ENTIRE LIVES VAIN TRYING TO FIND OUT WH HAPPENED TO MAYA.
THANKS TO MAR ENDERS, THE MA BALAM IS GOING EXHIBITED AT GO MUSEUM THE DAY TER TOMORROW
DARLING BELIEVES THAT RUPERT THORNE WILL TRY TO STEAL THE MASK.
SURELY YOU DON'T NEED ME FOR THAT?
WE'VE WORD THAT CATWOMAN AND THORNE ARE WORKING TOGETHER, SO I'LL NEED ALL THE HELP YOU CAN GIVE ME.
I'VE BEEN ABLE TO PROTECT THE MASK SO FAR, BUT IT WILL BE PARTICULARLY VULNERABLE HERE IN GOTHAM.
THAT'S WHY I PREFERRED TO BRIN IT ON AN UNSCHEDULED SHIP.
A FRIEND CONVINCED M THAT THAT T WAY OFFERED MORE PROTEC THAN OVER LA THROUGH MEX OR THROUGH T AIR WHERE A HIJACKING WAS ALL TOO POSSIBLE.
AND WOULD MAKE GORDON NERVOUS.
I'VE GOT NO BUDGET TO HIRE EXTRA GUARDS.
THE MUSEUM'S STATE-OF-THE-ART SECURITY WILL SURROUND THE MASK.
NEVERTHELESS, ELECTRONICS CAN BE DEFEATED.
EXACTLY! I CAN'T AFFORD THE RISK THAT THE MASK WILL BE STOLEN.
I KNOW A FAIR BIT ABOUT THE MAYA. WHAT MAKES THIS MASK SO VALUABLE?
IT'S THE ONLY MAJOR ARTIFACT FROM THE TIME OF THE END OF MAYA CIVILIZATION-- TWELFTH CENTURY A.D.
THE INSCRIPTIONS FOUND WITH IT TELL OF ITS BEING IN THE POSSESSION OF A PRIEST, BALAM, THE SAME NAME AS THE GOD IN WHOS IMAGE THE MASK WAS FASHIONED.

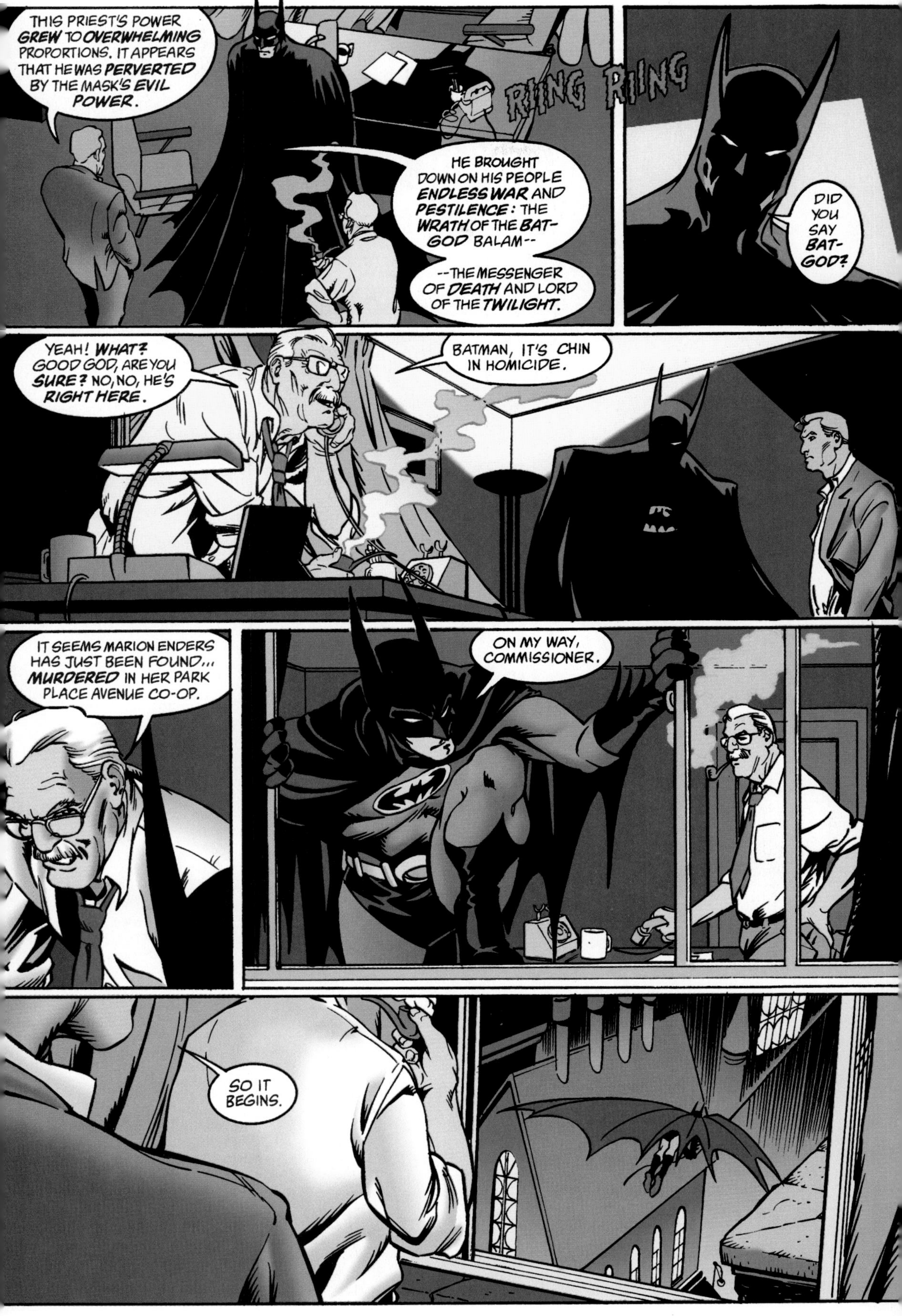
THIS PRIEST'S POWER GREW TO OVERWHELMING PROPORTIONS. IT APPEARS THAT HE WAS PERVERTED BY THE MASK'S EVIL POWER.
HE BROUGHT DOWN ON HIS PEOPLE ENDLESS WAR AND PESTILENCE: THE WRATH OF THE BAT-GOD BALAM--
--THE MESSENGER OF DEATH AND LORD OF THE TWILIGHT.
RIING RIING
DID YOU SAY BAT-GOD?
YEAH! WHAT? GOOD GOD, ARE YOU SURE? NO, NO, HE'S RIGHT HERE.
BATMAN, IT'S CHIN IN HOMICIDE.
IT SEEMS MARION ENDERS HAS JUST BEEN FOUND... MURDERED IN HER PARK PLACE AVENUE CO-OP.
ON MY WAY, COMMISSIONER.
SO IT BEGINS.

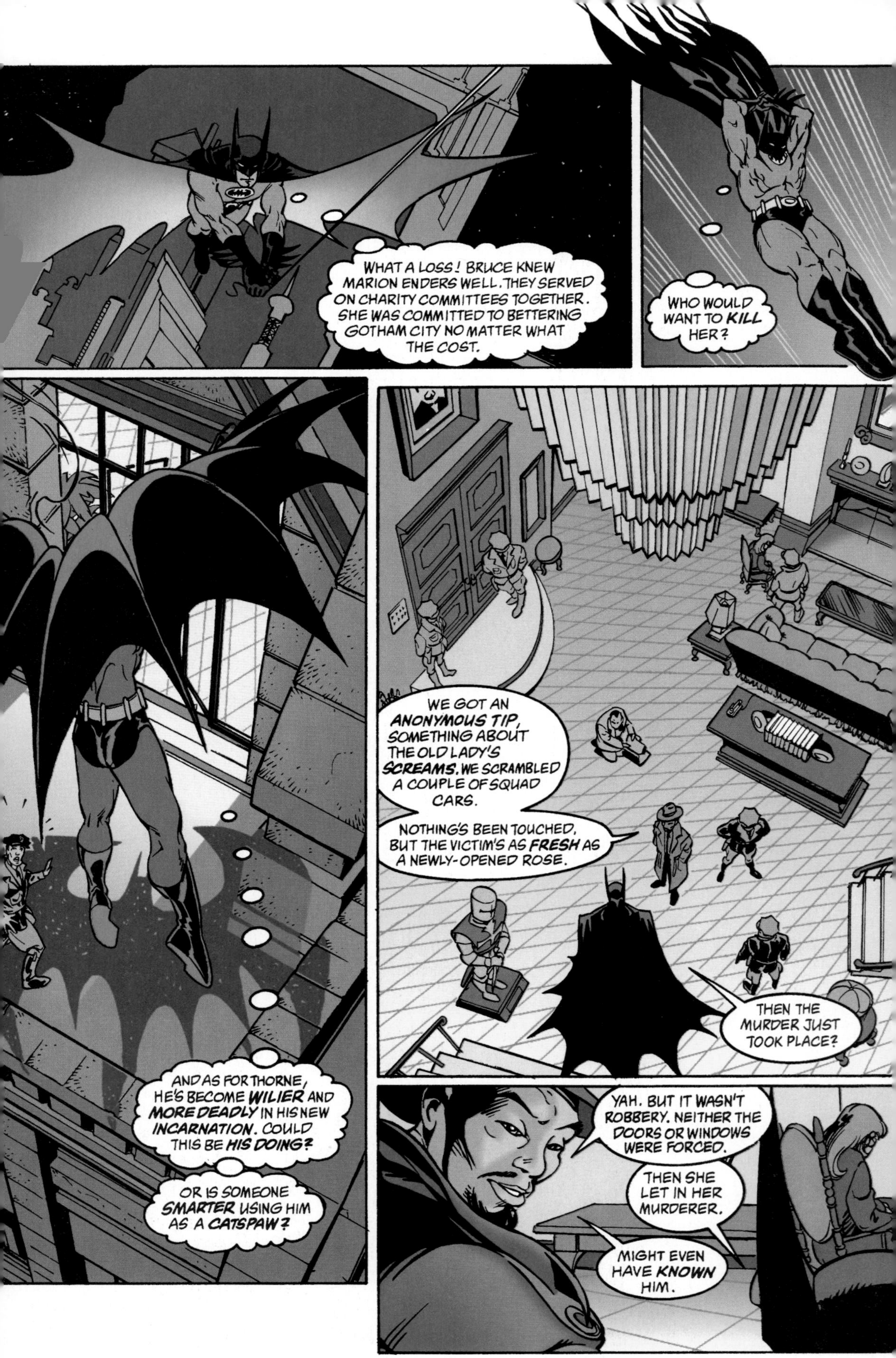
WHAT A LOSS! BRUCE KNEW MARION ENDERS WELL. THEY SERVED ON CHARITY COMMITTEES TOGETHER. SHE WAS COMMITTED TO BETTERING GOTHAM CITY NO MATTER WHAT THE COST.
WHO WOULD WANT TO KILL HER?
AND AS FOR THORNE, HE'S BECOME WILIER AND MORE DEADLY IN HIS NEW INCARNATION. COULD THIS BE HIS DOING?
OR IS SOMEONE SMARTER USING HIM AS A CATSPAW?
WE GOT AN ANONYMOUS TIP, SOMETHING ABOUT THE OLD LADY'S SCREAMS. WE SCRAMBLED A COUPLE OF SQUAD CARS.
NOTHING'S BEEN TOUCHED, BUT THE VICTIM'S AS FRESH AS A NEWLY-OPENED ROSE.
THEN THE MURDER JUST TOOK PLACE?
YAH. BUT IT WASN'T ROBBERY. NEITHER THE DOORS OR WINDOWS WERE FORCED.
THEN SHE LET IN HER MURDERER.
MIGHT EVEN HAVE KNOWN HIM.

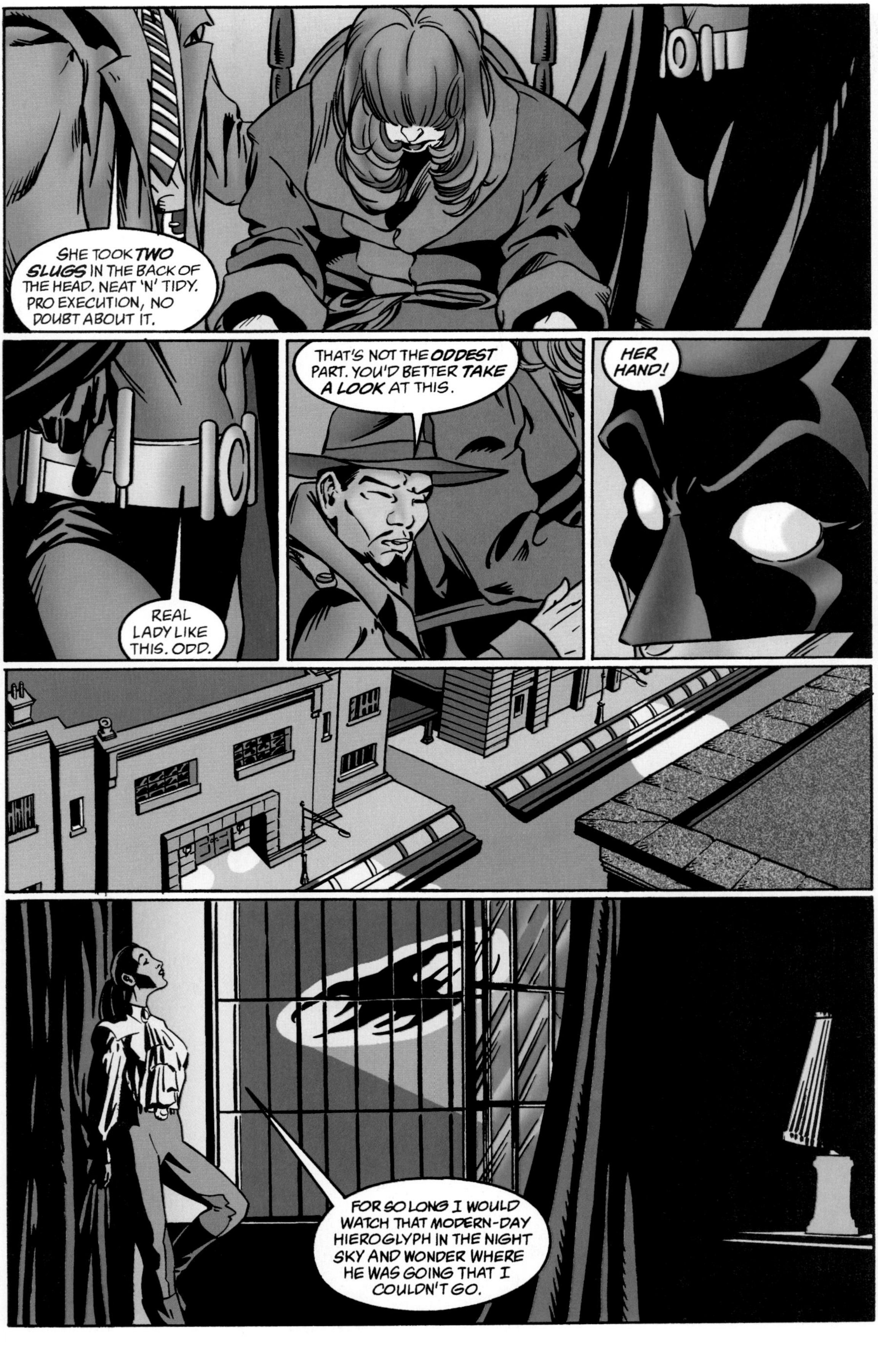
SHE TOOK TWO SLUGS IN THE BACK OF THE HEAD. NEAT 'N' TIDY. PRO EXECUTION, NO DOUBT ABOUT IT.
REAL LADY LIKE THIS. ODD.
THAT'S NOT THE ODDEST PART. YOU'D BETTER TAKE A LOOK AT THIS.
HER HAND!
FOR SO LONG I WOULD WATCH THAT MODERN-DAY HIEROGLYPH IN THE NIGHT SKY AND WONDER WHERE HE WAS GOING THAT I COULDN'T GO.

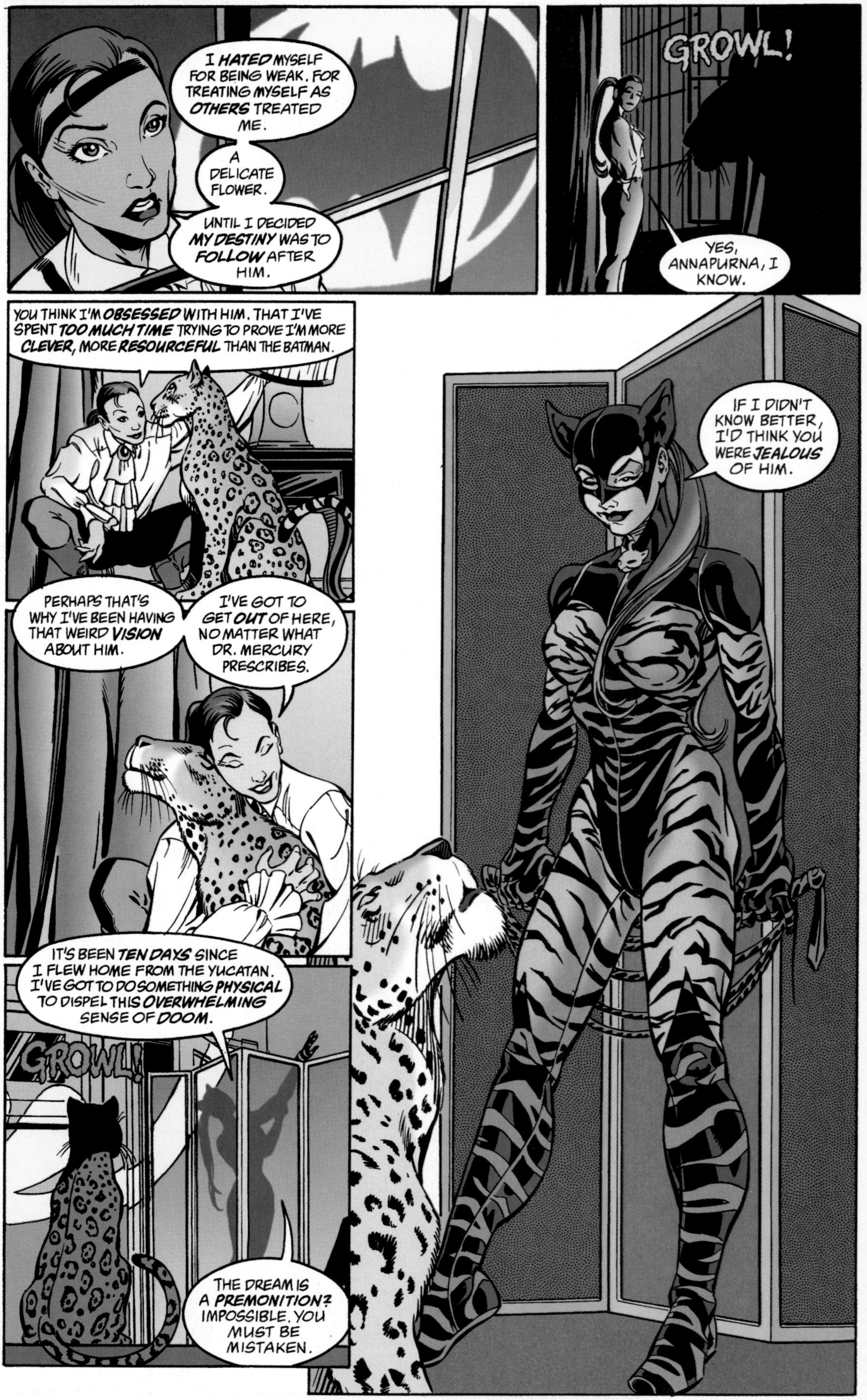
I HATED MYSELF FOR BEING WEAK. FOR TREATING MYSELF AS OTHERS TREATED ME.
A DELICATE FLOWER.
UNTIL I DECIDED MY DESTINY WAS TO FOLLOW AFTER HIM.
GROWL!
YES, ANNAPURNA, I KNOW.
YOU THINK I'M OBSESSED WITH HIM. THAT I'VE SPENT TOO MUCH TIME TRYING TO PROVE I'M MORE CLEVER, MORE RESOURCEFUL THAN THE BATMAN.
PERHAPS THAT'S WHY I'VE BEEN HAVING THAT WEIRD VISION ABOUT HIM.
I'VE GOT TO GET OUT OF HERE, NO MATTER WHAT DR. MERCURY PRESCRIBES.
IT'S BEEN TEN DAYS SINCE I FLEW HOME FROM THE YUCATAN. I'VE GOT TO DO SOMETHING PHYSICAL TO DISPEL THIS OVERWHELMING SENSE OF DOOM.
GROWL!
THE DREAM IS A PREMONITION? IMPOSSIBLE. YOU MUST BE MISTAKEN.
IF I DIDN'T KNOW BETTER, I'D THINK YOU WERE JEALOUS OF HIM.

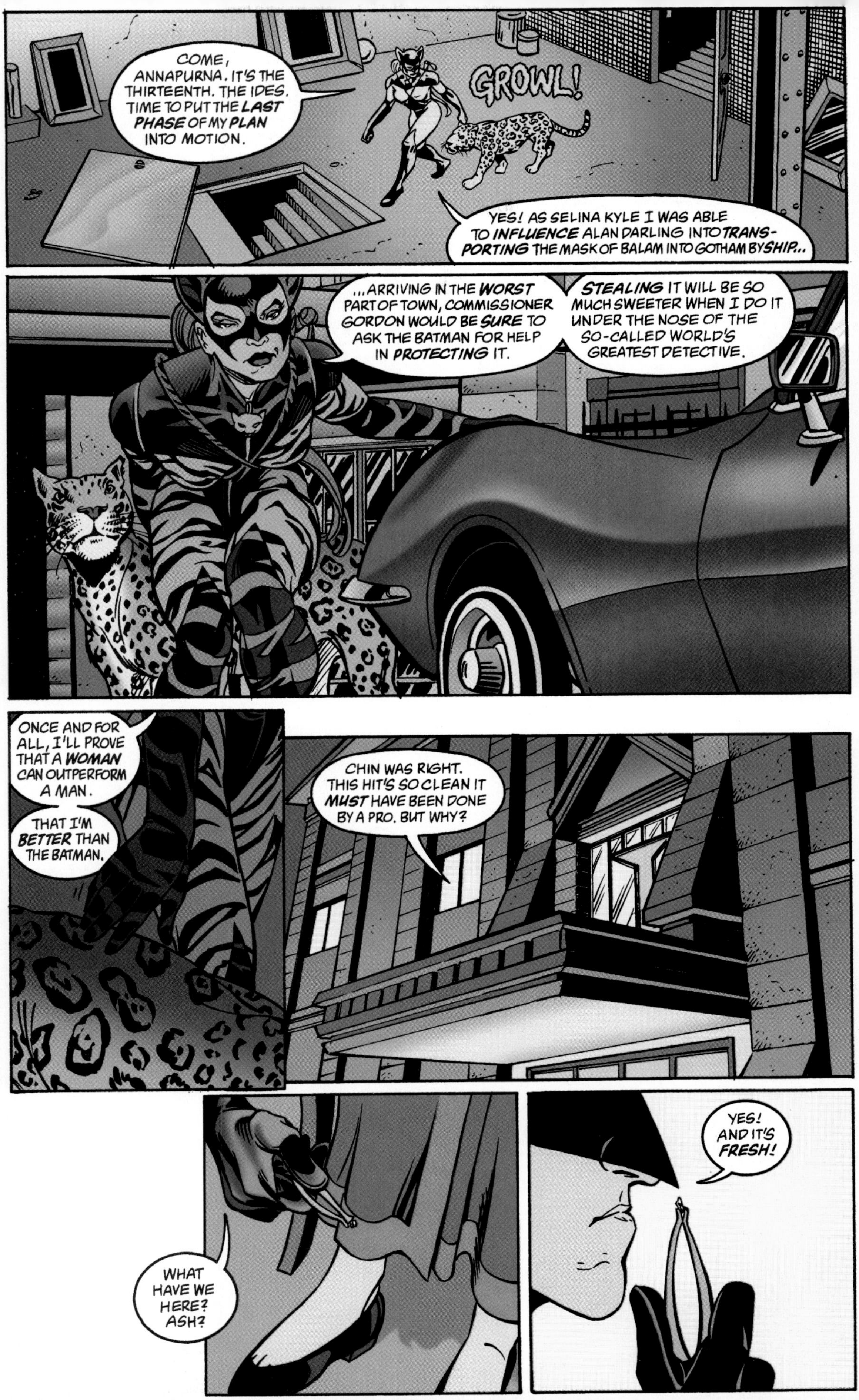
COME, ANNAPURNA. IT'S THE THIRTEENTH. THE IDES. TIME TO PUT THE LAST PHASE OF MY PLAN INTO MOTION.
GROWL!
YES! AS SELINA KYLE I WAS ABLE TO INFLUENCE ALAN DARLING INTO TRANS-PORTING THE MASK OF BALAM INTO GOTHAM BY SHIP...
...ARRIVING IN THE WORST PART OF TOWN, COMMISSIONER GORDON WOULD BE SURE TO ASK THE BATMAN FOR HELP IN PROTECTING IT.
STEALING IT WILL BE SO MUCH SWEETER WHEN I DO IT UNDER THE NOSE OF THE SO-CALLED WORLD'S GREATEST DETECTIVE.
ONCE AND FOR ALL, I'LL PROVE THAT A WOMAN CAN OUTPERFORM A MAN.
THAT I'M BETTER THAN THE BATMAN.
CHIN WAS RIGHT. THIS HIT'S SO CLEAN IT MUST HAVE BEEN DONE BY A PRO. BUT WHY?
WHAT HAVE WE HERE? ASH?
YES! AND IT'S FRESH!

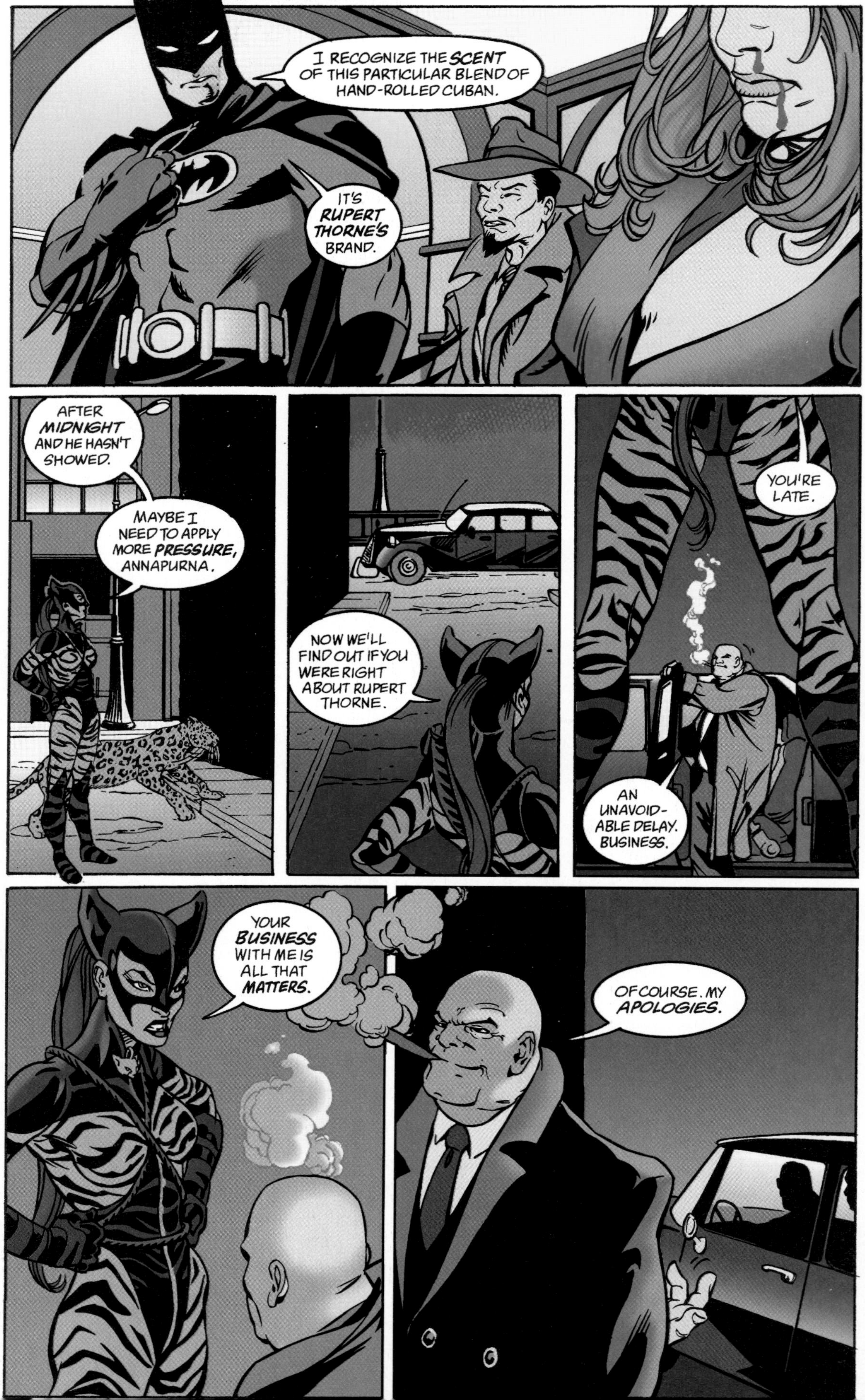
I RECOGNIZE THE SCENT OF THIS PARTICULAR BLEND OF HAND-ROLLED CUBAN.
IT'S RUPERT THORNE'S BRAND.
AFTER MIDNIGHT AND HE HASN'T SHOWED.
MAYBE I NEED TO APPLY MORE PRESSURE, ANNAPURNA.
NOW WE'LL FIND OUT IF YOU WERE RIGHT ABOUT RUPERT THORNE.
YOU'RE LATE.
AN UNAVOID-ABLE DELAY. BUSINESS.
YOUR BUSINESS WITH ME IS ALL THAT MATTERS.
OF COURSE. MY APOLOGIES.

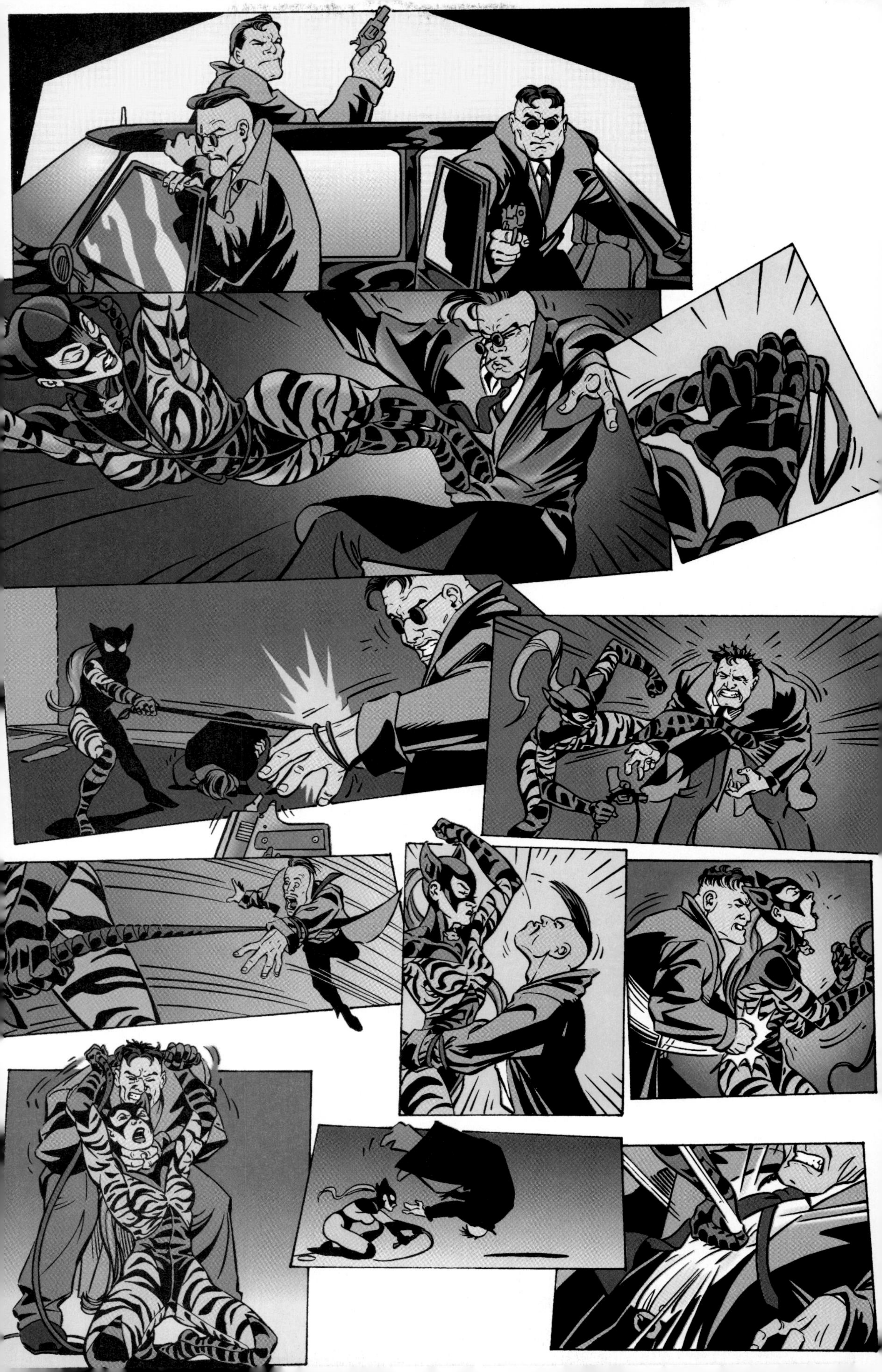

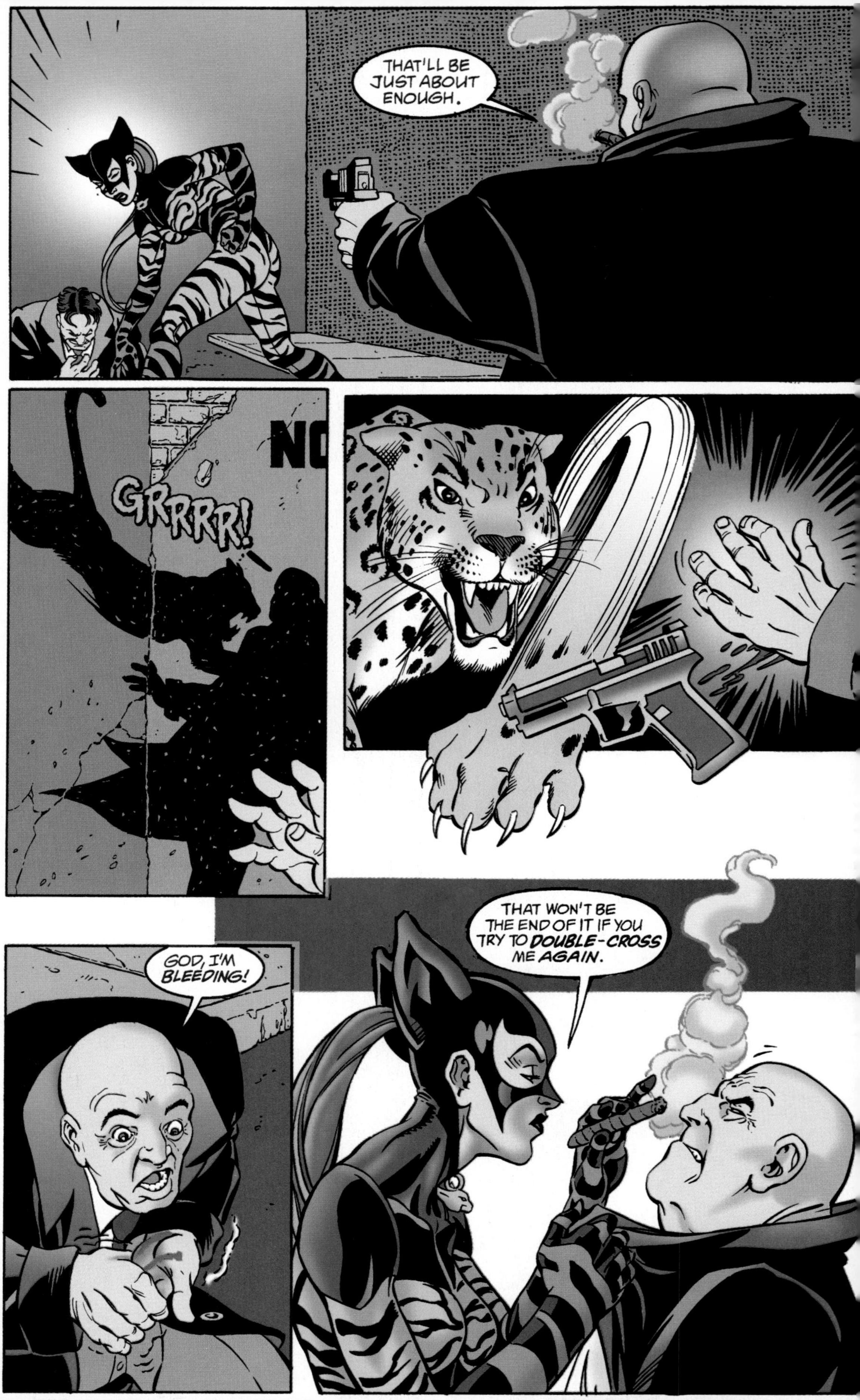
THAT'LL BE JUST ABOUT ENOUGH.
NO
GRRRR!
GOD, I'M BLEEDING!
THAT WON'T BE THE END OF IT IF YOU TRY TO DOUBLE-CROSS ME AGAIN.

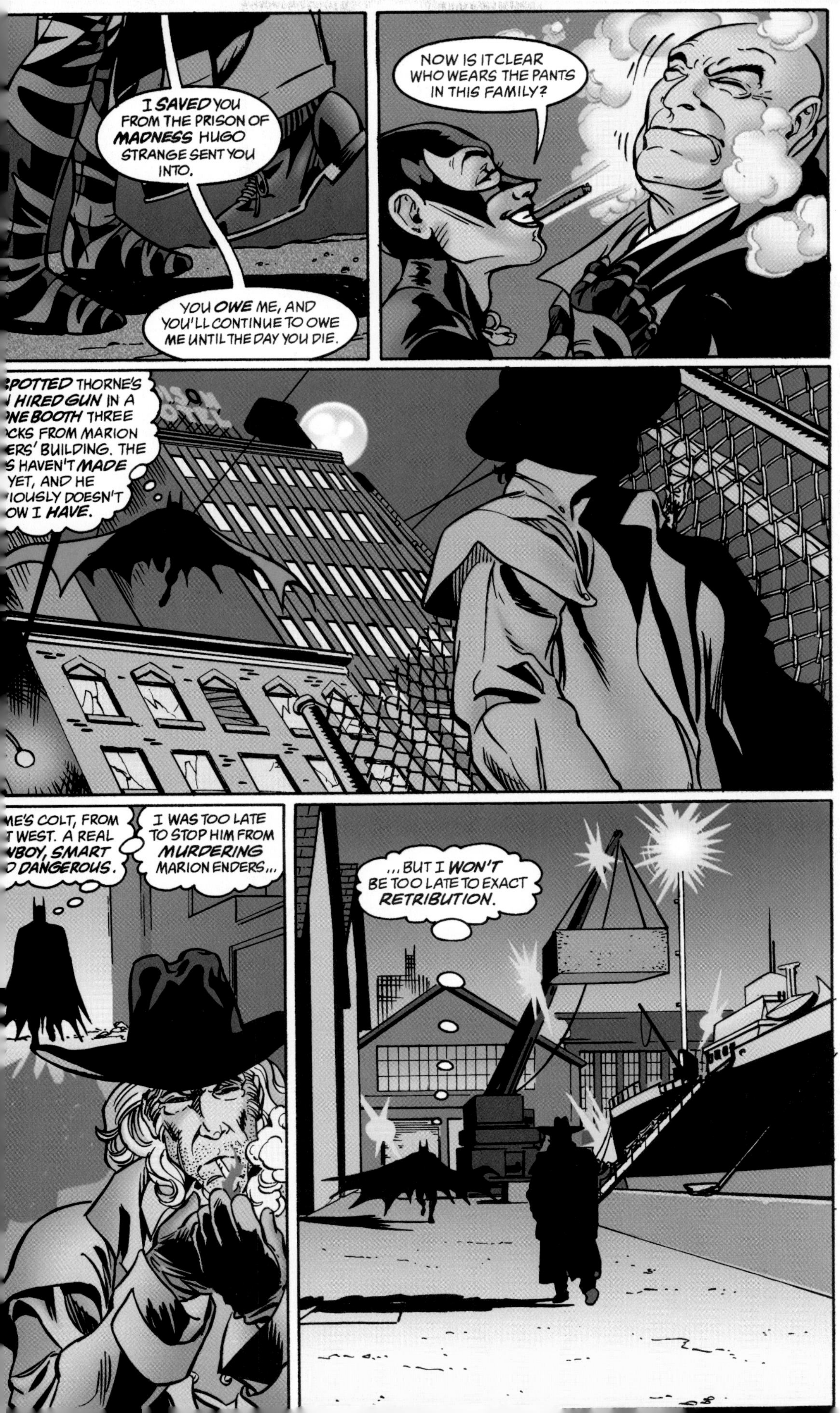

NOW IS IT CLEAR WHO WEARS THE PANTS IN THIS FAMILY?
I SAVED YOU FROM THE PRISON OF MADNESS HUGO STRANGE SENT YOU INTO.
YOU OWE ME, AND YOU'LL CONTINUE TO OWE ME UNTIL THE DAY YOU DIE.
SPOTTED THORNE'S HIRED GUN IN A NE BOOTH THREE CKS FROM MARION ERS' BUILDING. THE S HAVEN'T MADE YET, AND HE IOUSLY DOESN'T OW I HAVE.
ME'S COLT, FROM T WEST. A REAL WBOY, SMART D DANGEROUS.
I WAS TOO LATE TO STOP HIM FROM MURDERING MARION ENDERS...
...BUT I WON'T BE TOO LATE TO EXACT RETRIBUTION.

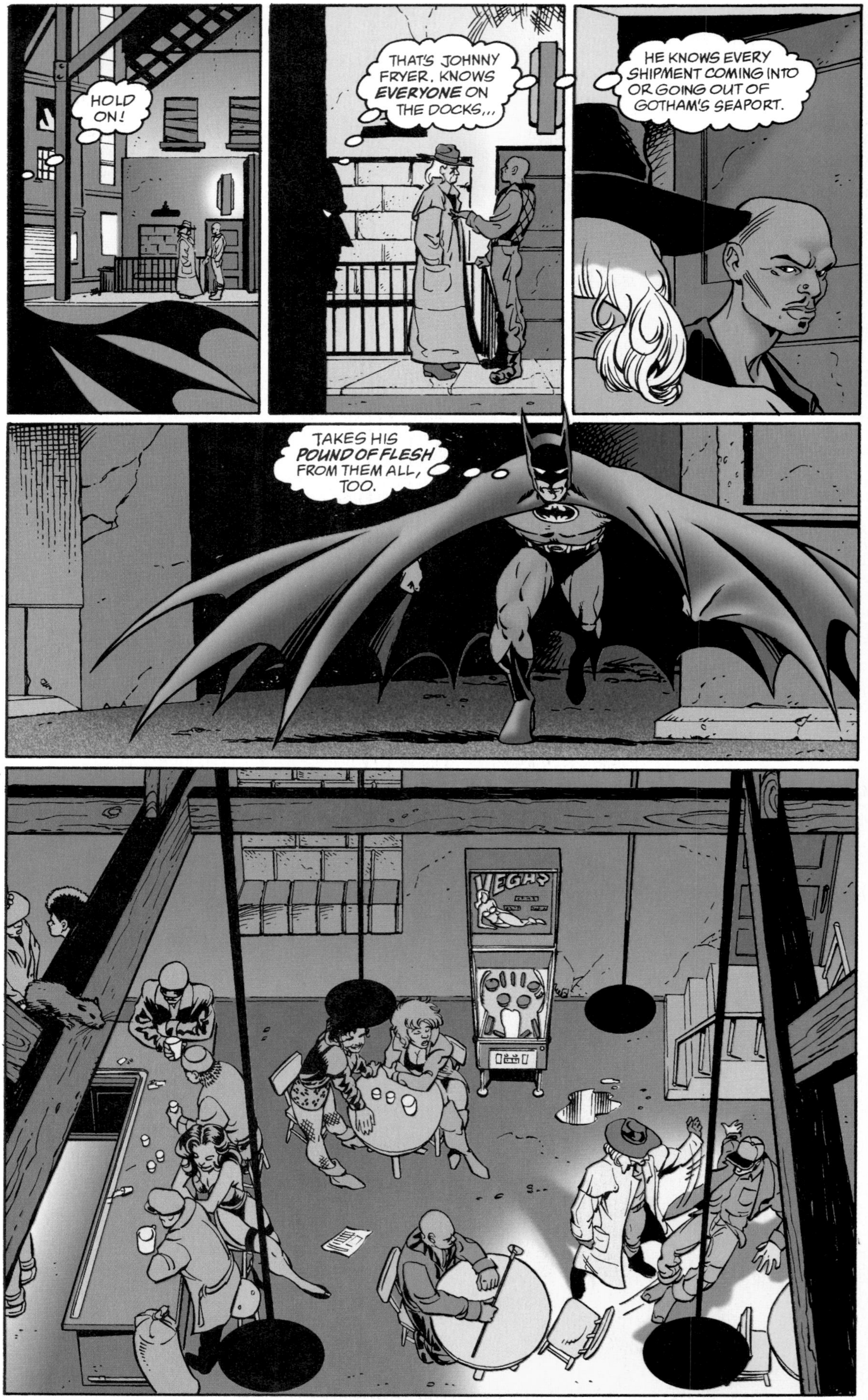
HOLD ON!
THAT'S JOHNNY FRYER. KNOWS EVERYONE ON THE DOCKS,..
HE KNOWS EVERY SHIPMENT COMING INTO OR GOING OUT OF GOTHAM'S SEAPORT.
TAKES HIS POUND OF FLESH FROM THEM ALL, TOO.

THAT'S **BETTER**. NOW WE CAN **TALK**.

IT ONLY MEANS A THING IF YOU SAY THE WORDS I WANT TO HEAR.

IT'S ALL TAKEN CARE OF. THE ENDERS WOMAN'S **ICED**. SHE WAS LONELY, AN **EASY MARK**. HA! SHE **LIKED** ME!

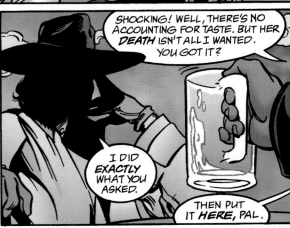

SHOCKING! WELL, THERE'S NO ACCOUNTING FOR TASTE. BUT HER **DEATH** ISN'T ALL I WANTED. YOU GOT IT?

I DID **EXACTLY** WHAT YOU ASKED.

THEN PUT IT **HERE**, PAL.

HOW CAN I BE OF **SERVICE?**

WHAT TIME WILL THE **CYRUS** DOCK TONIGHT AND WHICH SLIP WILL IT TIE UP AT?

LOOK IN THE **NEWSPAPER**. ALL SHIPPING ARRIVALS AND DEPARTURES ARE LISTED **DAILY**.

QUIT THE ACT. YOU KNOW **THIS** FREIGHTER'S **SPECIAL**.

UH-HUH. AND I ALSO KNOW THAT EVEN WITH **ALL** HIS SOURCES THORNE COULDN'T GET **THE** INFO. HE MAY **OWN** THE **INLAND** HALF OF GOTHAM CITY, BUT **I** OWN THE **REST**. SO YOU HAD TO MEET MY **PRICE**. WELL, I'VE **GOT** WHAT YOU WANT: MIDNIGHT. SLIP TWELVE.

I'VE **WANTED** THIS RING EVER SINCE I SAW IT AT AN **AUCTION** LAST YEAR.

I WOULDN'T BID FOR IT, THOUGH. I TRIED TO **STEAL** IT ONCE BUT RAN INTO THE BATMAN.

I WAS **SURPRISED.** IT **SLID** RIGHT OFF HER **FINGER.**

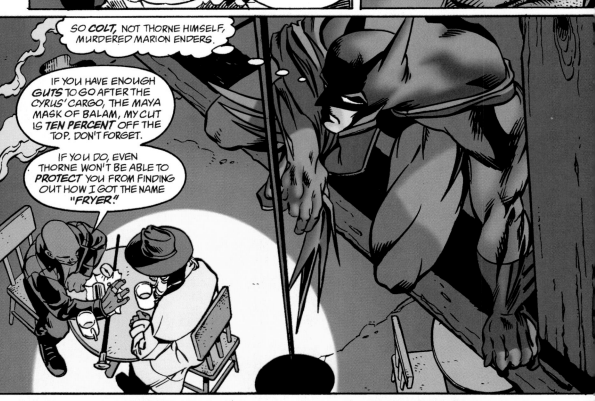

SO **COLT,** NOT THORNE HIMSELF, MURDERED MARION ENDERS.

IF YOU HAVE ENOUGH **GUTS** TO GO AFTER THE CYRUS' CARGO, THE MAYA MASK OF BALAM, MY CUT IS **TEN PERCENT** OFF THE TOP. DON'T FORGET.

IF YOU DO, EVEN THORNE WON'T BE ABLE TO **PROTECT** YOU FROM FINDING OUT HOW I GOT THE NAME "*FRYER*."

I **HATE** NIGHT WATCHES.

SURE. SHORT END OF THE STICK. EVERYONE ELSE IS **ASHORE** GETTING THE GIRLS AND THE DRINKS.

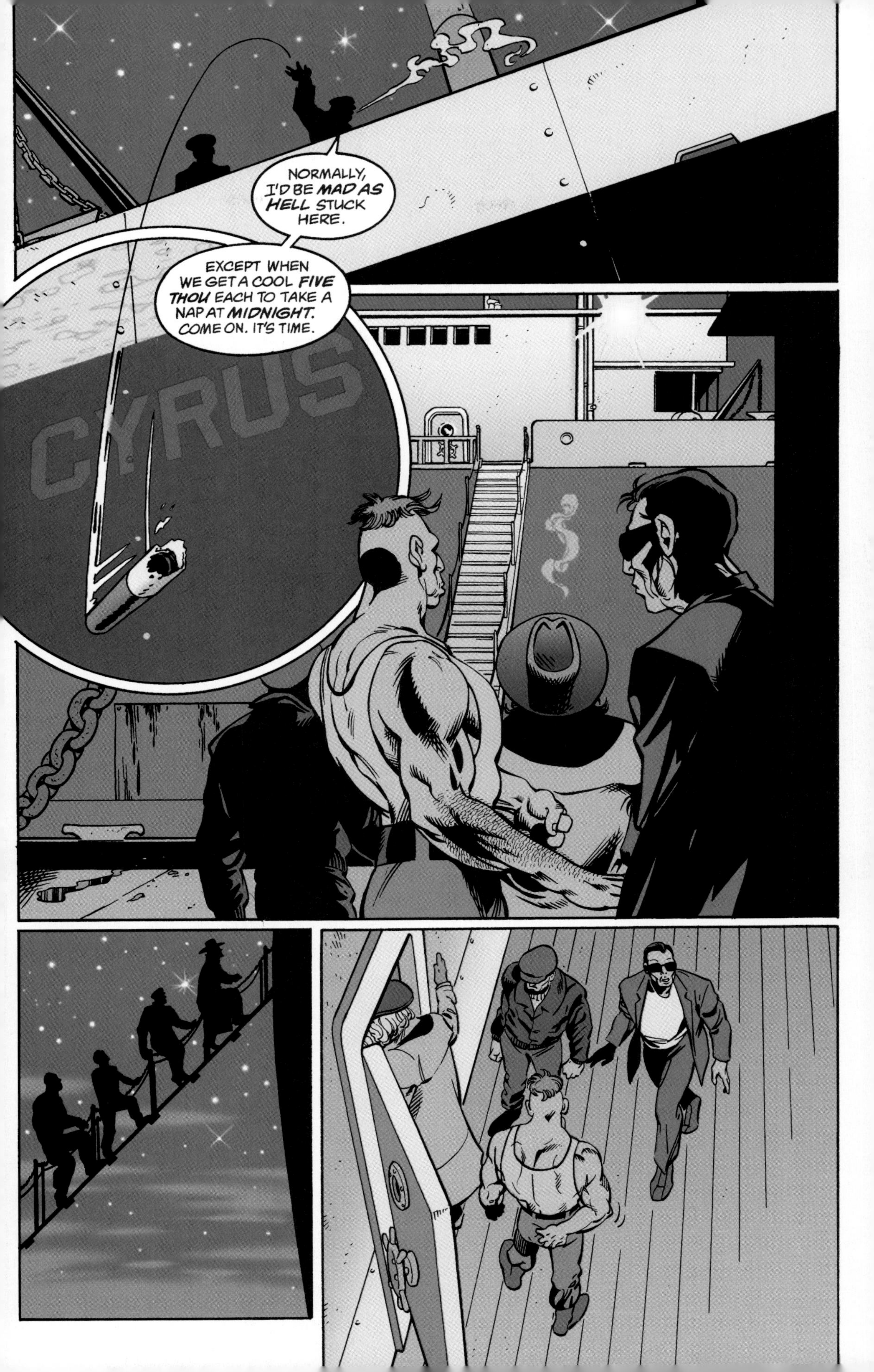
NORMALLY, I'D BE MAD AS HELL STUCK HERE.
EXCEPT WHEN WE GET A COOL FIVE THOU EACH TO TAKE A NAP AT MIDNIGHT. COME ON. IT'S TIME.
CYRUS

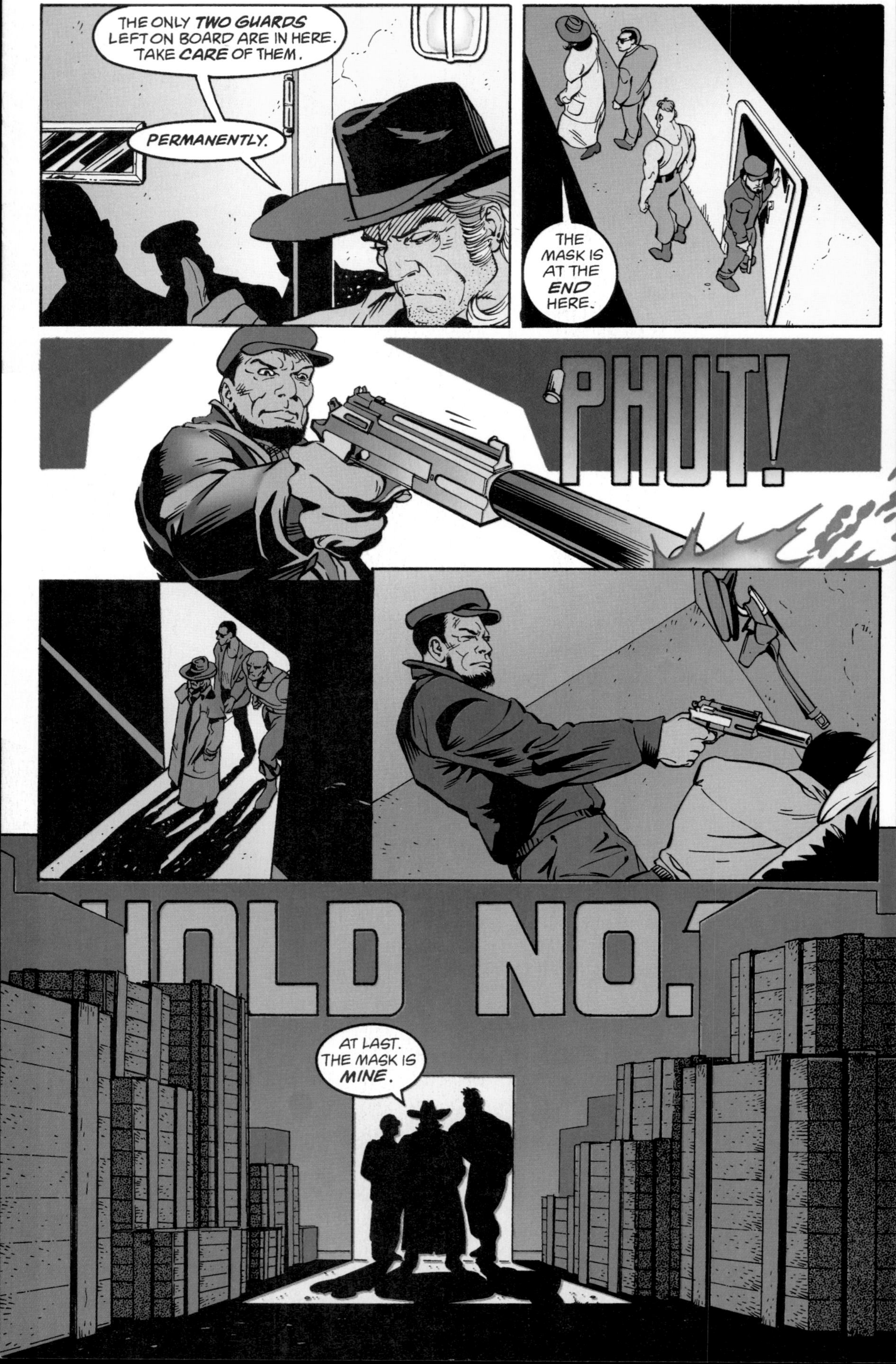
THE ONLY TWO GUARDS LEFT ON BOARD ARE IN HERE. TAKE CARE OF THEM.
PERMANENTLY.
THE MASK IS AT THE END HERE.
PHUT!
HOLD NO.
AT LAST. THE MASK IS MINE.

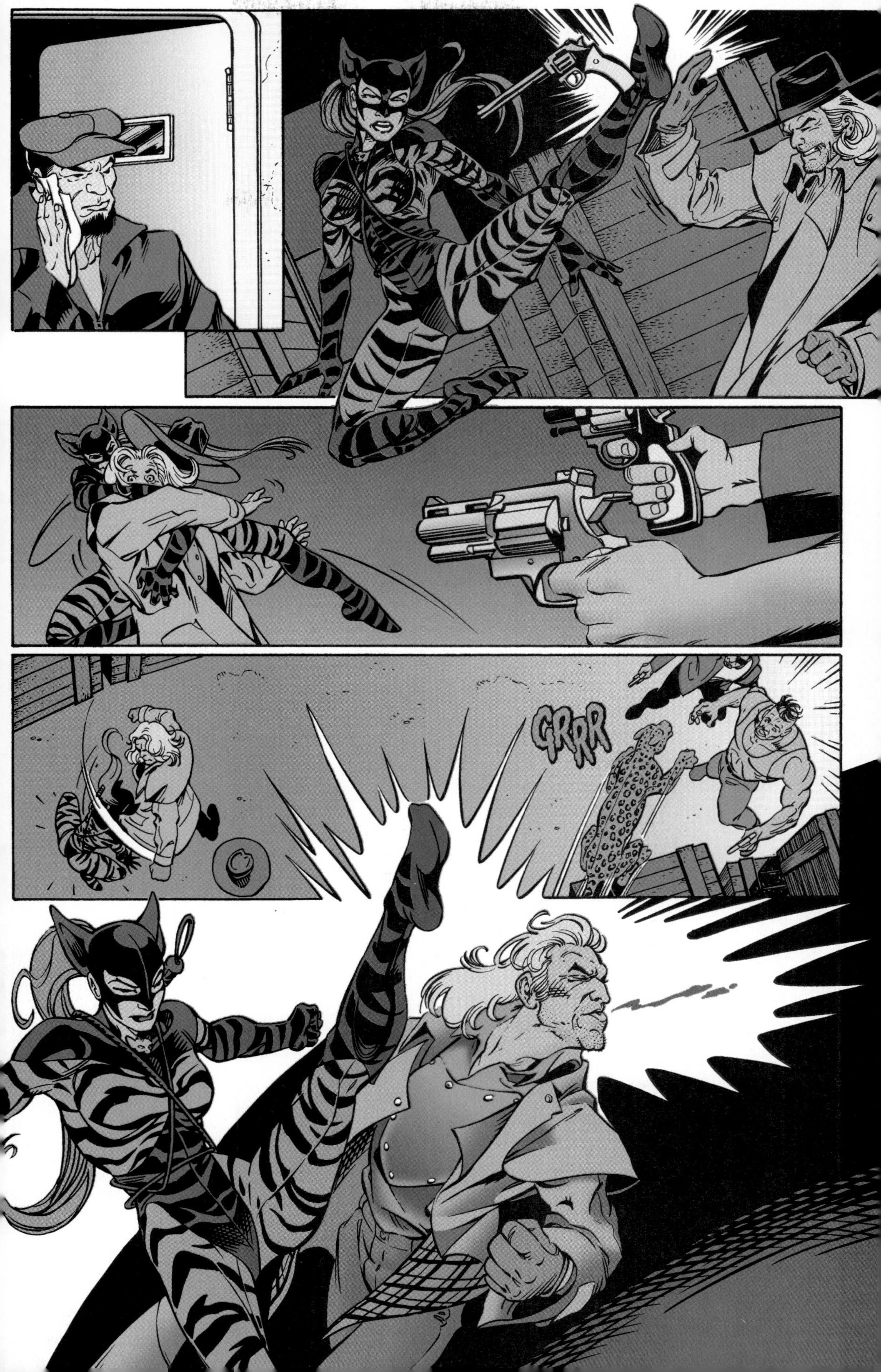
GRRR

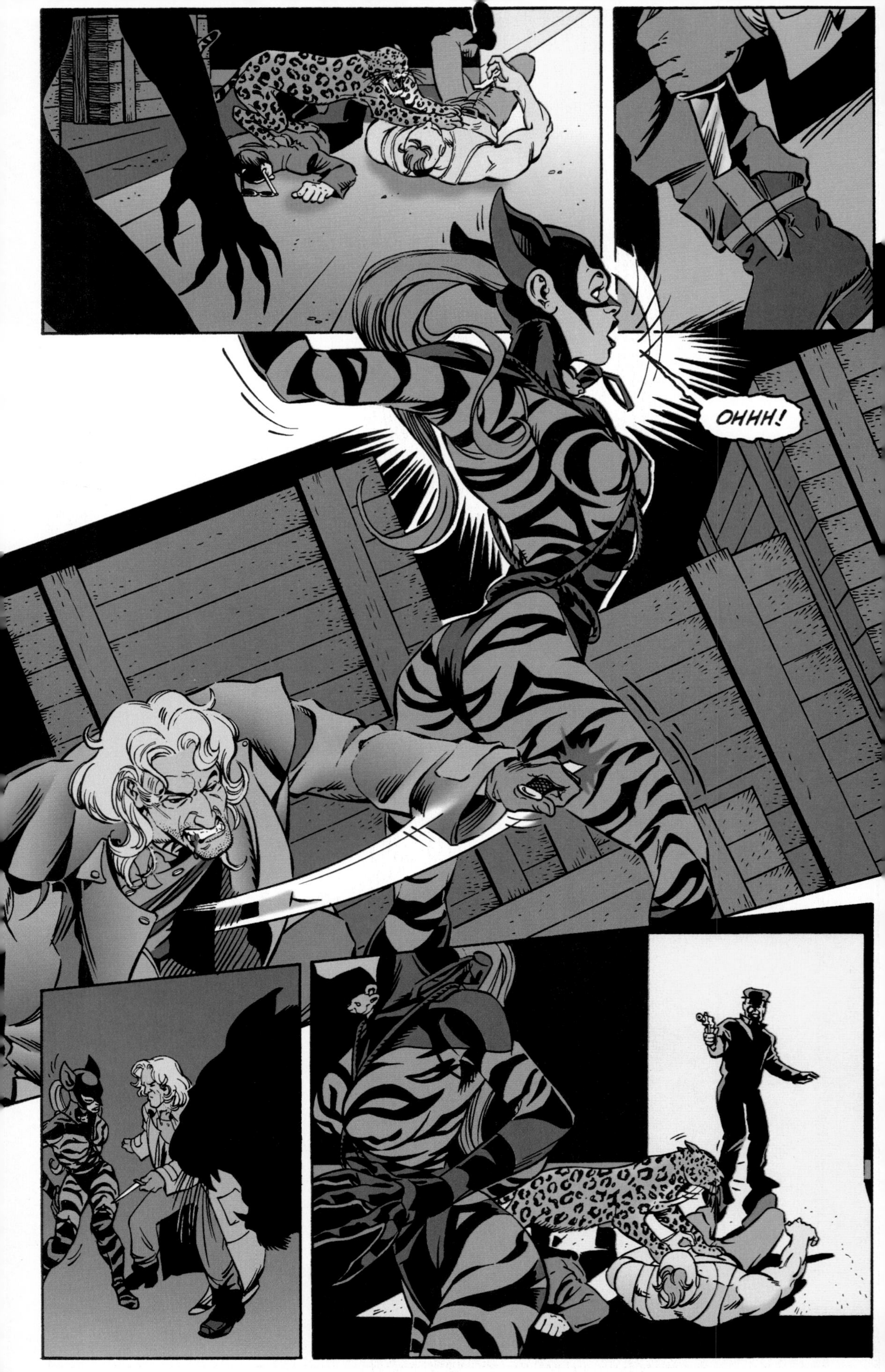
OHHH!

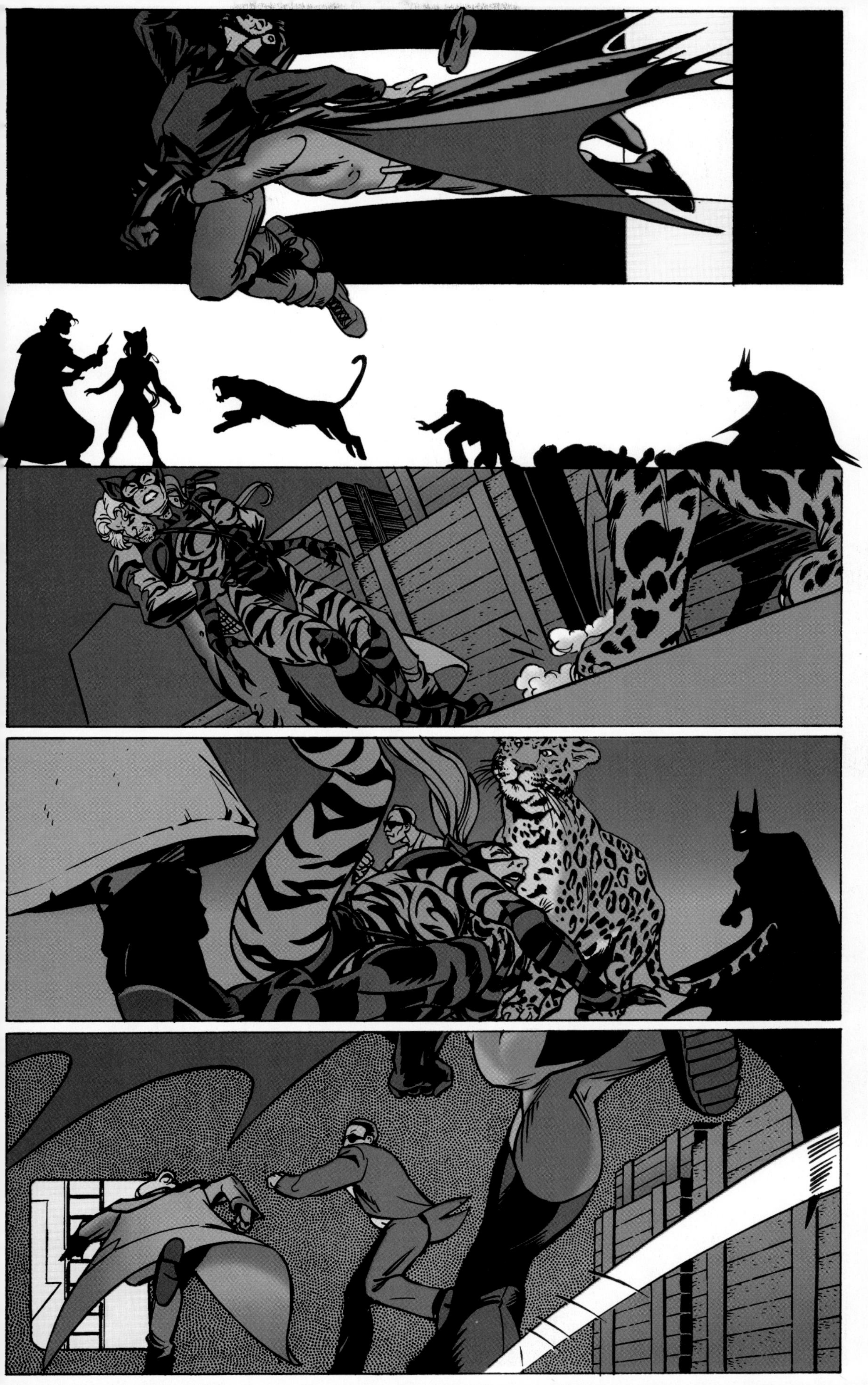

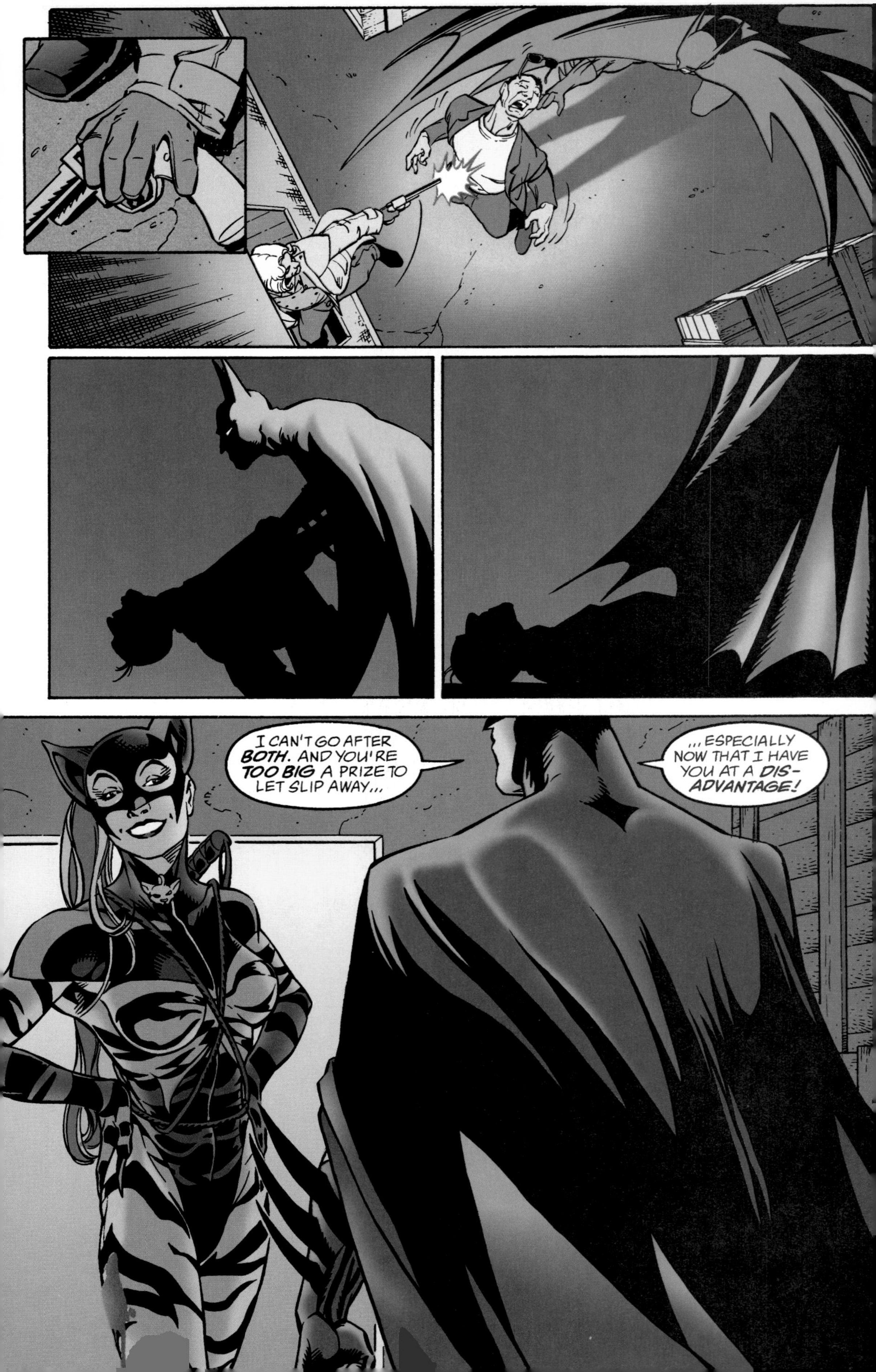
I CAN'T GO AFTER **BOTH**. AND YOU'RE **TOO BIG** A PRIZE TO LET SLIP AWAY...
...ESPECIALLY NOW THAT I HAVE YOU AT A ***DIS-ADVANTAGE!***

OUGH!
WHAT DISADVANTAGE, HANDSOME?
OH NO YOU DON'T!
EAT THIS, HANDSOME!

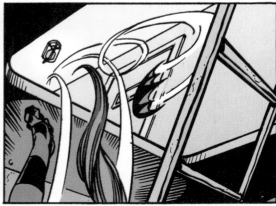

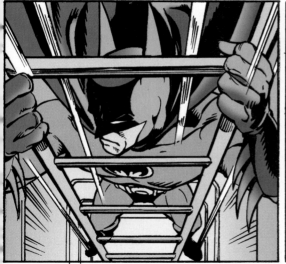

CATS HAVE **NINE** LIVES. HOW MANY DOES A **BATMAN** HAVE?

YOU THINK YOU CAN **STOP** ME SO **EASILY**, HANDSOME?

JUST BECAUSE I HAVE A **SOFT SPOT** IN MY HEART FOR YOU?

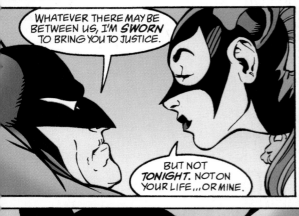

WHATEVER THERE MAY BE BETWEEN US, I'M **SWORN** TO BRING YOU TO JUSTICE.

BUT NOT **TONIGHT.** NOT ON YOUR LIFE... OR MINE.

YOU AND I HAVE SOME **OLD BUSINESS** TO FINISH...

PURRSONAL BUSINESS...

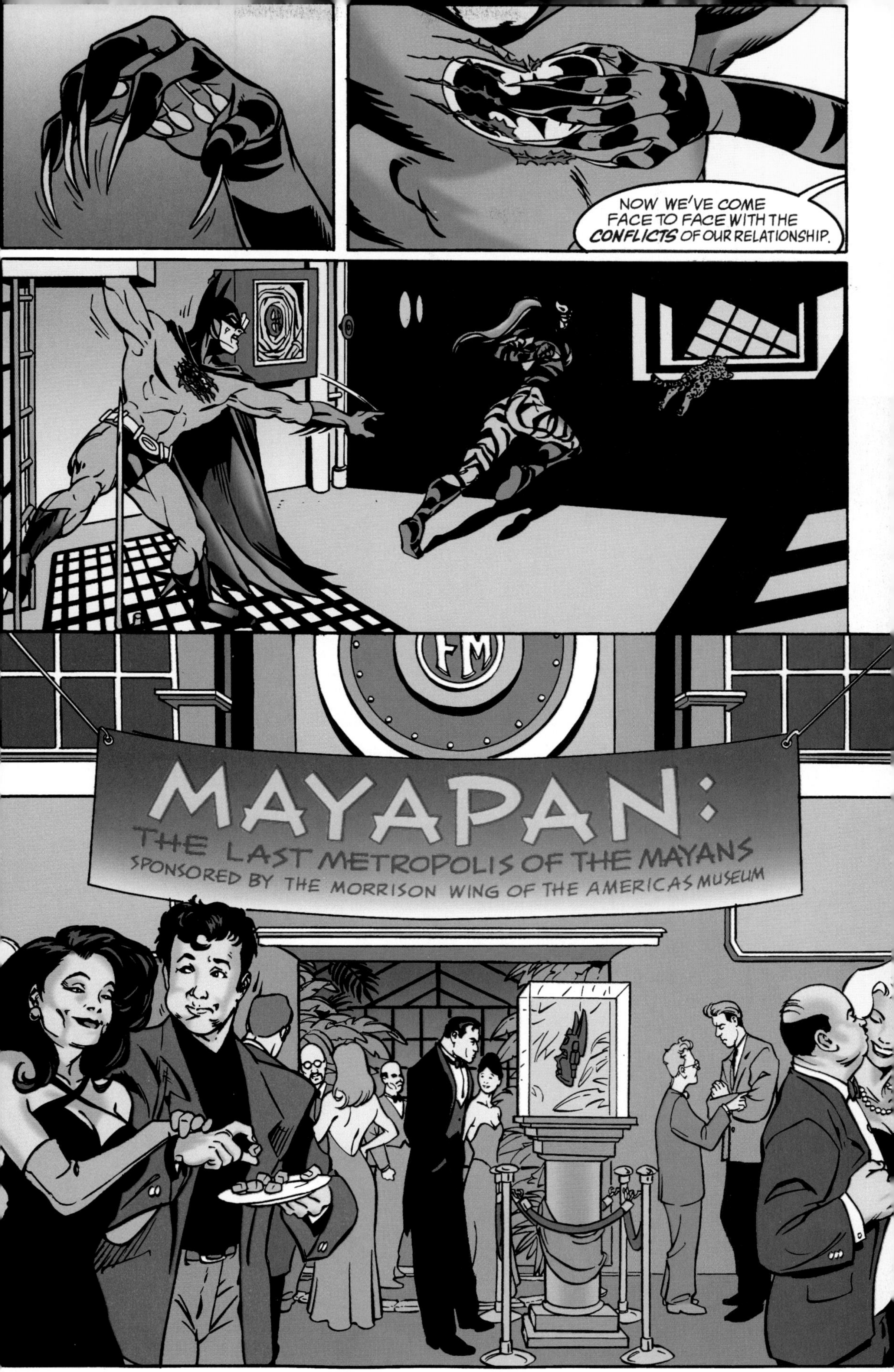
NOW WE'VE COME FACE TO FACE WITH THE CONFLICTS OF OUR RELATIONSHIP.
FM
MAYAPAN:
THE LAST METROPOLIS OF THE MAYANS
SPONSORED BY THE MORRISON WING OF THE AMERICAS MUSEUM

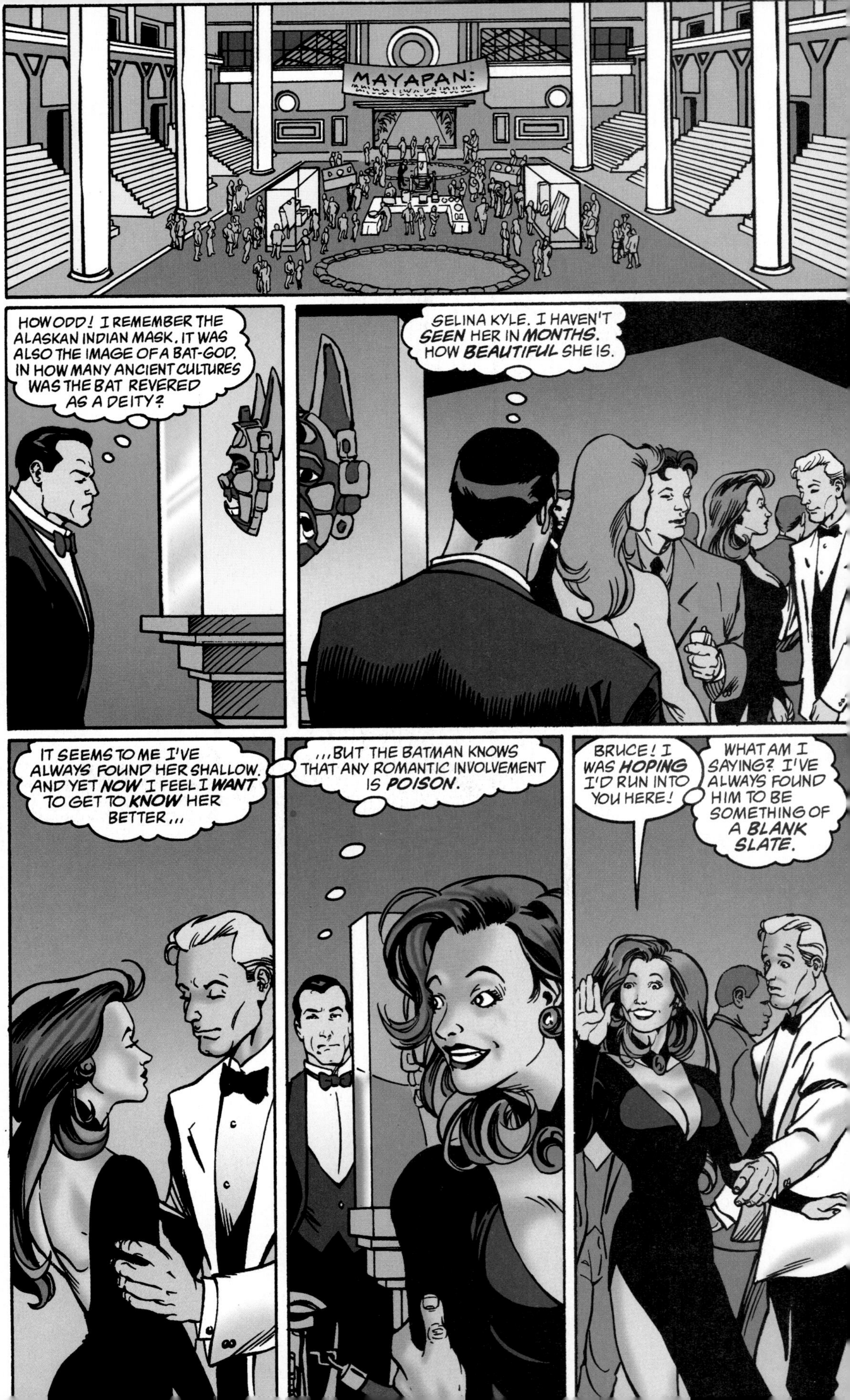
MAYAPAN:
HOW ODD! I REMEMBER THE ALASKAN INDIAN MASK. IT WAS ALSO THE IMAGE OF A BAT-GOD. IN HOW MANY ANCIENT CULTURES WAS THE BAT REVERED AS A DEITY?
SELINA KYLE. I HAVEN'T SEEN HER IN MONTHS. HOW BEAUTIFUL SHE IS.
IT SEEMS TO ME I'VE ALWAYS FOUND HER SHALLOW. AND YET NOW I FEEL I WANT TO GET TO KNOW HER BETTER...
...BUT THE BATMAN KNOWS THAT ANY ROMANTIC INVOLVEMENT IS POISON.
BRUCE! I WAS HOPING I'D RUN INTO YOU HERE!
WHAT AM I SAYING? I'VE ALWAYS FOUND HIM TO BE SOMETHING OF A BLANK SLATE.

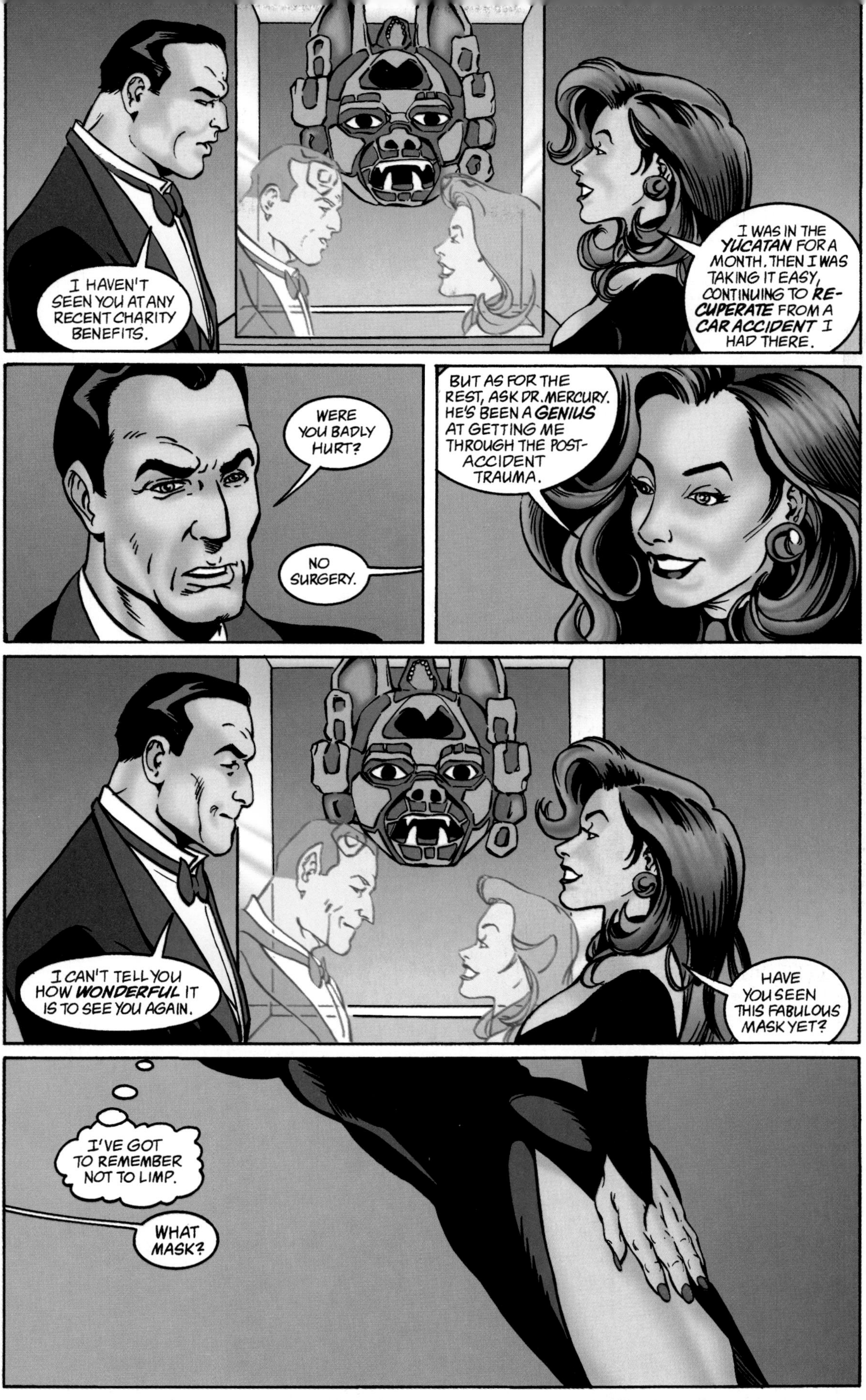
I HAVEN'T SEEN YOU AT ANY RECENT CHARITY BENEFITS.
I WAS IN THE YUCATAN FOR A MONTH. THEN I WAS TAKING IT EASY, CONTINUING TO RE-CUPERATE FROM A CAR ACCIDENT I HAD THERE.
WERE YOU BADLY HURT?
NO SURGERY.
BUT AS FOR THE REST, ASK DR. MERCURY. HE'S BEEN A GENIUS AT GETTING ME THROUGH THE POST-ACCIDENT TRAUMA.
I CAN'T TELL YOU HOW WONDERFUL IT IS TO SEE YOU AGAIN.
HAVE YOU SEEN THIS FABULOUS MASK YET?
I'VE GOT TO REMEMBER NOT TO LIMP.
WHAT MASK?

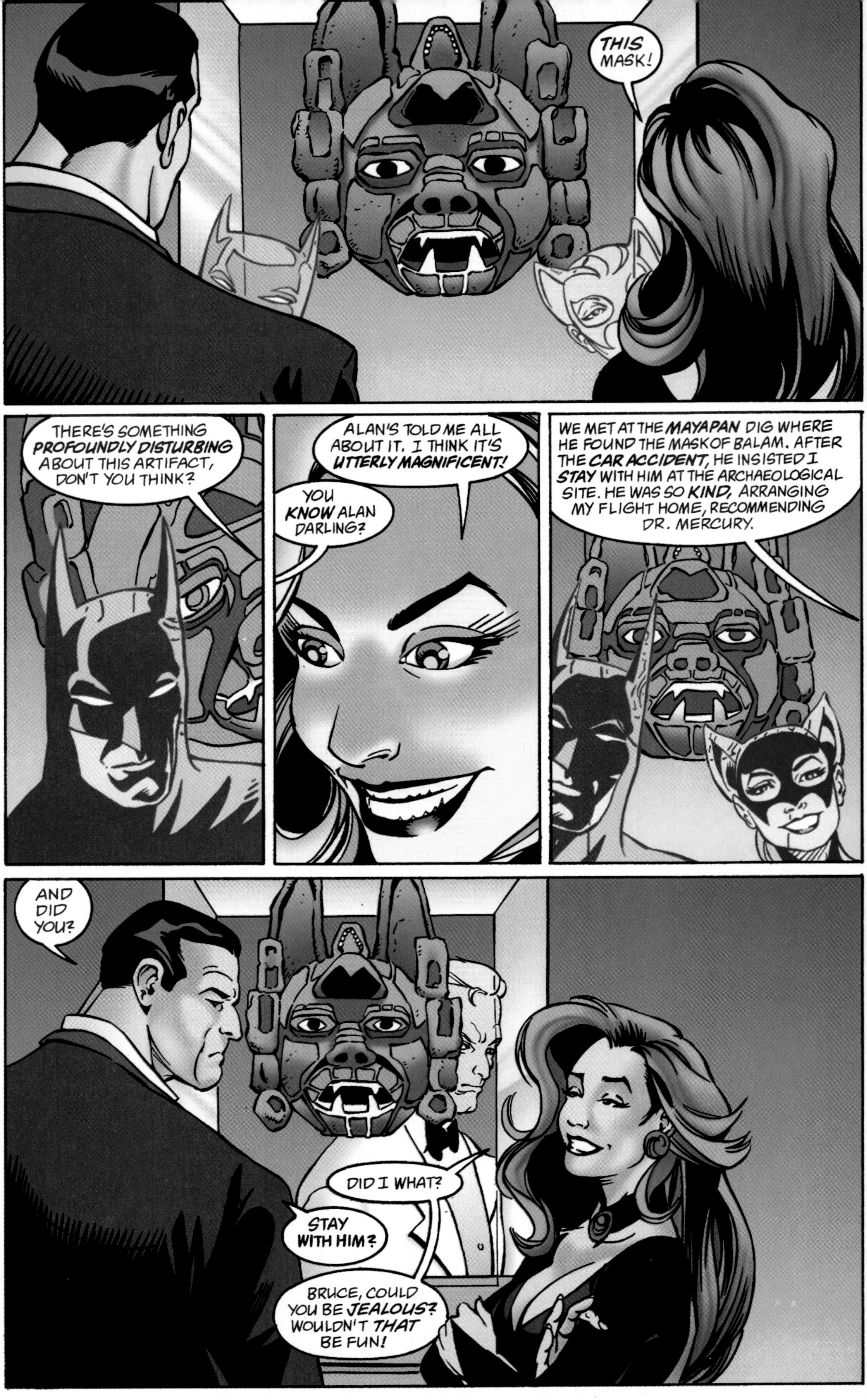
THIS MASK!
THERE'S SOMETHING PROFOUNDLY DISTURBING ABOUT THIS ARTIFACT, DON'T YOU THINK?
ALAN'S TOLD ME ALL ABOUT IT. I THINK IT'S UTTERLY MAGNIFICENT!
YOU KNOW ALAN DARLING?
WE MET AT THE MAYAPAN DIG WHERE HE FOUND THE MASK OF BALAM. AFTER THE CAR ACCIDENT, HE INSISTED I STAY WITH HIM AT THE ARCHAEOLOGICAL SITE. HE WAS SO KIND, ARRANGING MY FLIGHT HOME, RECOMMENDING DR. MERCURY.
AND DID YOU?
DID I WHAT?
STAY WITH HIM?
BRUCE, COULD YOU BE JEALOUS? WOULDN'T THAT BE FUN!

IT *WOULD?*

OF COURSE! I NEVER THOUGHT YOU'D TAKE AN INTEREST IN ME-- OR *ANY* OTHER WOMAN.

BRUCE WAYNE, THE ETERNAL BACHELOR!

IT'S TRUE. WOMEN NEVER HAD MUCH PLACE IN MY LIFE.

BUT WHY NOT?

TO TELL YOU THE *TRUTH,* I--

MAYOR KROL!

MISS KYLE! ALAN DARLING WANTS YOU TO CUT THE *CEREMONIAL CORD* MARKING THE PUBLIC *INTRODUCTION* OF THE MASK OF BALAM!

HURRY NOW, THE PRESS IS WAITING!

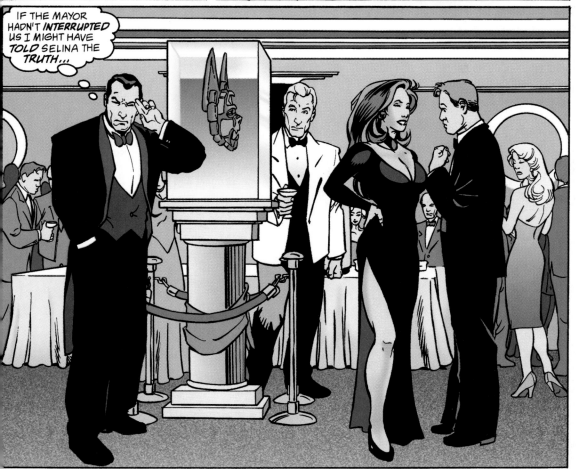

IF THE MAYOR HADN'T *INTERRUPTED* US I MIGHT HAVE *TOLD* SELINA THE *TRUTH...*

WHAT'S *COME OVER* ME? I'VE ALWAYS BEEN ABLE TO *MAINTAIN* THE *SEPARATION* OF CHURCH AND STATE...

... BRUCE WAYNE AND THE BATMAN...

BUT TONIGHT, FOR THE *FIRST TIME,* I FELT THE MASK I'VE LIVED WITH EVER SINCE I *BECAME* THE BATMAN *SLIP* OUT OF PLACE.

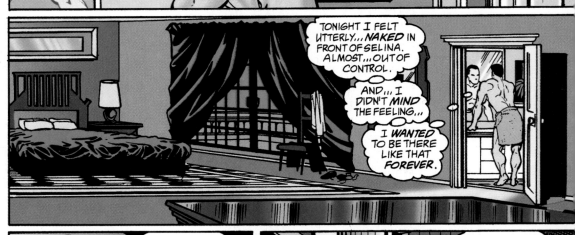

TONIGHT I FELT UTTERLY... *NAKED* IN FRONT OF SELINA. ALMOST... OUT OF CONTROL.

AND... I DIDN'T *MIND* THE FEELING...

I *WANTED* TO BE THERE LIKE THAT *FOREVER.*

OH, ALAN, THAT WAS FUNNY! YOU TELL THE *BEST* STORIES.

SELINA, I FIND YOU *CAPTIVATING.* THANK YOU--

Victoria's FINE FOOD

-- FOR SHARING MY TENT IN MAYAPAN.

AND THANK YOU FOR TAKING CARE OF ME AFTER THE ACCIDENT.

AND WHY NOT? IF MY PEOPLE HADN'T FOUND YOU IN THAT DITCH, *UNCONSCIOUS,* I DON'T KNOW WHAT WOULD HAVE *HAPPENED* TO YOU. MY TEAM HAD THE *ONLY* DOCTOR WITHIN MILES.

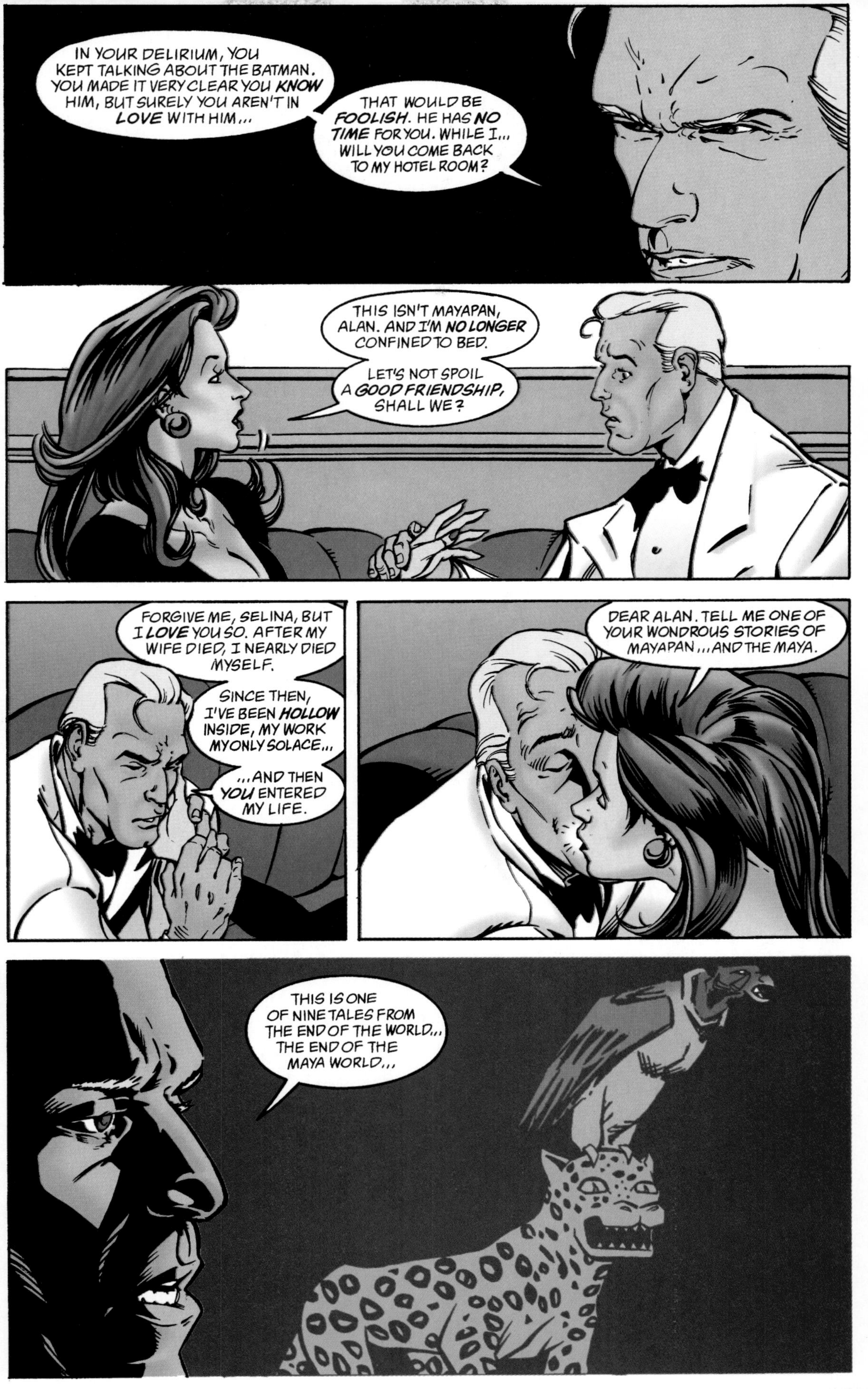
IN YOUR DELIRIUM, YOU KEPT TALKING ABOUT THE BATMAN. YOU MADE IT VERY CLEAR YOU KNOW HIM, BUT SURELY YOU AREN'T IN LOVE WITH HIM...
THAT WOULD BE FOOLISH. HE HAS NO TIME FOR YOU. WHILE I... WILL YOU COME BACK TO MY HOTEL ROOM?
THIS ISN'T MAYAPAN, ALAN. AND I'M NO LONGER CONFINED TO BED.
LET'S NOT SPOIL A GOOD FRIENDSHIP, SHALL WE?
FORGIVE ME, SELINA, BUT I LOVE YOU SO. AFTER MY WIFE DIED, I NEARLY DIED MYSELF.
SINCE THEN, I'VE BEEN HOLLOW INSIDE, MY WORK MY ONLY SOLACE...
...AND THEN YOU ENTERED MY LIFE.
DEAR ALAN. TELL ME ONE OF YOUR WONDROUS STORIES OF MAYAPAN... AND THE MAYA.
THIS IS ONE OF NINE TALES FROM THE END OF THE WORLD... THE END OF THE MAYA WORLD...

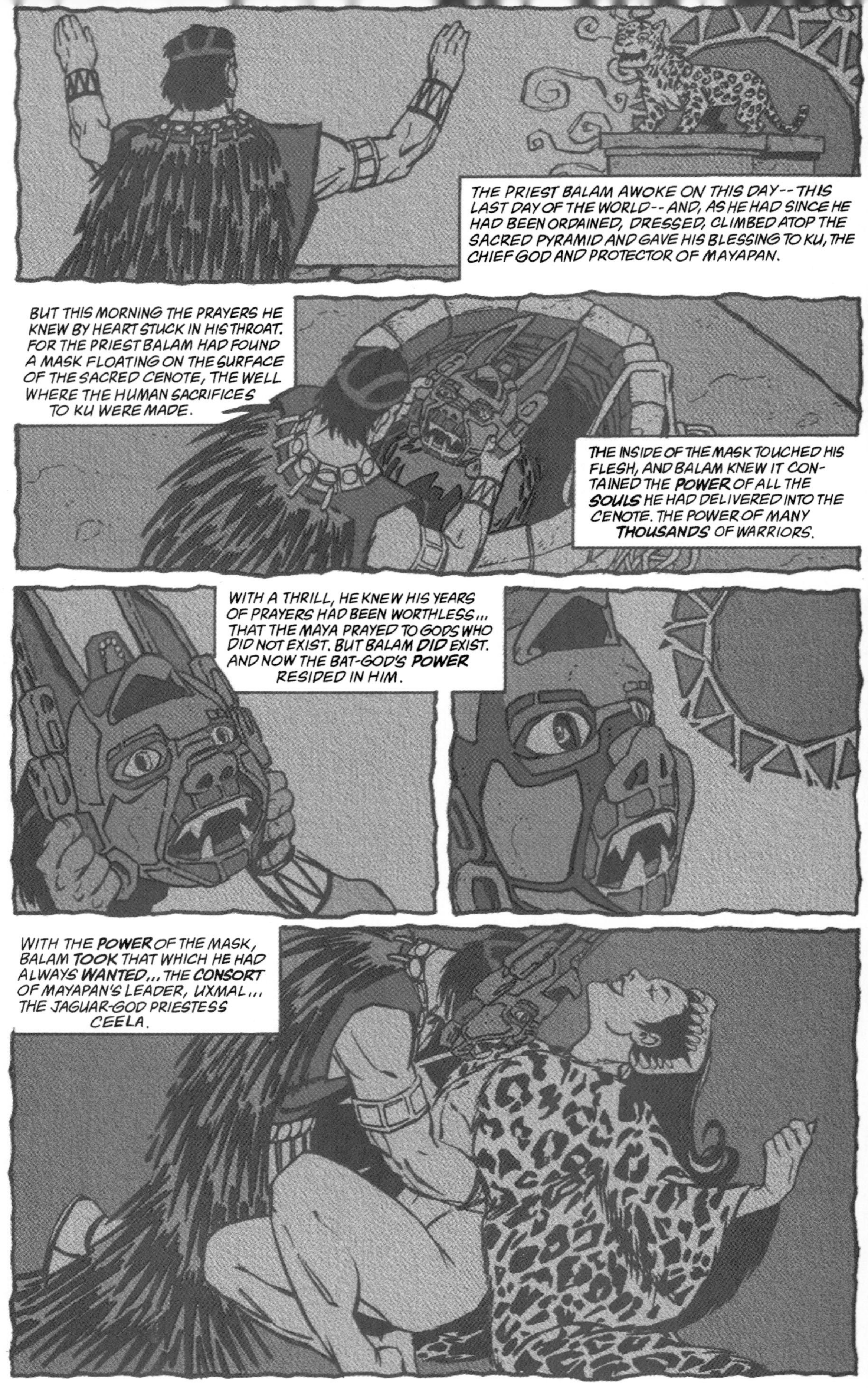
THE PRIEST BALAM AWOKE ON THIS DAY--THIS LAST DAY OF THE WORLD--AND, AS HE HAD SINCE HE HAD BEEN ORDAINED, DRESSED, CLIMBED ATOP THE SACRED PYRAMID AND GAVE HIS BLESSING TO KU, THE CHIEF GOD AND PROTECTOR OF MAYAPAN.
BUT THIS MORNING THE PRAYERS HE KNEW BY HEART STUCK IN HIS THROAT. FOR THE PRIEST BALAM HAD FOUND A MASK FLOATING ON THE SURFACE OF THE SACRED CENOTE, THE WELL WHERE THE HUMAN SACRIFICES TO KU WERE MADE.
THE INSIDE OF THE MASK TOUCHED HIS FLESH, AND BALAM KNEW IT CONTAINED THE POWER OF ALL THE SOULS HE HAD DELIVERED INTO THE CENOTE. THE POWER OF MANY THOUSANDS OF WARRIORS.
WITH A THRILL, HE KNEW HIS YEARS OF PRAYERS HAD BEEN WORTHLESS... THAT THE MAYA PRAYED TO GODS WHO DID NOT EXIST. BUT BALAM DID EXIST. AND NOW THE BAT-GOD'S POWER RESIDED IN HIM.
WITH THE POWER OF THE MASK, BALAM TOOK THAT WHICH HE HAD ALWAYS WANTED... THE CONSORT OF MAYAPAN'S LEADER, UXMAL... THE JAGUAR-GOD PRIESTESS CEELA.

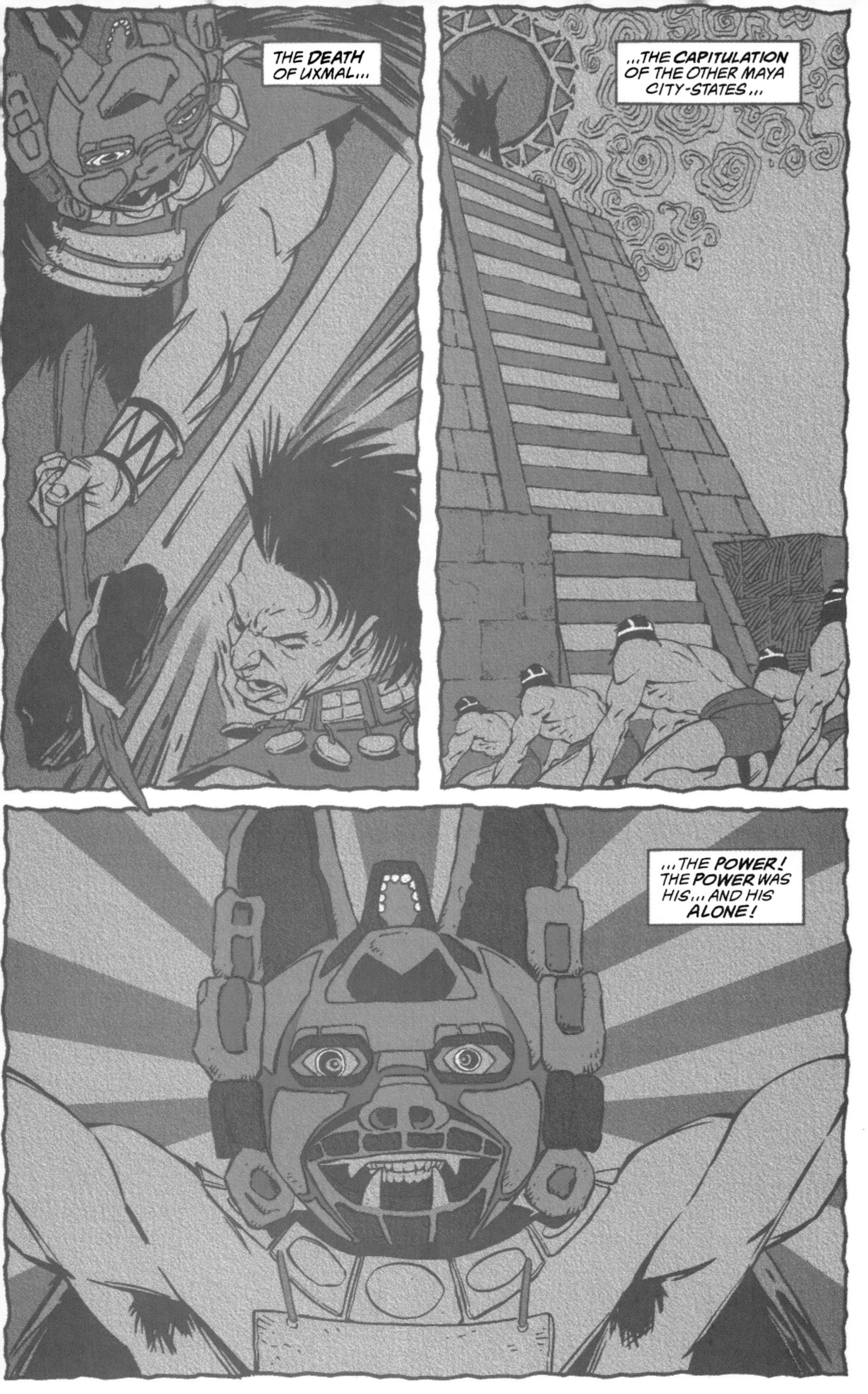
THE DEATH OF UXMAL...
...THE CAPITULATION OF THE OTHER MAYA CITY-STATES...
...THE POWER! THE POWER WAS HIS... AND HIS ALONE!

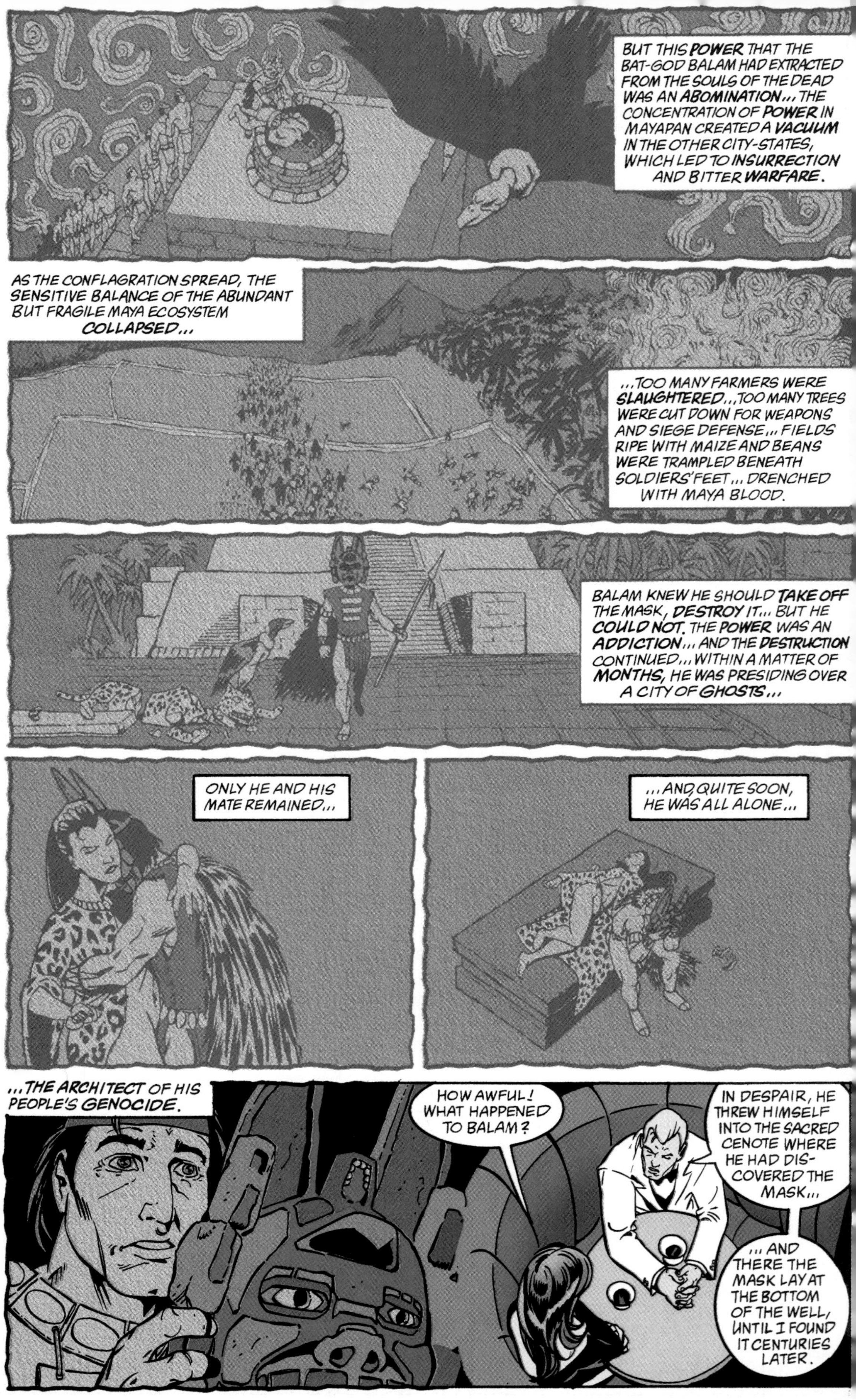
BUT THIS POWER THAT THE BAT-GOD BALAM HAD EXTRACTED FROM THE SOULS OF THE DEAD WAS AN ABOMINATION... THE CONCENTRATION OF POWER IN MAYAPAN CREATED A VACUUM IN THE OTHER CITY-STATES, WHICH LED TO INSURRECTION AND BITTER WARFARE.
AS THE CONFLAGRATION SPREAD, THE SENSITIVE BALANCE OF THE ABUNDANT BUT FRAGILE MAYA ECOSYSTEM COLLAPSED...
...TOO MANY FARMERS WERE SLAUGHTERED...TOO MANY TREES WERE CUT DOWN FOR WEAPONS AND SIEGE DEFENSE... FIELDS RIPE WITH MAIZE AND BEANS WERE TRAMPLED BENEATH SOLDIERS' FEET... DRENCHED WITH MAYA BLOOD.
BALAM KNEW HE SHOULD TAKE OFF THE MASK, DESTROY IT... BUT HE COULD NOT. THE POWER WAS AN ADDICTION... AND THE DESTRUCTION CONTINUED... WITHIN A MATTER OF MONTHS, HE WAS PRESIDING OVER A CITY OF GHOSTS...
ONLY HE AND HIS MATE REMAINED...
...AND, QUITE SOON, HE WAS ALL ALONE...
...THE ARCHITECT OF HIS PEOPLE'S GENOCIDE.
HOW AWFUL! WHAT HAPPENED TO BALAM?
IN DESPAIR, HE THREW HIMSELF INTO THE SACRED CENOTE WHERE HE HAD DIS-COVERED THE MASK...
...AND THERE THE MASK LAY AT THE BOTTOM OF THE WELL, UNTIL I FOUND IT CENTURIES LATER.

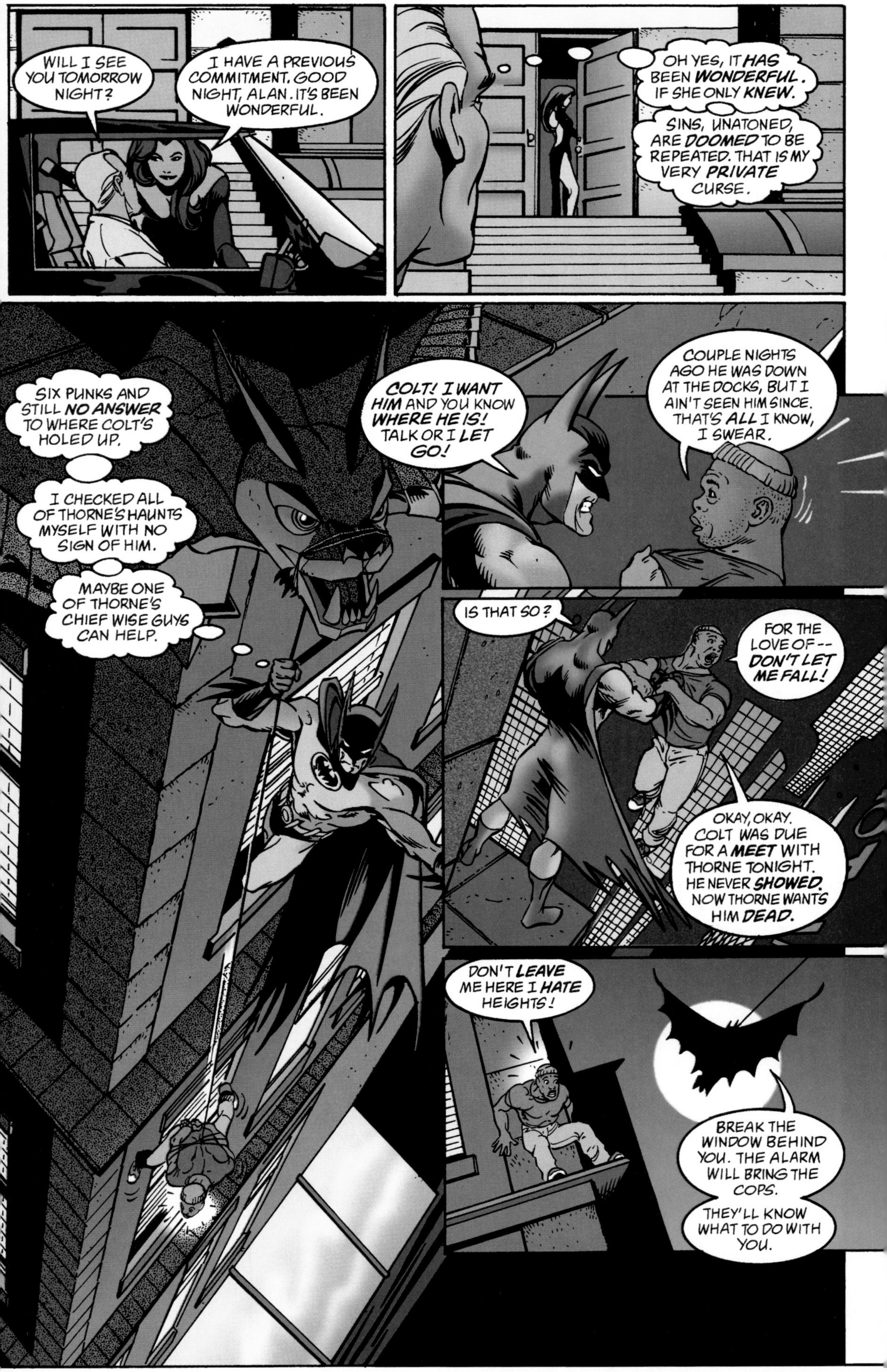
WILL I SEE YOU TOMORROW NIGHT?
I HAVE A PREVIOUS COMMITMENT. GOOD NIGHT, ALAN. IT'S BEEN WONDERFUL.
OH YES, IT HAS BEEN WONDERFUL. IF SHE ONLY KNEW.
SINS, UNATONED, ARE DOOMED TO BE REPEATED. THAT IS MY VERY PRIVATE CURSE.
SIX PUNKS AND STILL NO ANSWER TO WHERE COLT'S HOLED UP.
I CHECKED ALL OF THORNE'S HAUNTS MYSELF WITH NO SIGN OF HIM.
MAYBE ONE OF THORNE'S CHIEF WISE GUYS CAN HELP.
COLT! I WANT HIM AND YOU KNOW WHERE HE IS! TALK OR I LET GO!
COUPLE NIGHTS AGO HE WAS DOWN AT THE DOCKS, BUT I AIN'T SEEN HIM SINCE. THAT'S ALL I KNOW, I SWEAR.
IS THAT SO?
FOR THE LOVE OF -- DON'T LET ME FALL!
OKAY, OKAY. COLT WAS DUE FOR A MEET WITH THORNE TONIGHT. HE NEVER SHOWED. NOW THORNE WANTS HIM DEAD.
DON'T LEAVE ME HERE I HATE HEIGHTS!
BREAK THE WINDOW BEHIND YOU. THE ALARM WILL BRING THE COPS.
THEY'LL KNOW WHAT TO DO WITH YOU.

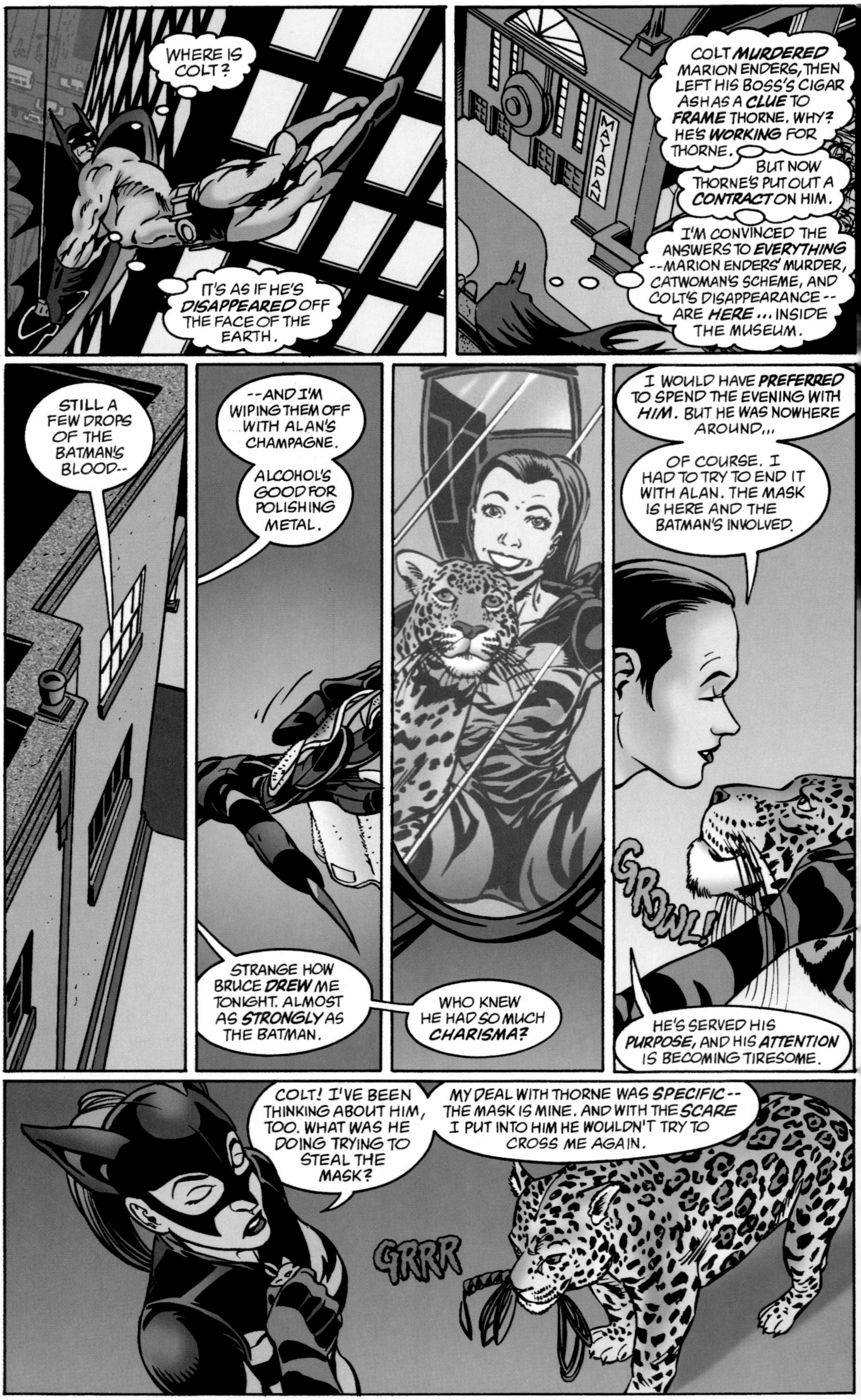

WHERE IS COLT?
IT'S AS IF HE'S DISAPPEARED OFF THE FACE OF THE EARTH.
COLT MURDERED MARION ENDERS, THEN LEFT HIS BOSS'S CIGAR ASH AS A CLUE TO FRAME THORNE. WHY? HE'S WORKING FOR THORNE.
BUT NOW THORNE'S PUT OUT A CONTRACT ON HIM.
I'M CONVINCED THE ANSWERS TO EVERYTHING --MARION ENDERS' MURDER, CATWOMAN'S SCHEME, AND COLT'S DISAPPEARANCE -- ARE HERE... INSIDE THE MUSEUM.
MAYAPAN
STILL A FEW DROPS OF THE BATMAN'S BLOOD--
--AND I'M WIPING THEM OFF WITH ALAN'S CHAMPAGNE.
ALCOHOL'S GOOD FOR POLISHING METAL.
STRANGE HOW BRUCE DREW ME TONIGHT. ALMOST AS STRONGLY AS THE BATMAN.
WHO KNEW HE HAD SO MUCH CHARISMA?
I WOULD HAVE PREFERRED TO SPEND THE EVENING WITH HIM. BUT HE WAS NOWHERE AROUND...
OF COURSE. I HAD TO TRY TO END IT WITH ALAN. THE MASK IS HERE AND THE BATMAN'S INVOLVED.
GROWL!
HE'S SERVED HIS PURPOSE, AND HIS ATTENTION IS BECOMING TIRESOME.
COLT! I'VE BEEN THINKING ABOUT HIM, TOO. WHAT WAS HE DOING TRYING TO STEAL THE MASK?
MY DEAL WITH THORNE WAS SPECIFIC-- THE MASK IS MINE. AND WITH THE SCARE I PUT INTO HIM HE WOULDN'T TRY TO CROSS ME AGAIN.
GRRR

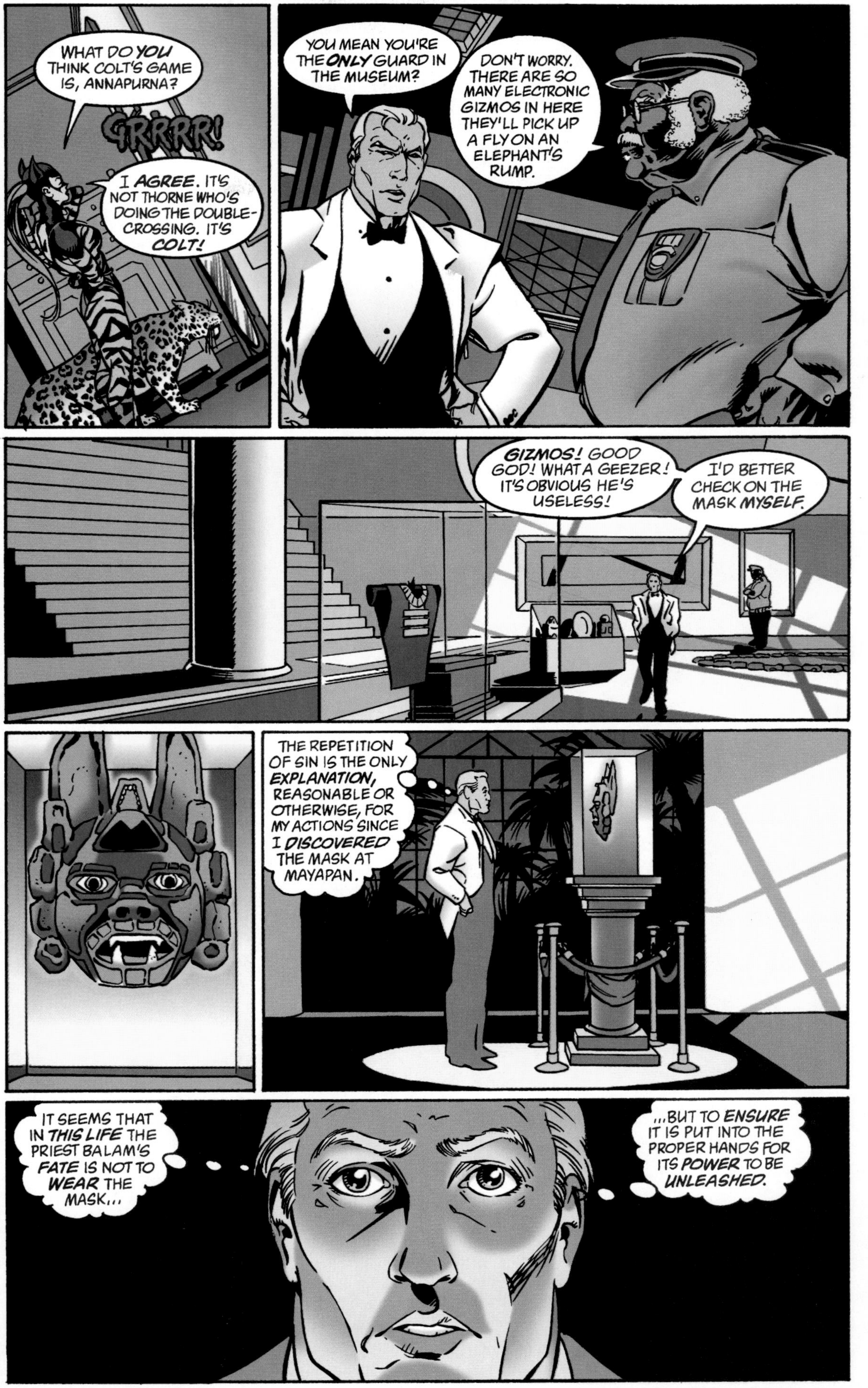
WHAT DO YOU THINK COLT'S GAME IS, ANNAPURNA?
GRRRR!
I AGREE. IT'S NOT THORNE WHO'S DOING THE DOUBLE-CROSSING. IT'S COLT!
YOU MEAN YOU'RE THE ONLY GUARD IN THE MUSEUM?
DON'T WORRY. THERE ARE SO MANY ELECTRONIC GIZMOS IN HERE THEY'LL PICK UP A FLY ON AN ELEPHANT'S RUMP.
GIZMOS! GOOD GOD! WHAT A GEEZER! IT'S OBVIOUS HE'S USELESS!
I'D BETTER CHECK ON THE MASK MYSELF.
THE REPETITION OF SIN IS THE ONLY EXPLANATION, REASONABLE OR OTHERWISE, FOR MY ACTIONS SINCE I DISCOVERED THE MASK AT MAYAPAN.
IT SEEMS THAT IN THIS LIFE THE PRIEST BALAM'S FATE IS NOT TO WEAR THE MASK...
...BUT TO ENSURE IT IS PUT INTO THE PROPER HANDS FOR ITS POWER TO BE UNLEASHED.

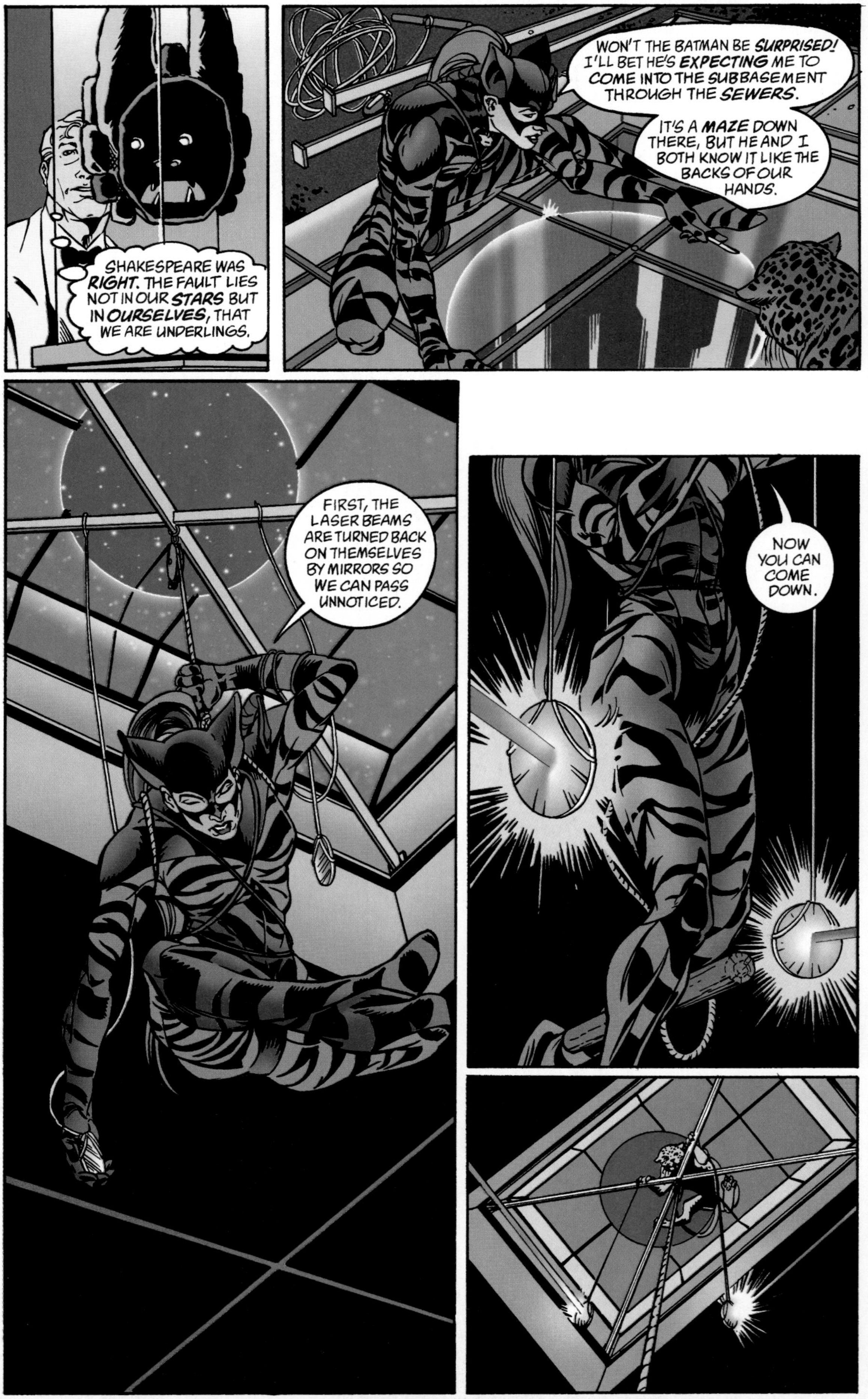
SHAKESPEARE WAS RIGHT. THE FAULT LIES NOT IN OUR STARS BUT IN OURSELVES, THAT WE ARE UNDERLINGS.
WON'T THE BATMAN BE SURPRISED! I'LL BET HE'S EXPECTING ME TO COME INTO THE SUBBASEMENT THROUGH THE SEWERS.
IT'S A MAZE DOWN THERE, BUT HE AND I BOTH KNOW IT LIKE THE BACKS OF OUR HANDS.
FIRST, THE LASER BEAMS ARE TURNED BACK ON THEMSELVES BY MIRRORS SO WE CAN PASS UNNOTICED.
NOW YOU CAN COME DOWN.

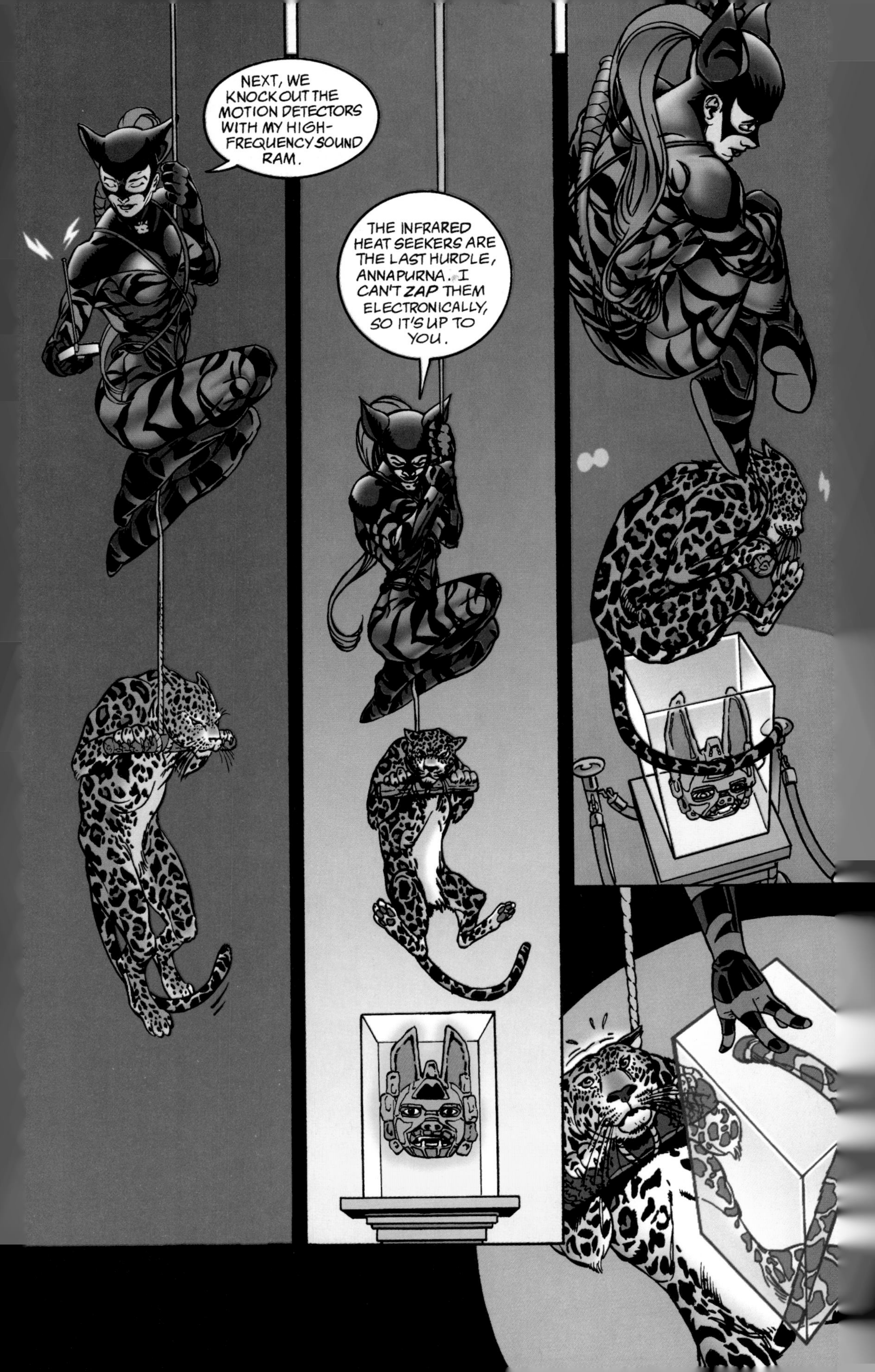
NEXT, WE KNOCK OUT THE MOTION DETECTORS WITH MY HIGH-FREQUENCY SOUND RAM.
THE INFRARED HEAT SEEKERS ARE THE LAST HURDLE, ANNAPURNA. I CAN'T ZAP THEM ELECTRONICALLY, SO IT'S UP TO YOU.

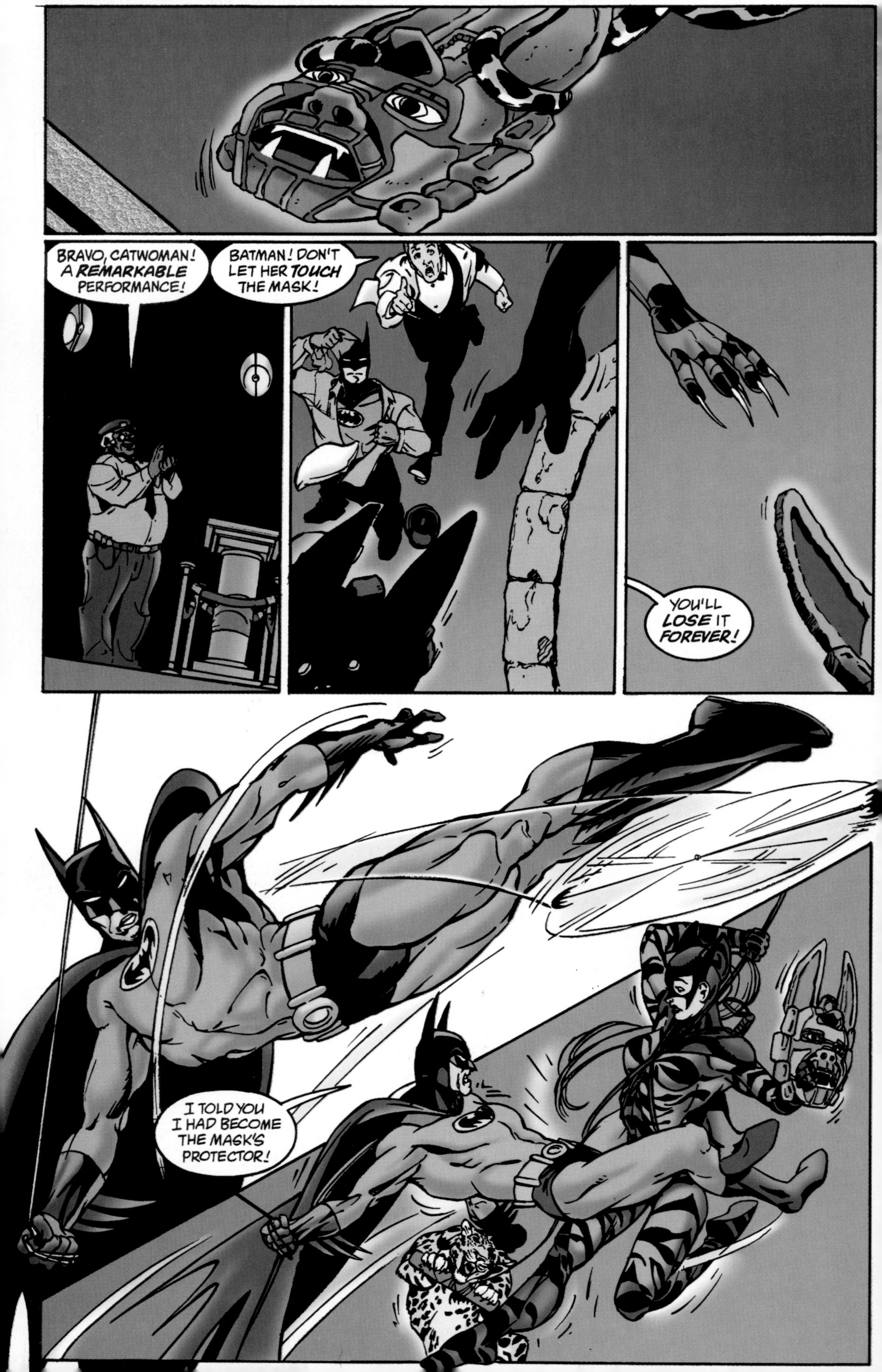
BRAVO, CATWOMAN! A REMARKABLE PERFORMANCE!
BATMAN! DON'T LET HER TOUCH THE MASK!
YOU'LL LOSE IT FOREVER!
I TOLD YOU I HAD BECOME THE MASK'S PROTECTOR!

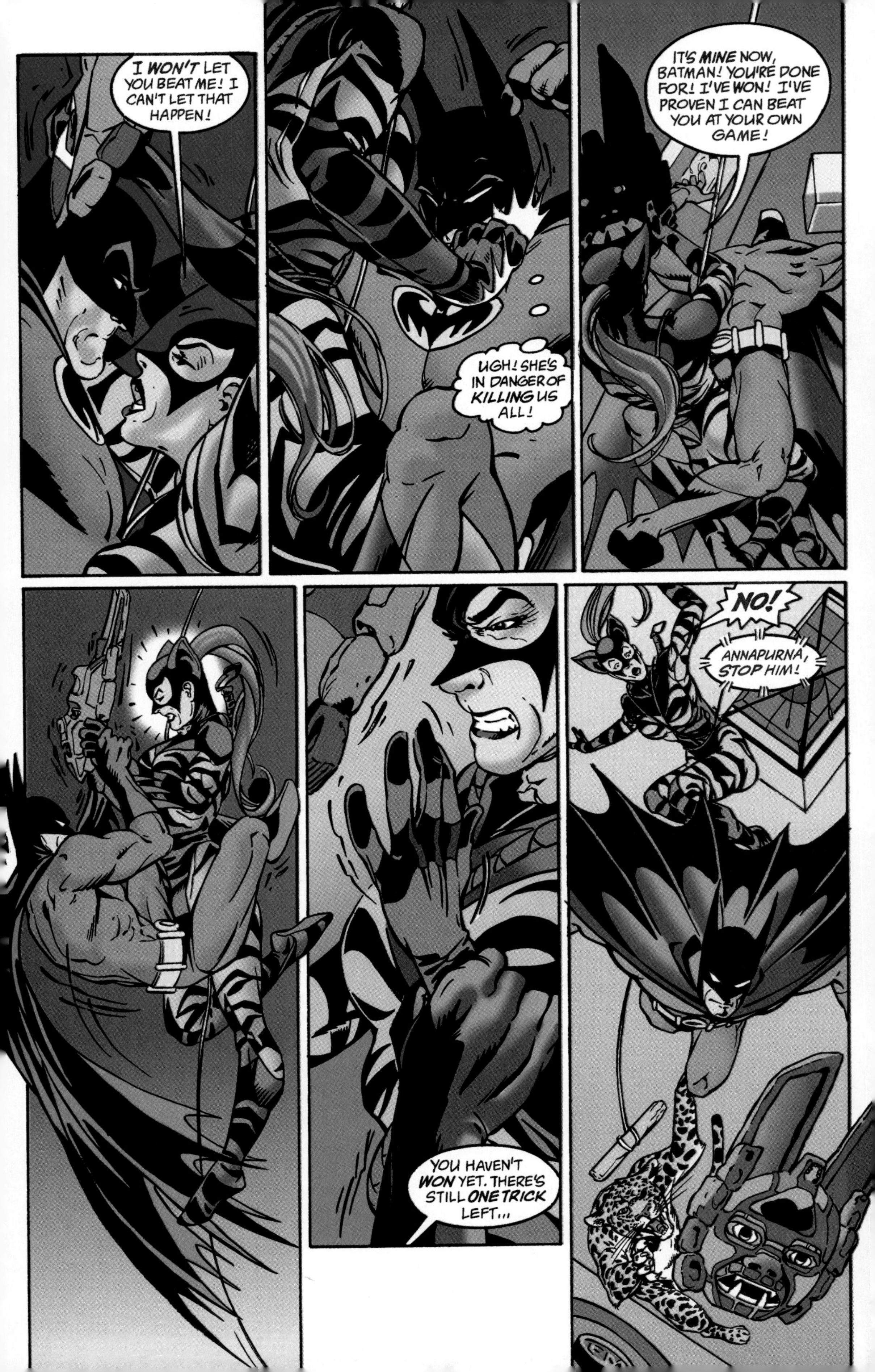
I WON'T LET YOU BEAT ME! I CAN'T LET THAT HAPPEN!
UGH! SHE'S IN DANGER OF KILLING US ALL!
IT'S MINE NOW, BATMAN! YOU'RE DONE FOR! I'VE WON! I'VE PROVEN I CAN BEAT YOU AT YOUR OWN GAME!
YOU HAVEN'T WON YET. THERE'S STILL ONE TRICK LEFT...
NO!
ANNAPURNA, STOP HIM!

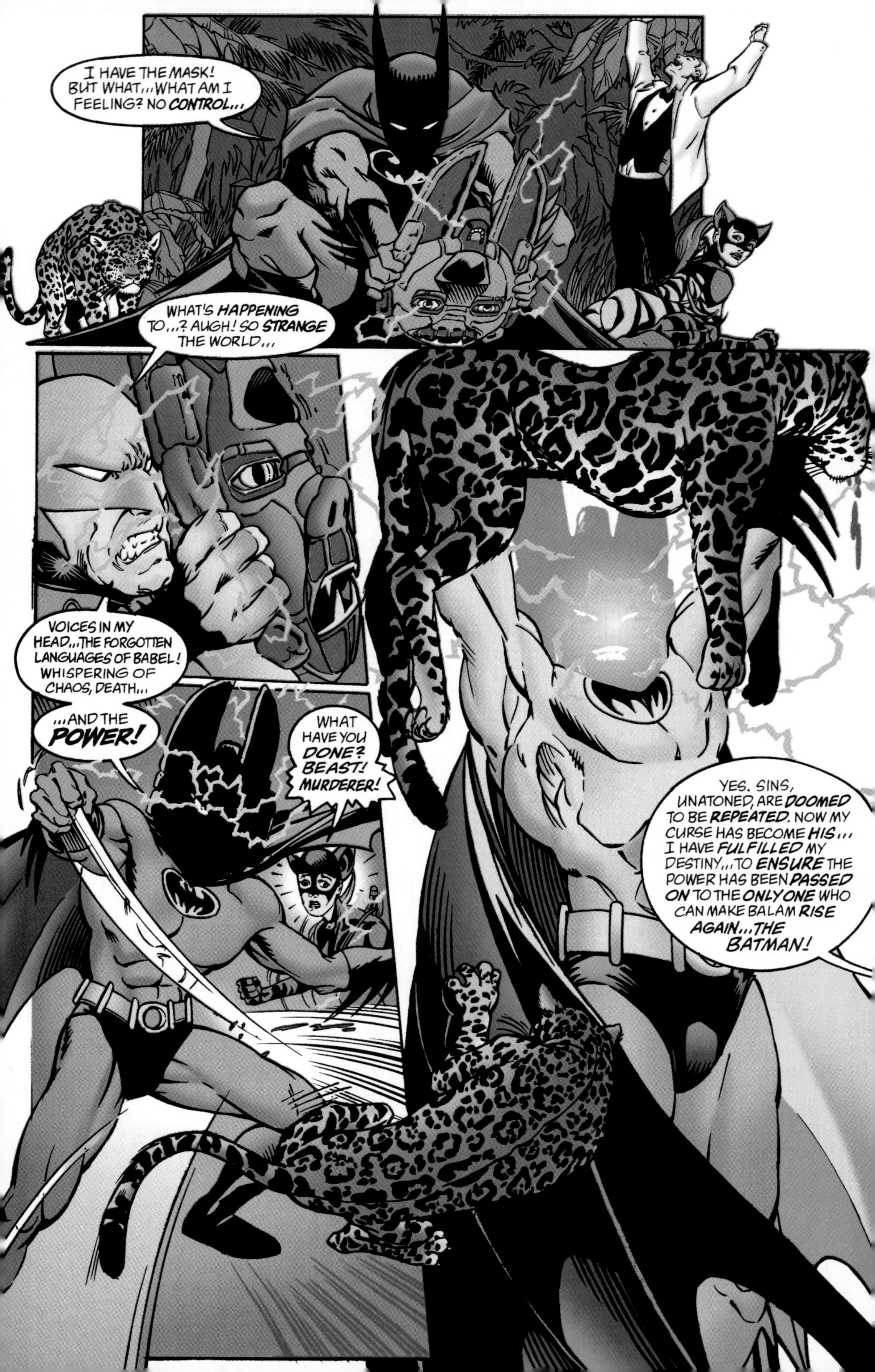
I HAVE THE MASK! BUT WHAT... WHAT AM I FEELING? NO CONTROL...
WHAT'S HAPPENING TO...? AUGH! SO STRANGE THE WORLD...
VOICES IN MY HEAD... THE FORGOTTEN LANGUAGES OF BABEL! WHISPERING OF CHAOS, DEATH...
...AND THE POWER!
WHAT HAVE YOU DONE? BEAST! MURDERER!
YES. SINS, UNATONED, ARE DOOMED TO BE REPEATED. NOW MY CURSE HAS BECOME HIS... I HAVE FULFILLED MY DESTINY... TO ENSURE THE POWER HAS BEEN PASSED ON TO THE ONLY ONE WHO CAN MAKE BALAM RISE AGAIN... THE BATMAN!

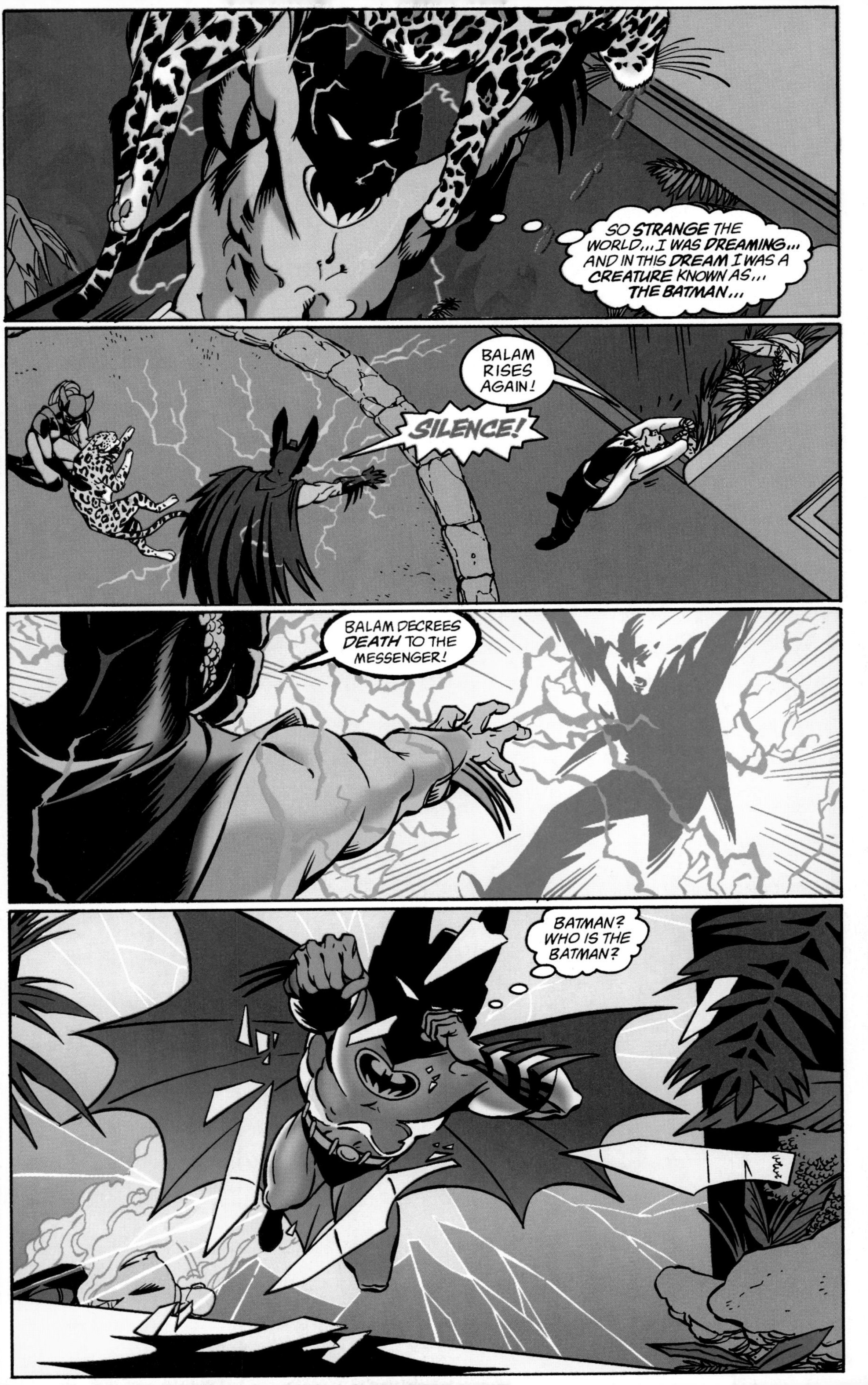
SO STRANGE THE WORLD... I WAS DREAMING... AND IN THIS DREAM I WAS A CREATURE KNOWN AS... THE BATMAN...
BALAM RISES AGAIN!
SILENCE!
BALAM DECREES DEATH TO THE MESSENGER!
BATMAN? WHO IS THE BATMAN?

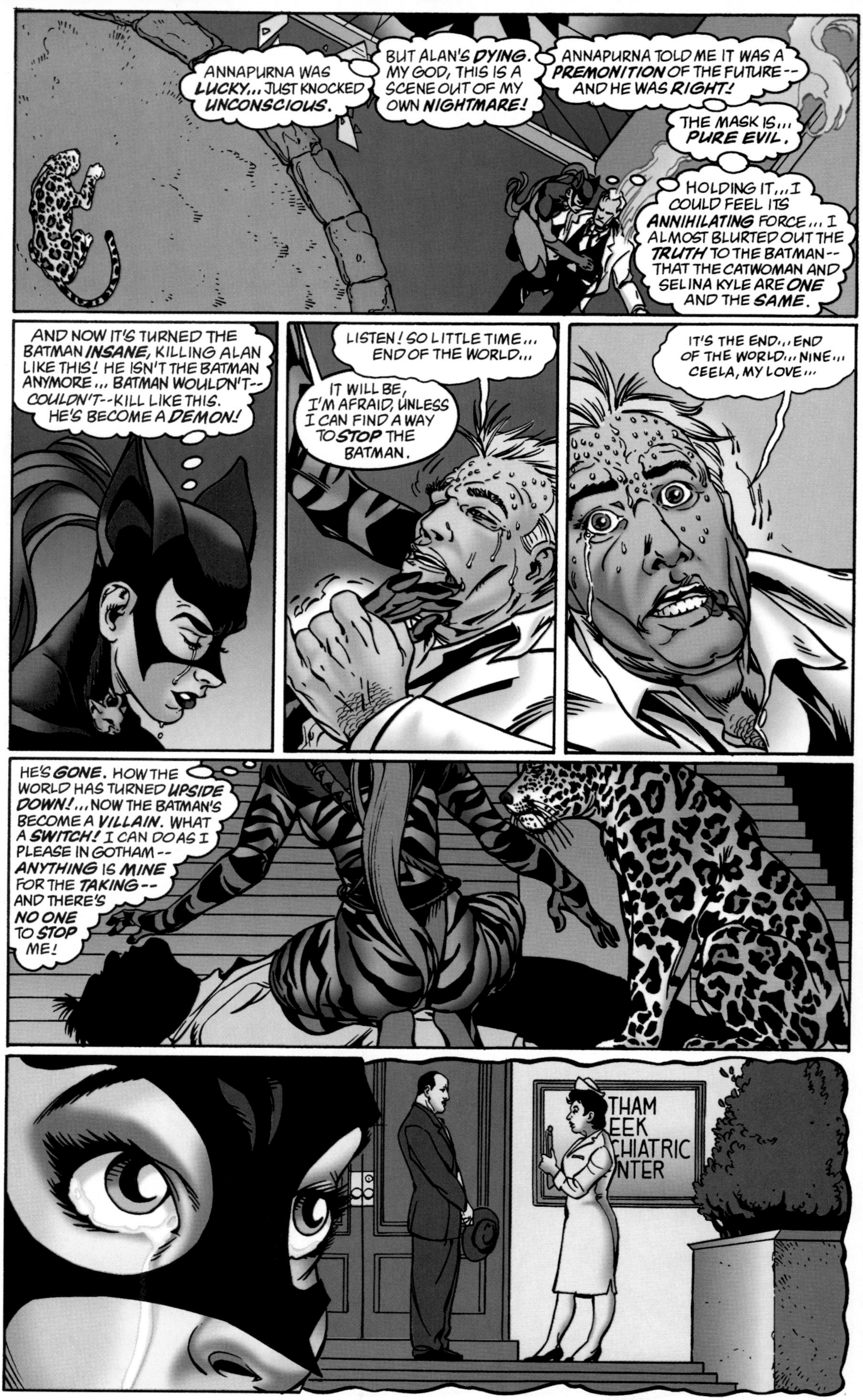
ANNAPURNA WAS LUCKY... JUST KNOCKED UNCONSCIOUS.
BUT ALAN'S DYING. MY GOD, THIS IS A SCENE OUT OF MY OWN NIGHTMARE!
ANNAPURNA TOLD ME IT WAS A PREMONITION OF THE FUTURE-- AND HE WAS RIGHT!
THE MASK IS... PURE EVIL.
HOLDING IT... I COULD FEEL ITS ANNIHILATING FORCE... I ALMOST BLURTED OUT THE TRUTH TO THE BATMAN-- THAT THE CATWOMAN AND SELINA KYLE ARE ONE AND THE SAME.
AND NOW IT'S TURNED THE BATMAN INSANE, KILLING ALAN LIKE THIS! HE ISN'T THE BATMAN ANYMORE... BATMAN WOULDN'T-- COULDN'T--KILL LIKE THIS. HE'S BECOME A DEMON!
LISTEN! SO LITTLE TIME... END OF THE WORLD...
IT WILL BE, I'M AFRAID, UNLESS I CAN FIND A WAY TO STOP THE BATMAN.
IT'S THE END... END OF THE WORLD... NINE... CEELA, MY LOVE...
HE'S GONE. HOW THE WORLD HAS TURNED UPSIDE DOWN!... NOW THE BATMAN'S BECOME A VILLAIN. WHAT A SWITCH! I CAN DO AS I PLEASE IN GOTHAM -- ANYTHING IS MINE FOR THE TAKING -- AND THERE'S NO ONE TO STOP ME!
THAM
EEK
CHIATRIC
NTER

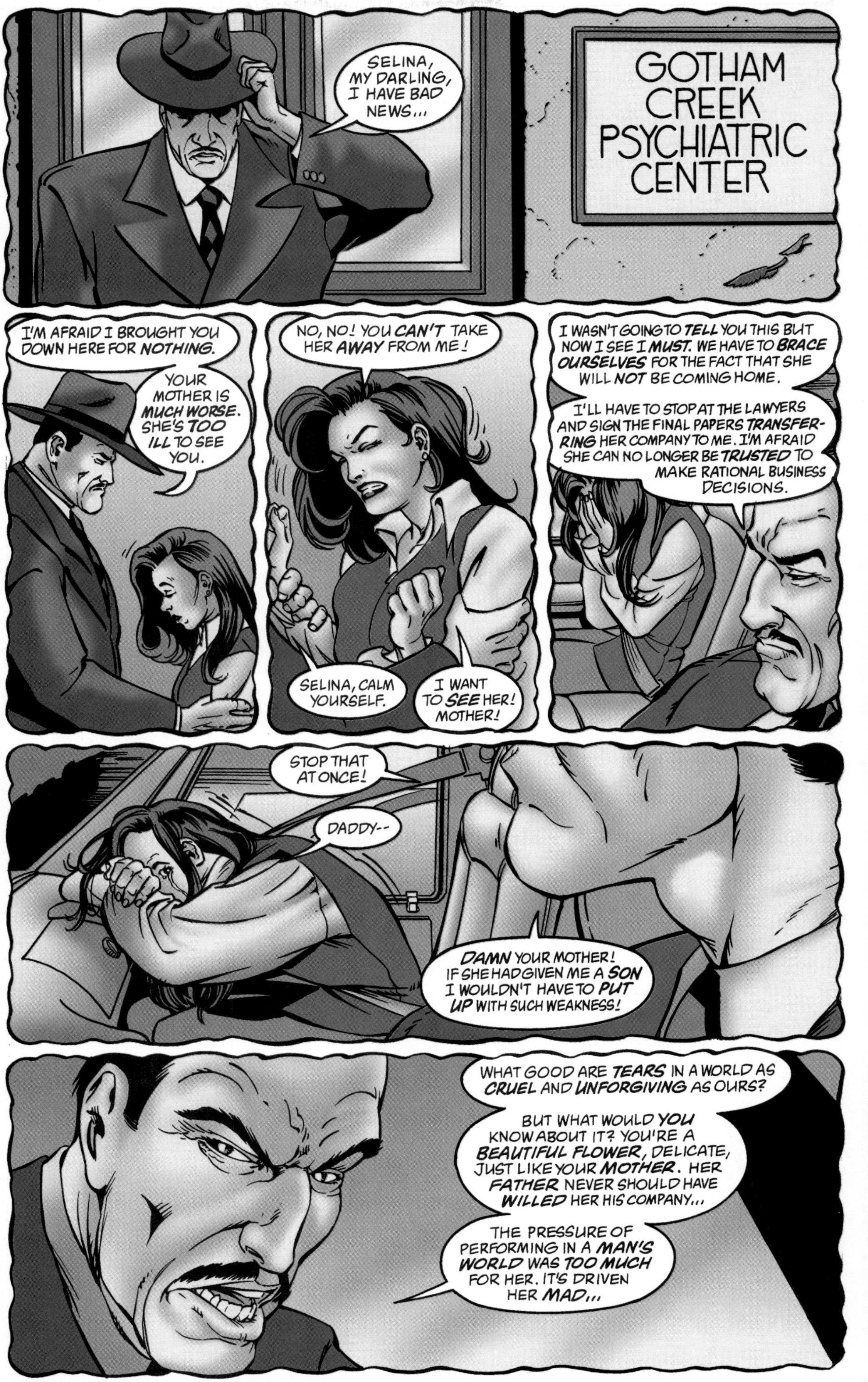
SELINA, MY DARLING, I HAVE BAD NEWS...
GOTHAM CREEK PSYCHIATRIC CENTER
I'M AFRAID I BROUGHT YOU DOWN HERE FOR NOTHING.
YOUR MOTHER IS MUCH WORSE. SHE'S TOO ILL TO SEE YOU.
NO, NO! YOU CAN'T TAKE HER AWAY FROM ME!
SELINA, CALM YOURSELF.
I WANT TO SEE HER! MOTHER!
I WASN'T GOING TO TELL YOU THIS BUT NOW I SEE I MUST. WE HAVE TO BRACE OURSELVES FOR THE FACT THAT SHE WILL NOT BE COMING HOME.
I'LL HAVE TO STOP AT THE LAWYERS AND SIGN THE FINAL PAPERS TRANSFERRING HER COMPANY TO ME. I'M AFRAID SHE CAN NO LONGER BE TRUSTED TO MAKE RATIONAL BUSINESS DECISIONS.
STOP THAT AT ONCE!
DADDY--
DAMN YOUR MOTHER! IF SHE HAD GIVEN ME A SON I WOULDN'T HAVE TO PUT UP WITH SUCH WEAKNESS!
WHAT GOOD ARE TEARS IN A WORLD AS CRUEL AND UNFORGIVING AS OURS?
BUT WHAT WOULD YOU KNOW ABOUT IT? YOU'RE A BEAUTIFUL FLOWER, DELICATE, JUST LIKE YOUR MOTHER. HER FATHER NEVER SHOULD HAVE WILLED HER HIS COMPANY...
THE PRESSURE OF PERFORMING IN A MAN'S WORLD WAS TOO MUCH FOR HER. IT'S DRIVEN HER MAD...

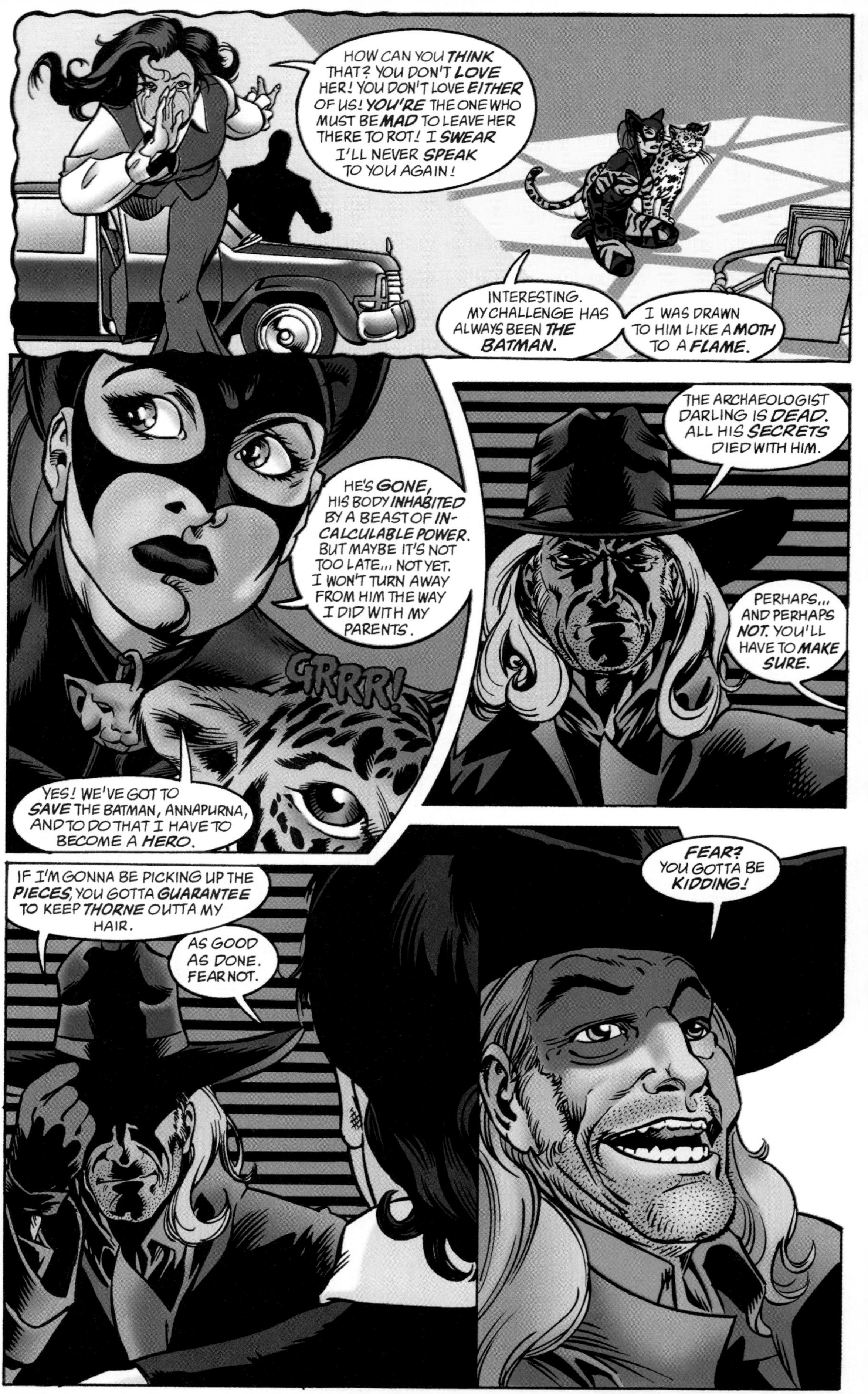
HOW CAN YOU THINK THAT? YOU DON'T LOVE HER! YOU DON'T LOVE EITHER OF US! YOU'RE THE ONE WHO MUST BE MAD TO LEAVE HER THERE TO ROT! I SWEAR I'LL NEVER SPEAK TO YOU AGAIN!
INTERESTING. MY CHALLENGE HAS ALWAYS BEEN THE BATMAN.
I WAS DRAWN TO HIM LIKE A MOTH TO A FLAME.
HE'S GONE, HIS BODY INHABITED BY A BEAST OF INCALCULABLE POWER. BUT MAYBE IT'S NOT TOO LATE... NOT YET. I WON'T TURN AWAY FROM HIM THE WAY I DID WITH MY PARENTS.
GRRRR!
YES! WE'VE GOT TO SAVE THE BATMAN, ANNAPURNA, AND TO DO THAT I HAVE TO BECOME A HERO.
THE ARCHAEOLOGIST DARLING IS DEAD. ALL HIS SECRETS DIED WITH HIM.
PERHAPS... AND PERHAPS NOT. YOU'LL HAVE TO MAKE SURE.
IF I'M GONNA BE PICKING UP THE PIECES, YOU GOTTA GUARANTEE TO KEEP THORNE OUTTA MY HAIR.
AS GOOD AS DONE. FEAR NOT.
FEAR? YOU GOTTA BE KIDDING!

POSITIVELY NO SMOKING!

NOT A *PRETTY* SIGHT, EDWARDS. WHAT *KILLED* HIM?

GOOD QUESTION. DO YOU HAVE ANOTHER ONE FOR ME TO ANSWER?

IS THAT A *JOKE?*

ONLY IN A MANNER OF SPEAKING.

I HAVE *NO* IDEA WHAT *KILLED* HIM. UNLESS, OF COURSE, HE PUT HIS FACE IN AN *OVERHEATED* OVEN.

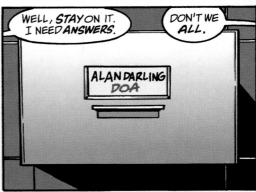

WELL, *STAY* ON IT. I NEED *ANSWERS.*

DON'T WE *ALL.*

ALAN DARLING
DOA

BOO

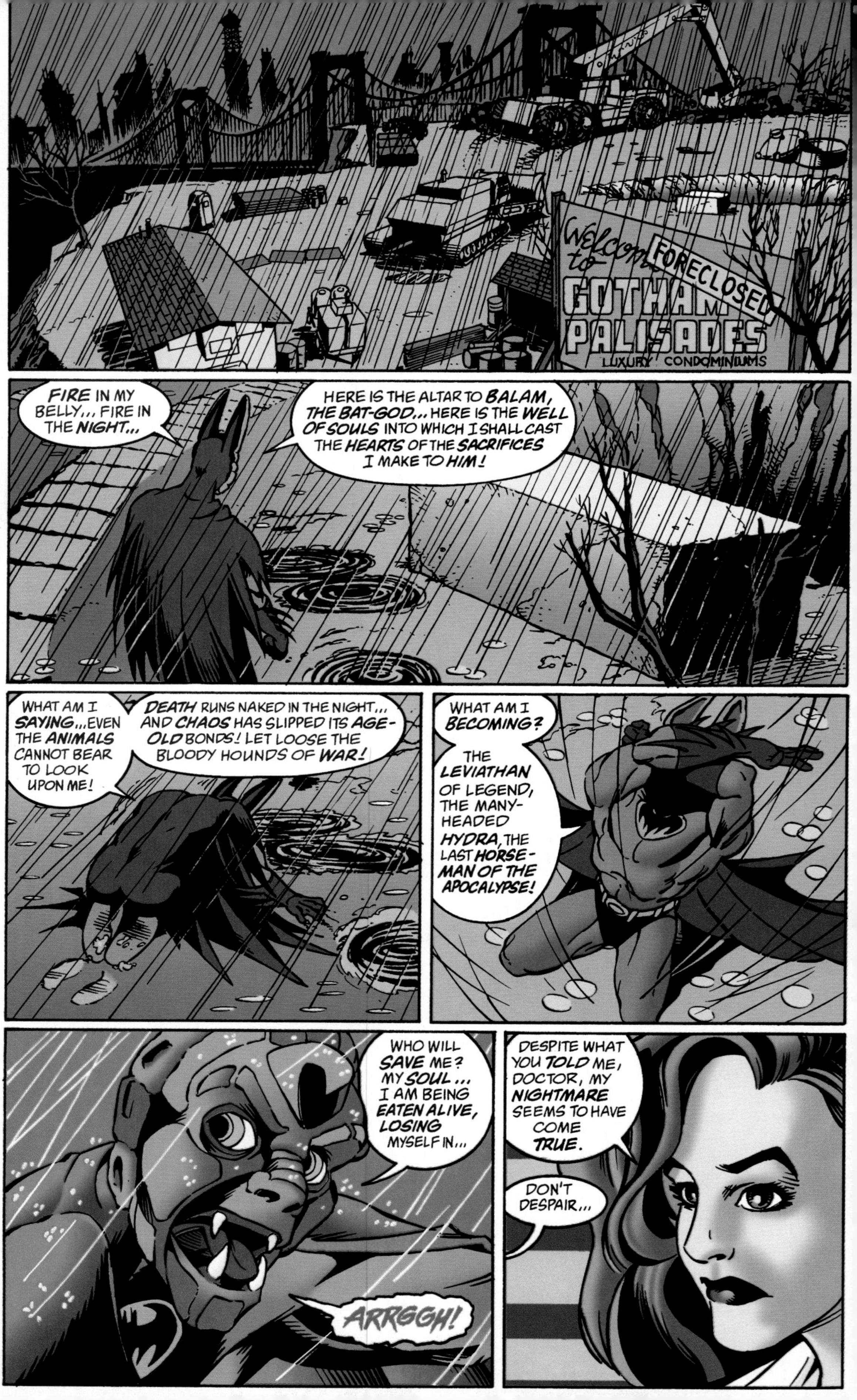
Welcome to
FORECLOSED
GOTHAM PALISADES
LUXURY CONDOMINIUMS
FIRE IN MY BELLY... FIRE IN THE NIGHT...
HERE IS THE ALTAR TO BALAM, THE BAT-GOD... HERE IS THE WELL OF SOULS INTO WHICH I SHALL CAST THE HEARTS OF THE SACRIFICES I MAKE TO HIM!
WHAT AM I SAYING... EVEN THE ANIMALS CANNOT BEAR TO LOOK UPON ME!
DEATH RUNS NAKED IN THE NIGHT... AND CHAOS HAS SLIPPED ITS AGE-OLD BONDS! LET LOOSE THE BLOODY HOUNDS OF WAR!
WHAT AM I BECOMING?
THE LEVIATHAN OF LEGEND, THE MANY-HEADED HYDRA, THE LAST HORSE-MAN OF THE APOCALYPSE!
WHO WILL SAVE ME? MY SOUL... I AM BEING EATEN ALIVE, LOSING MYSELF IN...
ARRGGH!
DESPITE WHAT YOU TOLD ME, DOCTOR, MY NIGHTMARE SEEMS TO HAVE COME TRUE.
DON'T DESPAIR...

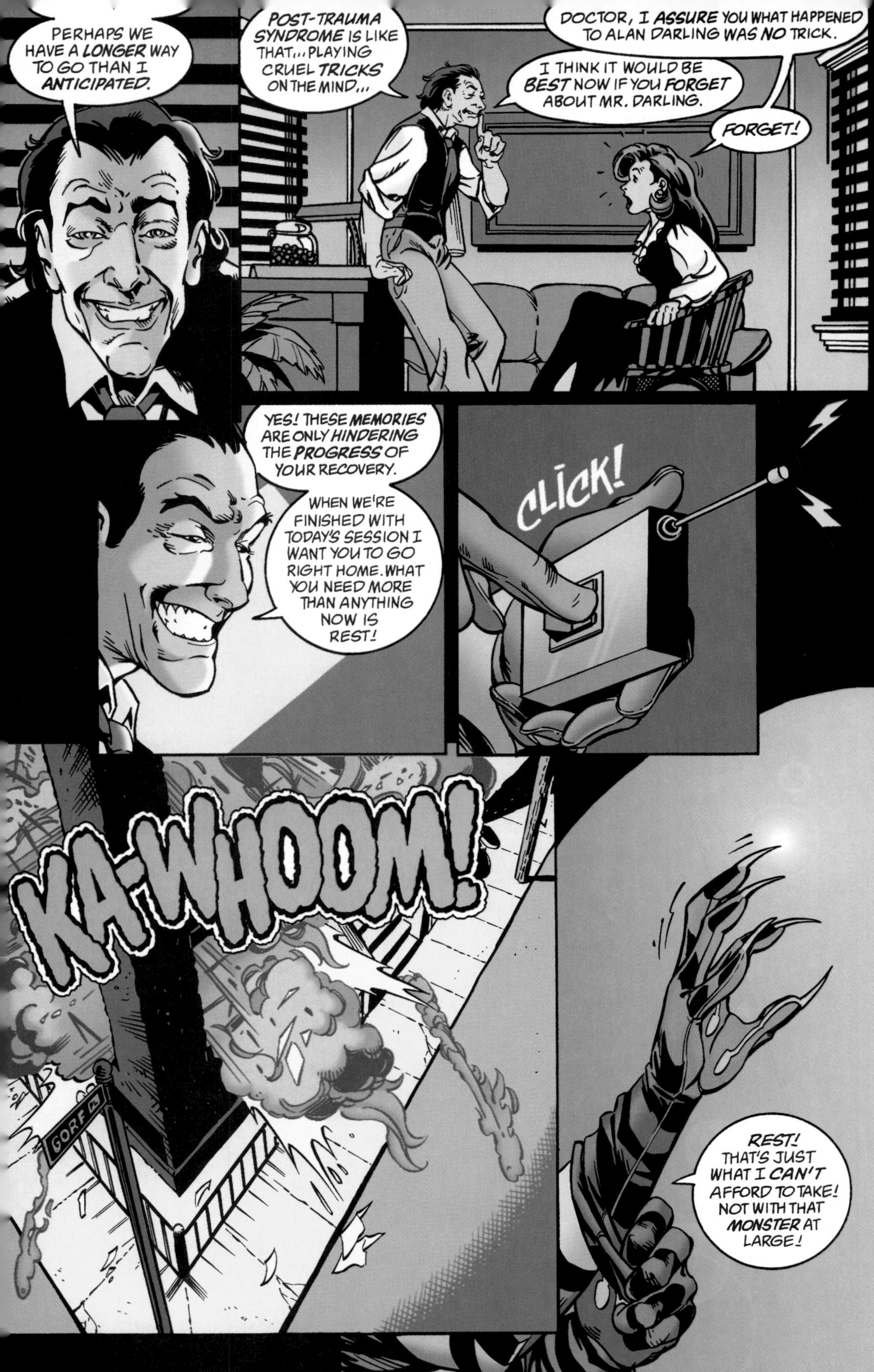
PERHAPS WE HAVE A LONGER WAY TO GO THAN I ANTICIPATED.
POST-TRAUMA SYNDROME IS LIKE THAT... PLAYING CRUEL TRICKS ON THE MIND...
DOCTOR, I ASSURE YOU WHAT HAPPENED TO ALAN DARLING WAS NO TRICK.
I THINK IT WOULD BE BEST NOW IF YOU FORGET ABOUT MR. DARLING.
FORGET!
YES! THESE MEMORIES ARE ONLY HINDERING THE PROGRESS OF YOUR RECOVERY.
WHEN WE'RE FINISHED WITH TODAY'S SESSION I WANT YOU TO GO RIGHT HOME. WHAT YOU NEED MORE THAN ANYTHING NOW IS REST!
CLICK!
KA-WHOOM!
GORF PL
REST! THAT'S JUST WHAT I CAN'T AFFORD TO TAKE! NOT WITH THAT MONSTER AT LARGE!

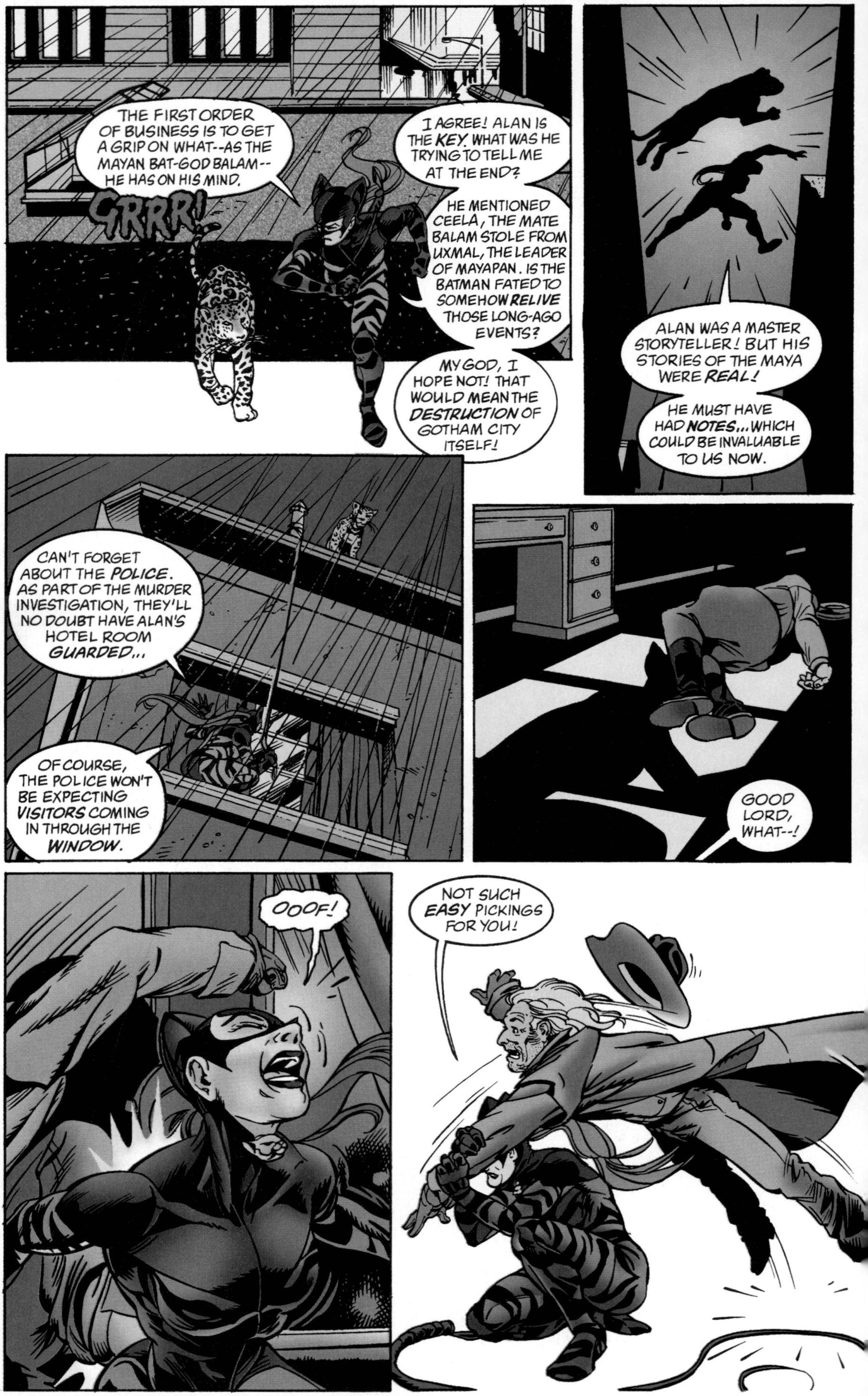
THE FIRST ORDER OF BUSINESS IS TO GET A GRIP ON WHAT--AS THE MAYAN BAT-GOD BALAM--HE HAS ON HIS MIND.
GRRR!
I AGREE! ALAN IS THE KEY. WHAT WAS HE TRYING TO TELL ME AT THE END?
HE MENTIONED CEELA, THE MATE BALAM STOLE FROM UXMAL, THE LEADER OF MAYAPAN. IS THE BATMAN FATED TO SOMEHOW RELIVE THOSE LONG-AGO EVENTS?
MY GOD, I HOPE NOT! THAT WOULD MEAN THE DESTRUCTION OF GOTHAM CITY ITSELF!
ALAN WAS A MASTER STORYTELLER! BUT HIS STORIES OF THE MAYA WERE REAL!
HE MUST HAVE HAD NOTES... WHICH COULD BE INVALUABLE TO US NOW.
CAN'T FORGET ABOUT THE POLICE. AS PART OF THE MURDER INVESTIGATION, THEY'LL NO DOUBT HAVE ALAN'S HOTEL ROOM GUARDED...
OF COURSE, THE POLICE WON'T BE EXPECTING VISITORS COMING IN THROUGH THE WINDOW.
GOOD LORD, WHAT--!
OOOF!
NOT SUCH EASY PICKINGS FOR YOU!

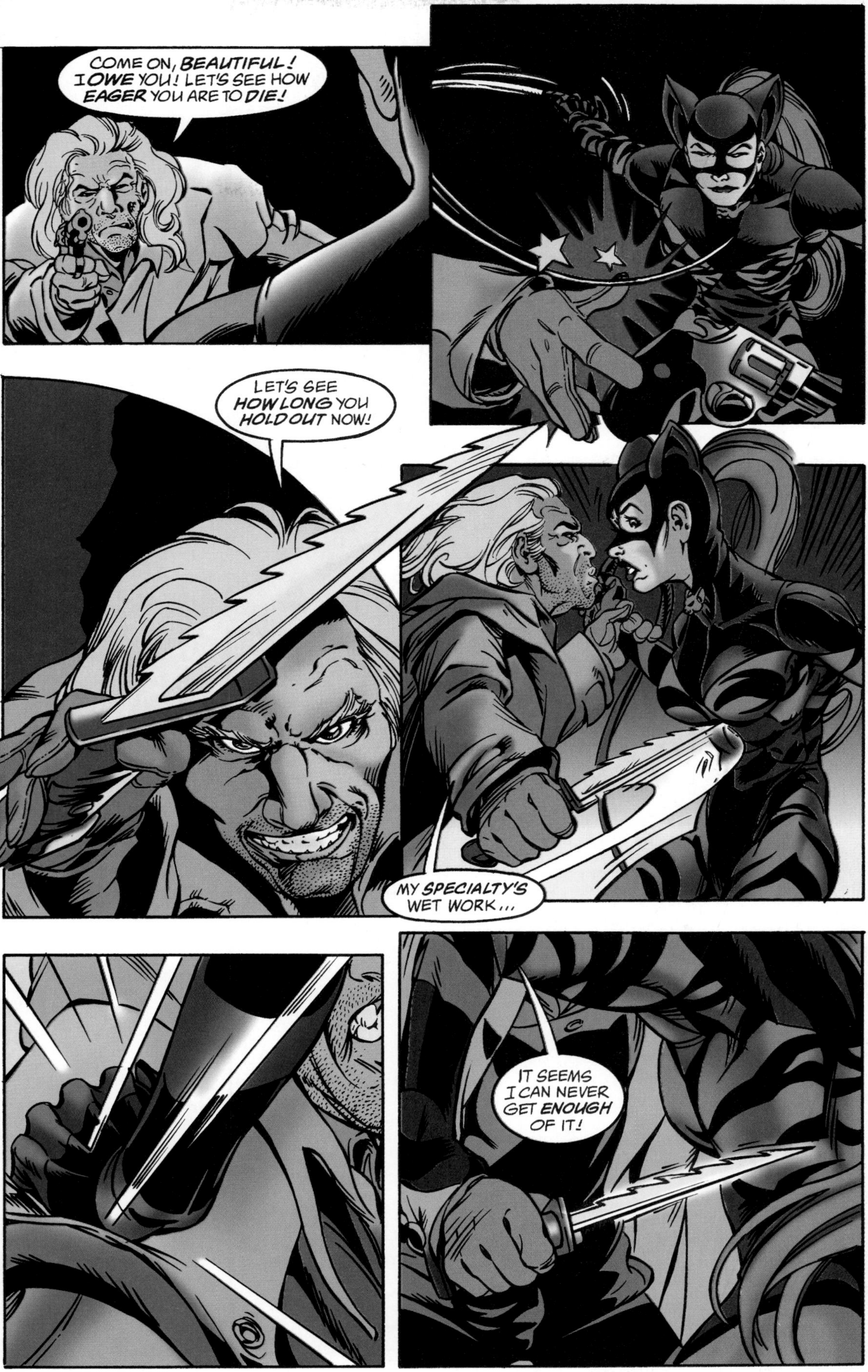
COME ON, BEAUTIFUL! I OWE YOU! LET'S SEE HOW EAGER YOU ARE TO DIE!
LET'S SEE HOW LONG YOU HOLD OUT NOW!
MY SPECIALTY'S WET WORK...
IT SEEMS I CAN NEVER GET ENOUGH OF IT!

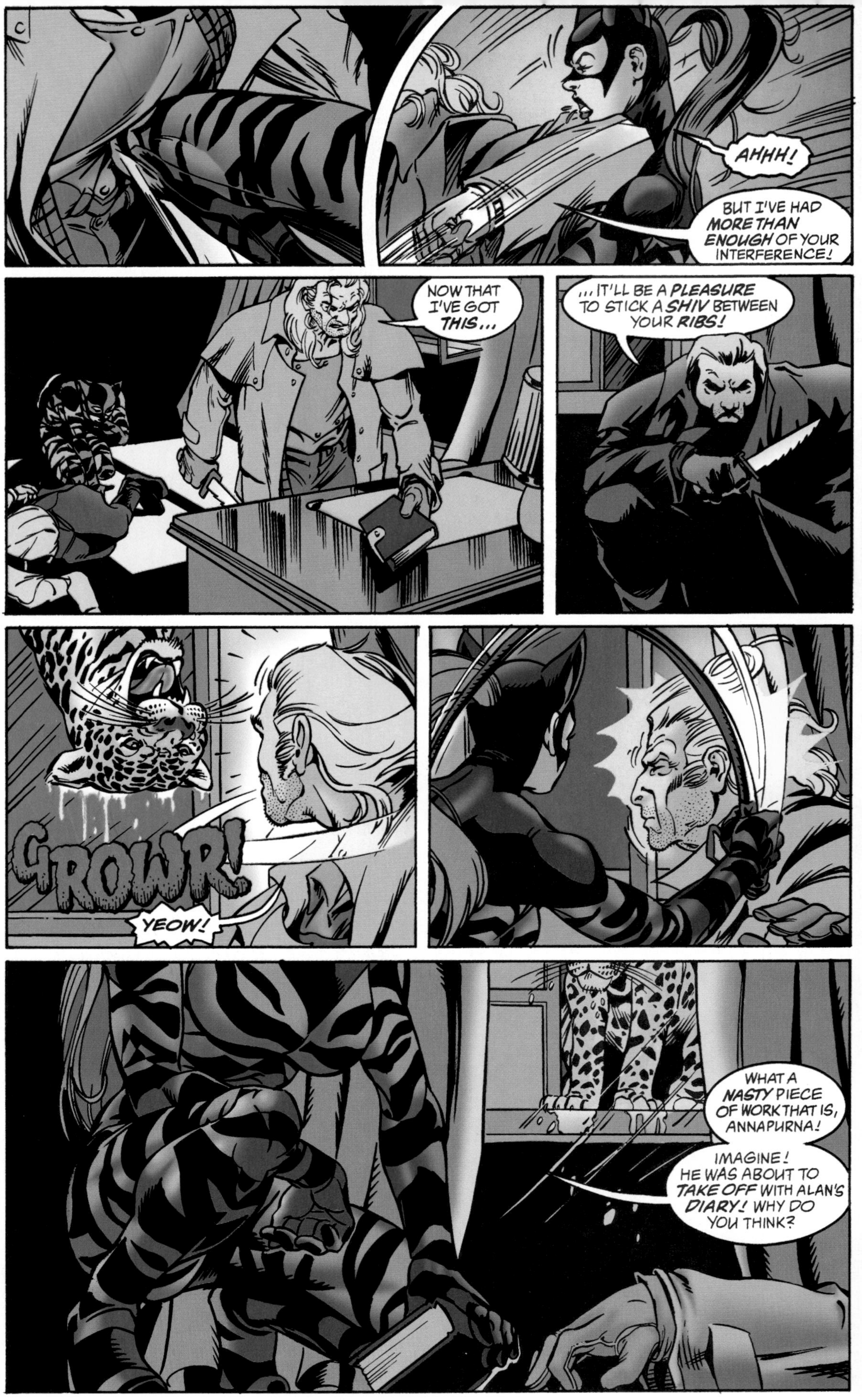
AHHH!
BUT I'VE HAD MORE THAN ENOUGH OF YOUR INTERFERENCE!
NOW THAT I'VE GOT THIS...
...IT'LL BE A PLEASURE TO STICK A SHIV BETWEEN YOUR RIBS!
GROWR!
YEOW!
WHAT A NASTY PIECE OF WORK THAT IS, ANNAPURNA!
IMAGINE! HE WAS ABOUT TO TAKE OFF WITH ALAN'S DIARY! WHY DO YOU THINK?

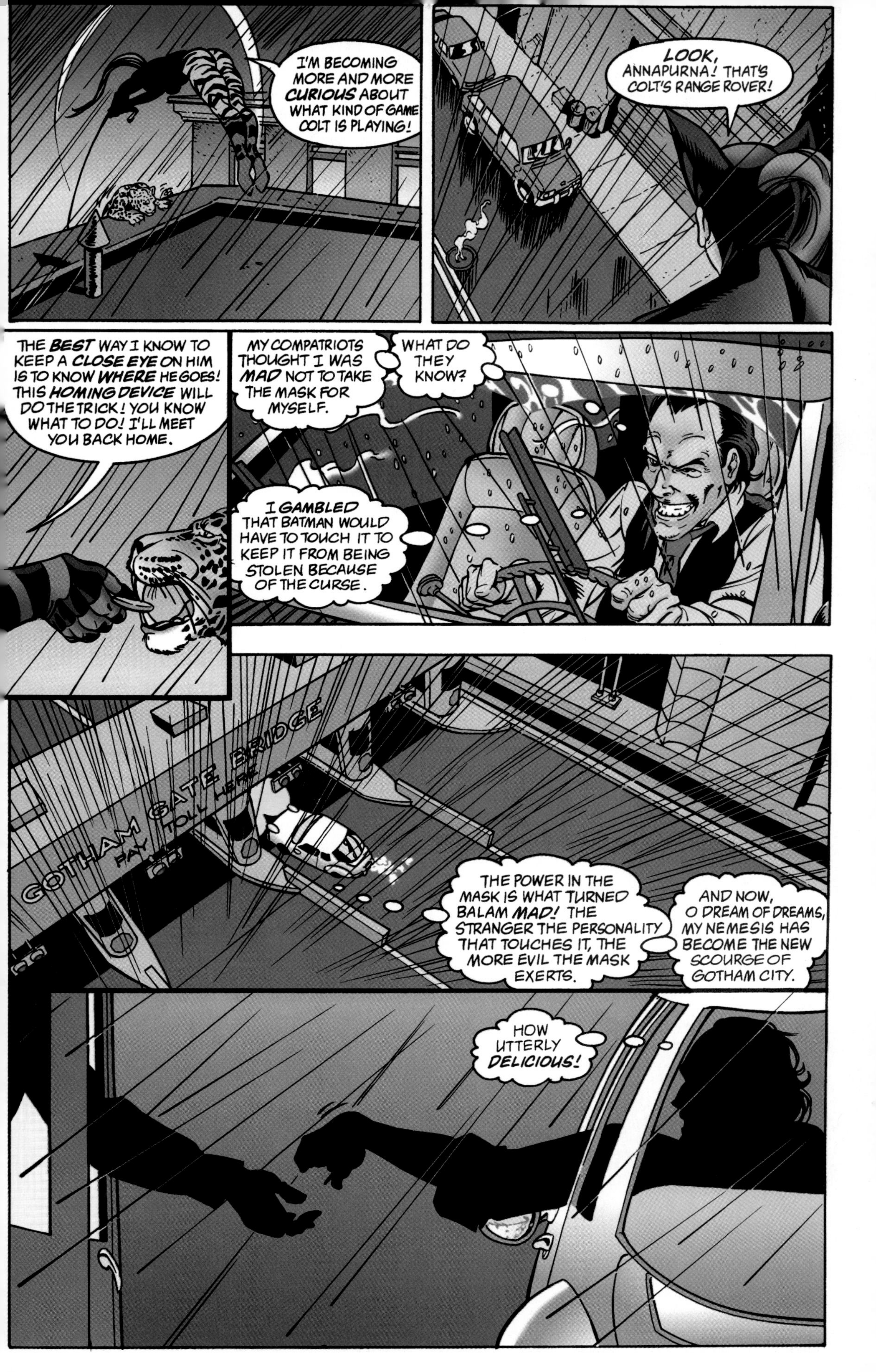
I'M BECOMING MORE AND MORE CURIOUS ABOUT WHAT KIND OF GAME COLT IS PLAYING!
LOOK, ANNAPURNA! THAT'S COLT'S RANGE ROVER!
THE BEST WAY I KNOW TO KEEP A CLOSE EYE ON HIM IS TO KNOW WHERE HE GOES! THIS HOMING DEVICE WILL DO THE TRICK! YOU KNOW WHAT TO DO! I'LL MEET YOU BACK HOME.
MY COMPATRIOTS THOUGHT I WAS MAD NOT TO TAKE THE MASK FOR MYSELF.
WHAT DO THEY KNOW?
I GAMBLED THAT BATMAN WOULD HAVE TO TOUCH IT TO KEEP IT FROM BEING STOLEN BECAUSE OF THE CURSE.
GOTHAM GATE BRIDGE
PAY TOLL HERE
THE POWER IN THE MASK IS WHAT TURNED BALAM MAD! THE STRANGER THE PERSONALITY THAT TOUCHES IT, THE MORE EVIL THE MASK EXERTS.
AND NOW, O DREAM OF DREAMS, MY NEMESIS HAS BECOME THE NEW SCOURGE OF GOTHAM CITY.
HOW UTTERLY DELICIOUS!

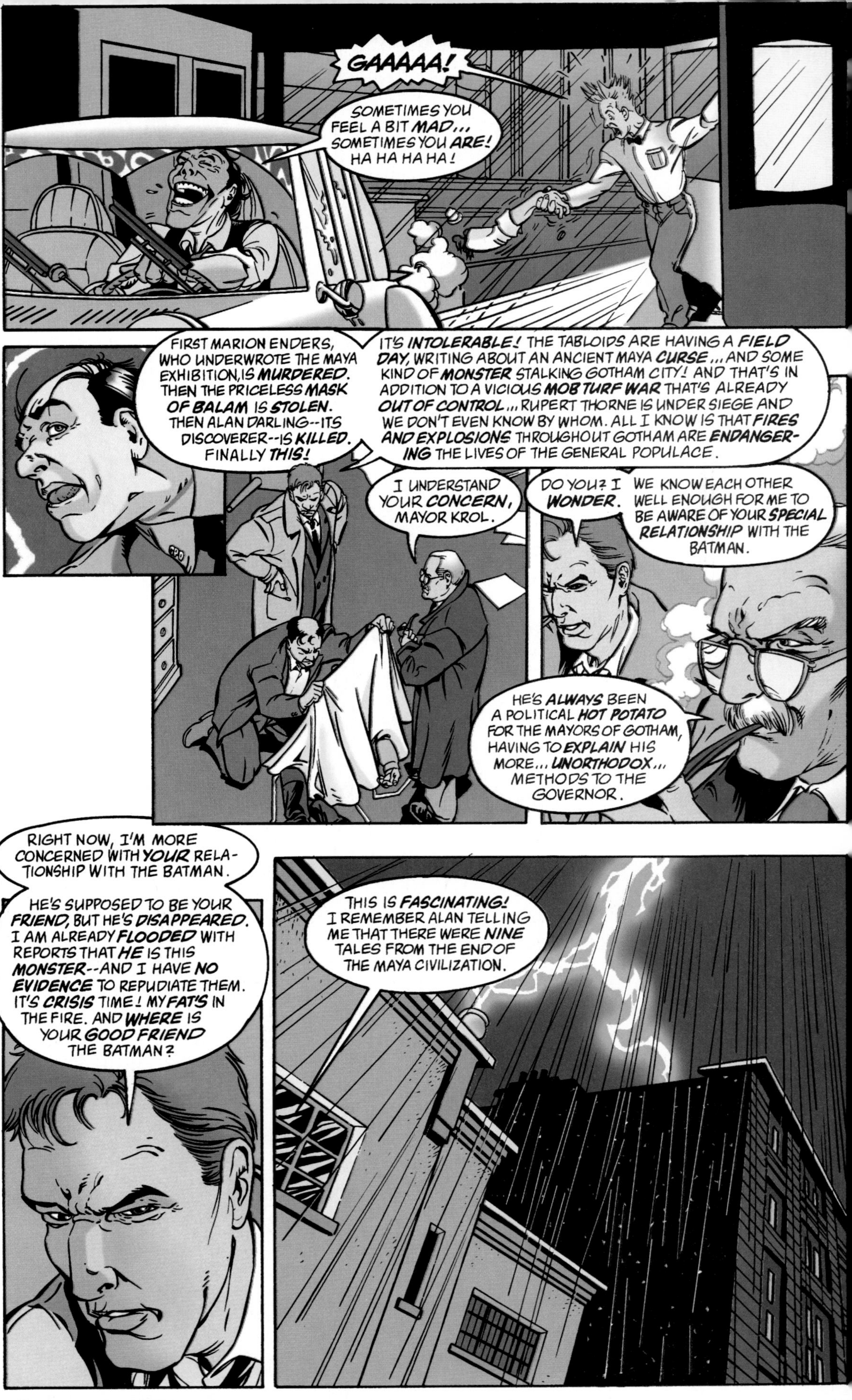
GAAAAA!
SOMETIMES YOU FEEL A BIT MAD... SOMETIMES YOU ARE! HA HA HA HA!
FIRST MARION ENDERS, WHO UNDERWROTE THE MAYA EXHIBITION, IS MURDERED. THEN THE PRICELESS MASK OF BALAM IS STOLEN. THEN ALAN DARLING--ITS DISCOVERER--IS KILLED. FINALLY THIS!
IT'S INTOLERABLE! THE TABLOIDS ARE HAVING A FIELD DAY, WRITING ABOUT AN ANCIENT MAYA CURSE... AND SOME KIND OF MONSTER STALKING GOTHAM CITY! AND THAT'S IN ADDITION TO A VICIOUS MOB TURF WAR THAT'S ALREADY OUT OF CONTROL... RUPERT THORNE IS UNDER SIEGE AND WE DON'T EVEN KNOW BY WHOM. ALL I KNOW IS THAT FIRES AND EXPLOSIONS THROUGHOUT GOTHAM ARE ENDANGERING THE LIVES OF THE GENERAL POPULACE.
I UNDERSTAND YOUR CONCERN, MAYOR KROL.
DO YOU? I WONDER.
WE KNOW EACH OTHER WELL ENOUGH FOR ME TO BE AWARE OF YOUR SPECIAL RELATIONSHIP WITH THE BATMAN.
HE'S ALWAYS BEEN A POLITICAL HOT POTATO FOR THE MAYORS OF GOTHAM, HAVING TO EXPLAIN HIS MORE... UNORTHODOX... METHODS TO THE GOVERNOR.
RIGHT NOW, I'M MORE CONCERNED WITH YOUR RELATIONSHIP WITH THE BATMAN.
HE'S SUPPOSED TO BE YOUR FRIEND, BUT HE'S DISAPPEARED. I AM ALREADY FLOODED WITH REPORTS THAT HE IS THIS MONSTER--AND I HAVE NO EVIDENCE TO REPUDIATE THEM. IT'S CRISIS TIME! MY FAT'S IN THE FIRE. AND WHERE IS YOUR GOOD FRIEND THE BATMAN?
THIS IS FASCINATING! I REMEMBER ALAN TELLING ME THAT THERE WERE NINE TALES FROM THE END OF THE MAYA CIVILIZATION.

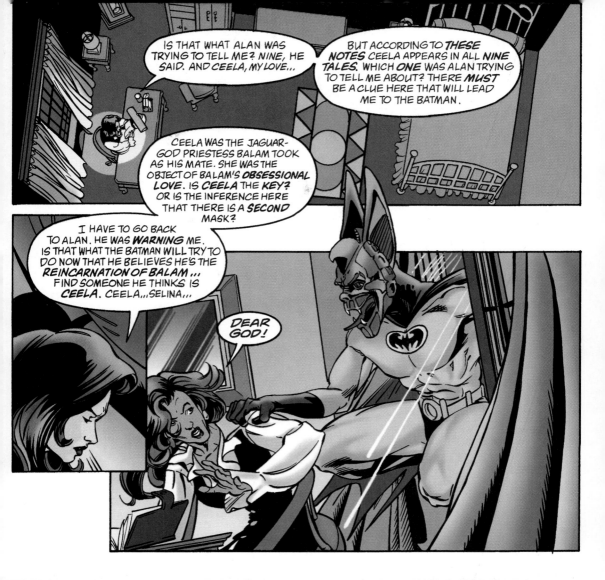

IS THAT WHAT ALAN WAS TRYING TO TELL ME? NINE, HE SAID. AND CEELA, MY LOVE...

BUT ACCORDING TO *THESE NOTES* CEELA APPEARS IN ALL *NINE TALES*. WHICH *ONE* WAS ALAN TRYING TO TELL ME ABOUT? THERE *MUST* BE A CLUE HERE THAT WILL LEAD ME TO THE BATMAN.

CEELA WAS THE JAGUAR-GOD PRIESTESS BALAM TOOK AS HIS MATE. SHE WAS THE OBJECT OF BALAM'S *OBSESSIONAL LOVE*. IS *CEELA* THE *KEY*? OR IS THE INFERENCE HERE THAT THERE IS A *SECOND MASK*?

I HAVE TO GO BACK TO ALAN. HE WAS *WARNING* ME. IS THAT WHAT THE BATMAN WILL TRY TO DO NOW THAT HE BELIEVES HE'S THE *REINCARNATION OF BALAM*... FIND SOMEONE HE THINKS IS *CEELA*. CEELA...SELINA...

DEAR GOD!

THIS IS WAR, I TELL YOU! WAR!

WE ARE BEING *DECIMATED* ON ALL *FRONTS* BY WHAT AMOUNTS TO GUERRILLA TACTICS!

FIRST MY *NUMBERS JOINT* ON THE WEST SIDE *GETS HIT* BY AN *ARSONIST*, THEN AN *EXPLOSION DESTROYS* MY *DRUG* FACTORY ON THE EAST SIDE.

THERE'S ONLY *ONE* CONCLUSION...*SOMEONE'S* LOOKING TO TAKE OVER MY *TERRITORY*!

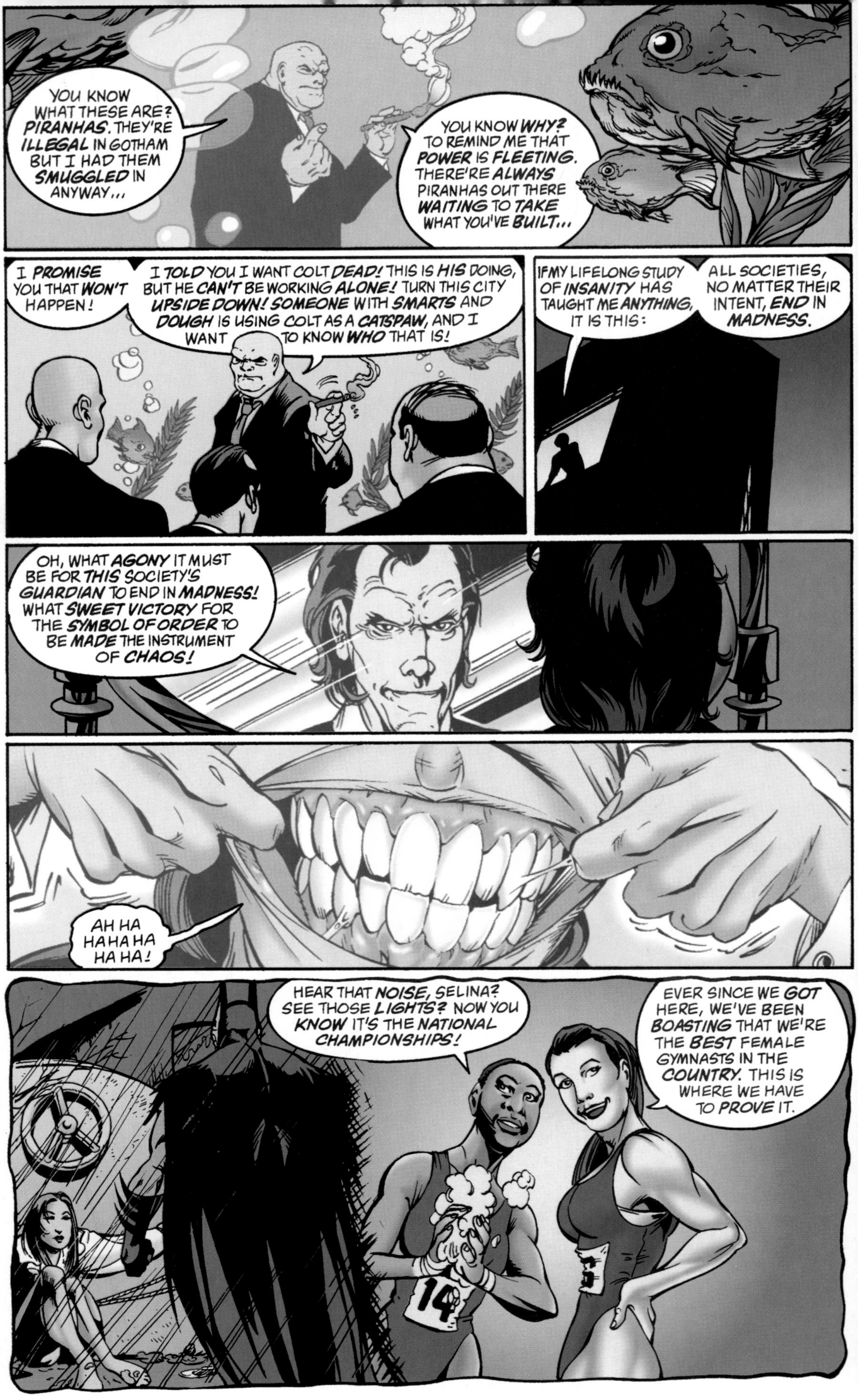
YOU KNOW WHAT THESE ARE? PIRANHAS. THEY'RE ILLEGAL IN GOTHAM BUT I HAD THEM SMUGGLED IN ANYWAY...
YOU KNOW WHY? TO REMIND ME THAT POWER IS FLEETING. THERE'RE ALWAYS PIRANHAS OUT THERE WAITING TO TAKE WHAT YOU'VE BUILT...
I PROMISE YOU THAT WON'T HAPPEN!
I TOLD YOU I WANT COLT DEAD! THIS IS HIS DOING, BUT HE CAN'T BE WORKING ALONE! TURN THIS CITY UPSIDE DOWN! SOMEONE WITH SMARTS AND DOUGH IS USING COLT AS A CATSPAW, AND I WANT TO KNOW WHO THAT IS!
IF MY LIFELONG STUDY OF INSANITY HAS TAUGHT ME ANYTHING, IT IS THIS:
ALL SOCIETIES, NO MATTER THEIR INTENT, END IN MADNESS.
OH, WHAT AGONY IT MUST BE FOR THIS SOCIETY'S GUARDIAN TO END IN MADNESS! WHAT SWEET VICTORY FOR THE SYMBOL OF ORDER TO BE MADE THE INSTRUMENT OF CHAOS!
AH HA HA HA HA HA HA!
HEAR THAT NOISE, SELINA? SEE THOSE LIGHTS? NOW YOU KNOW IT'S THE NATIONAL CHAMPIONSHIPS!
EVER SINCE WE GOT HERE, WE'VE BEEN BOASTING THAT WE'RE THE BEST FEMALE GYMNASTS IN THE COUNTRY. THIS IS WHERE WE HAVE TO PROVE IT.
14
5

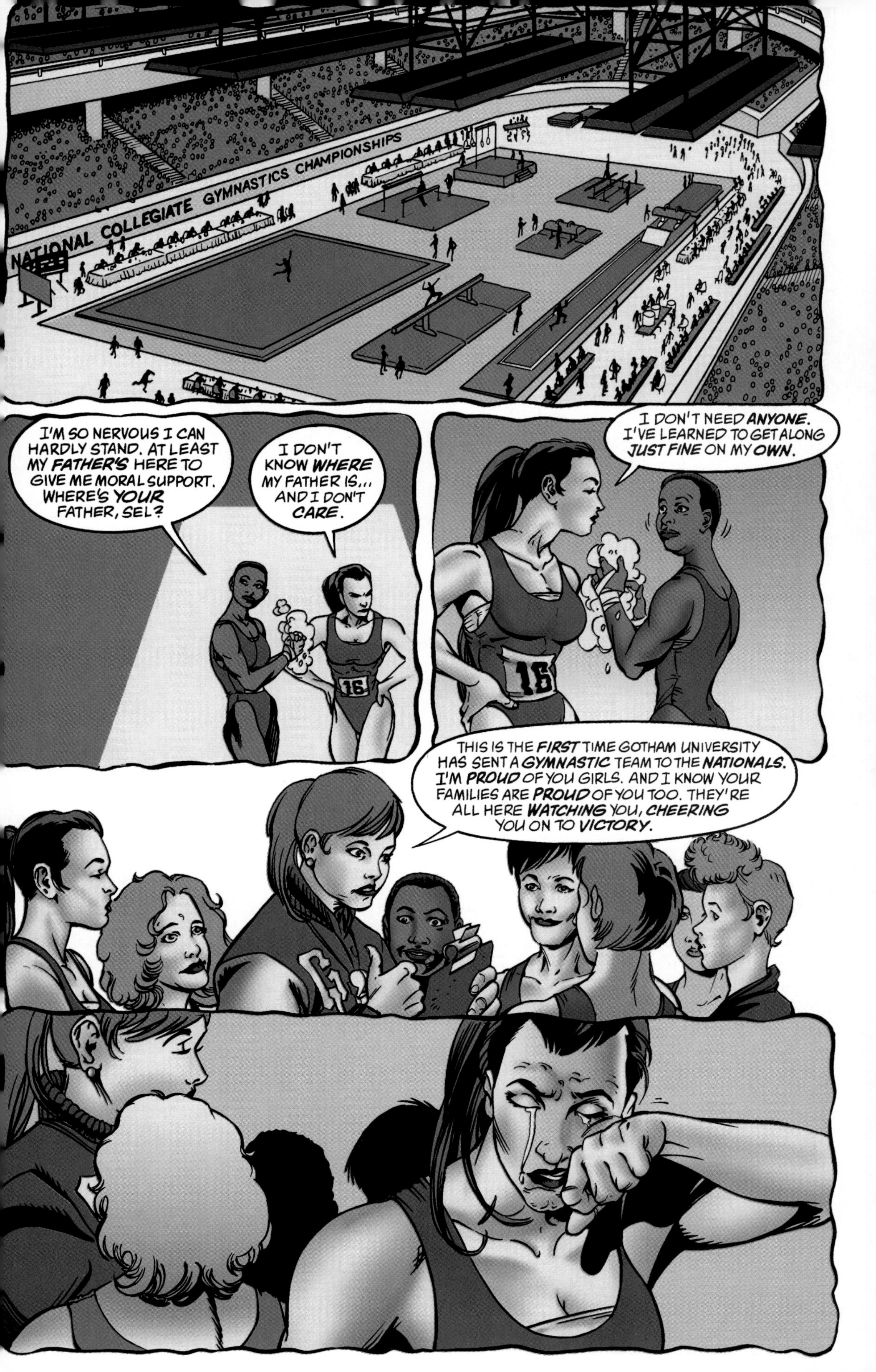
NATIONAL COLLEGIATE GYMNASTICS CHAMPIONSHIPS
I'M SO NERVOUS I CAN HARDLY STAND. AT LEAST MY FATHER'S HERE TO GIVE ME MORAL SUPPORT. WHERE'S YOUR FATHER, SEL?
I DON'T KNOW WHERE MY FATHER IS... AND I DON'T CARE.
I DON'T NEED ANYONE. I'VE LEARNED TO GET ALONG JUST FINE ON MY OWN.
THIS IS THE FIRST TIME GOTHAM UNIVERSITY HAS SENT A GYMNASTIC TEAM TO THE NATIONALS. I'M PROUD OF YOU GIRLS. AND I KNOW YOUR FAMILIES ARE PROUD OF YOU TOO. THEY'RE ALL HERE WATCHING YOU, CHEERING YOU ON TO VICTORY.

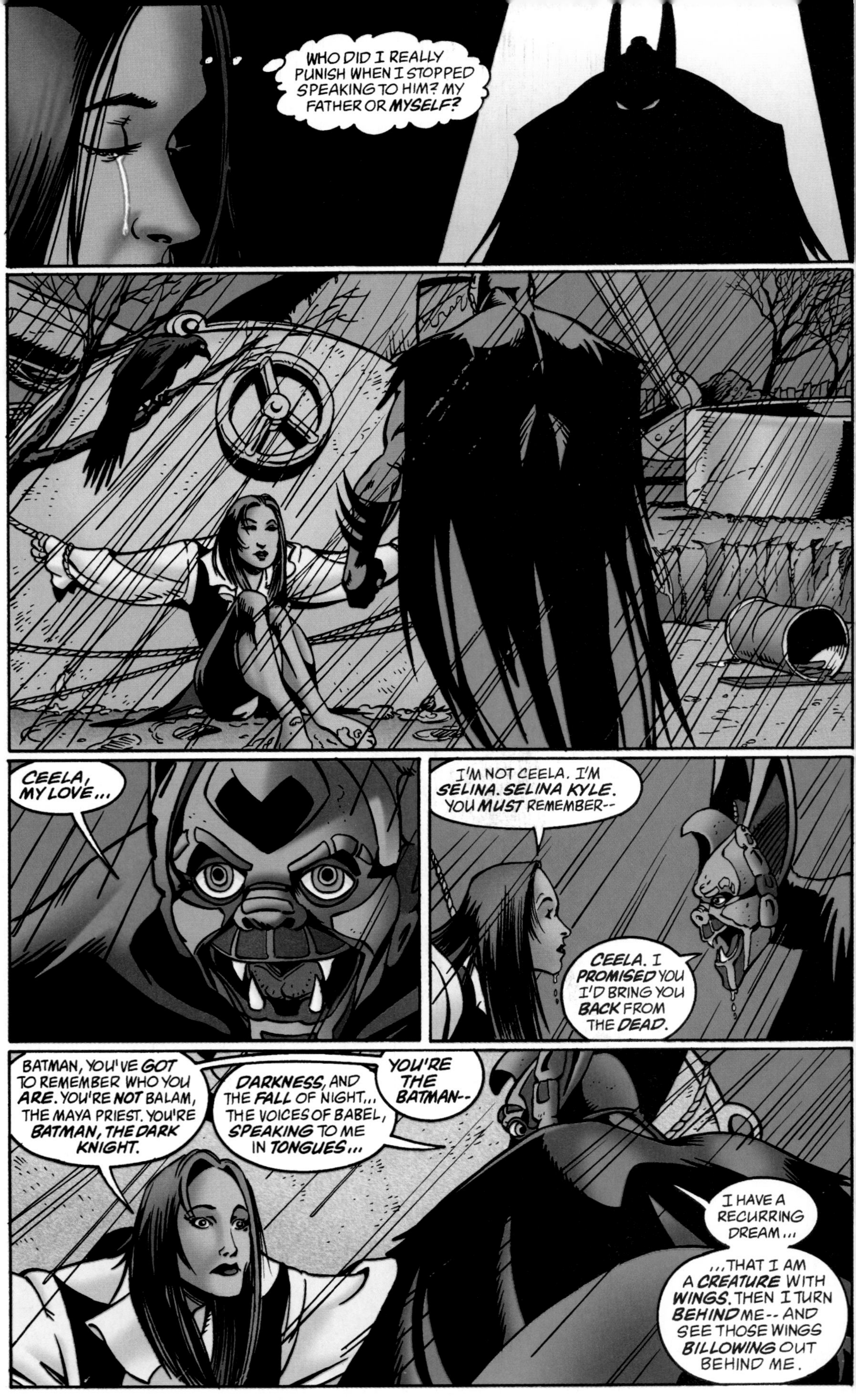

WHO DID I REALLY PUNISH WHEN I STOPPED SPEAKING TO HIM? MY FATHER OR MYSELF?
CEELA, MY LOVE...
I'M NOT CEELA. I'M SELINA. SELINA KYLE. YOU MUST REMEMBER--
CEELA. I PROMISED YOU I'D BRING YOU BACK FROM THE DEAD.
BATMAN, YOU'VE GOT TO REMEMBER WHO YOU ARE. YOU'RE NOT BALAM, THE MAYA PRIEST. YOU'RE BATMAN, THE DARK KNIGHT.
DARKNESS, AND THE FALL OF NIGHT... THE VOICES OF BABEL, SPEAKING TO ME IN TONGUES...
YOU'RE THE BATMAN--
I HAVE A RECURRING DREAM...
...THAT I AM A CREATURE WITH WINGS. THEN I TURN BEHIND ME-- AND SEE THOSE WINGS BILLOWING OUT BEHIND ME.

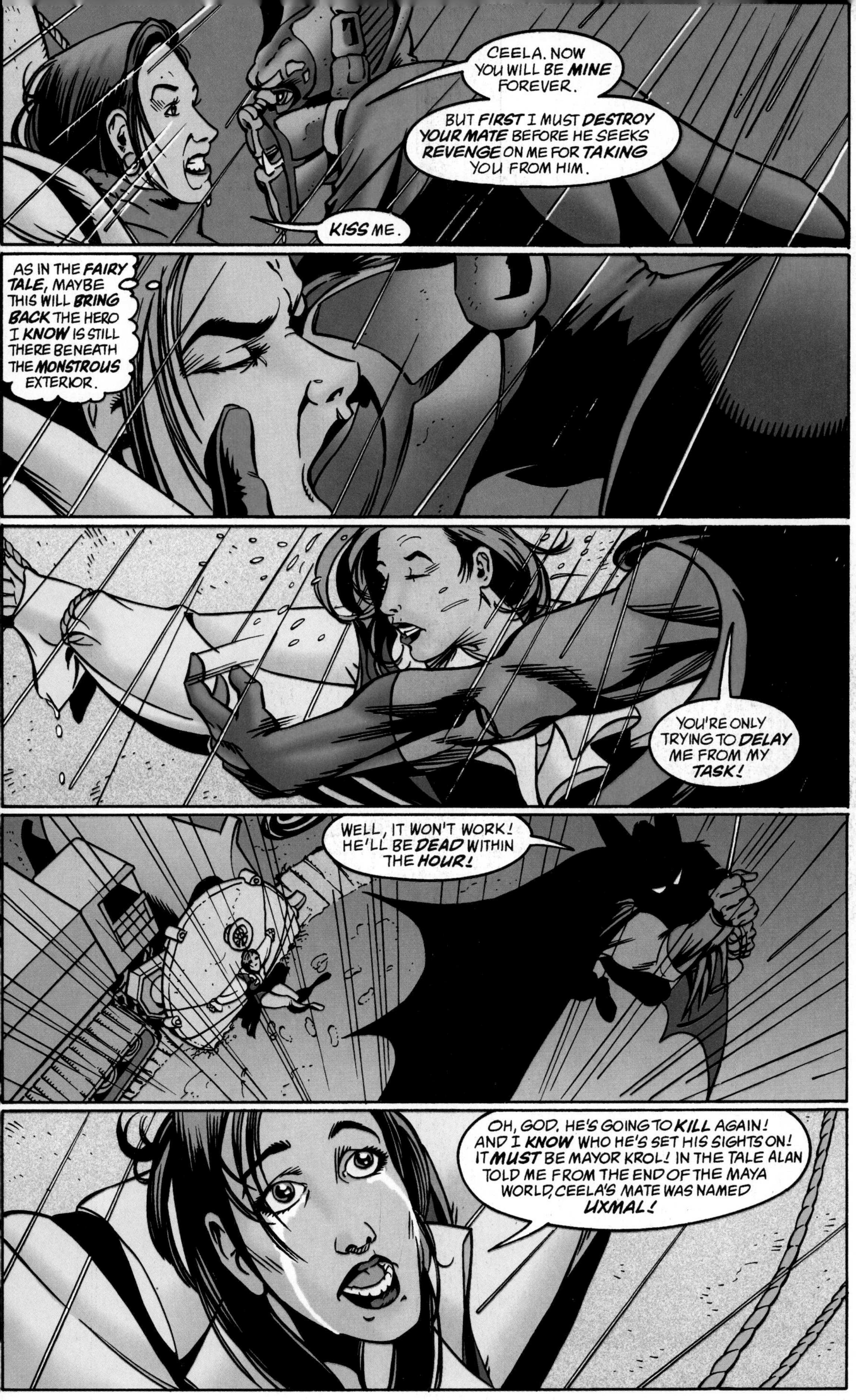
CEELA. NOW YOU WILL BE MINE FOREVER.
BUT FIRST I MUST DESTROY YOUR MATE BEFORE HE SEEKS REVENGE ON ME FOR TAKING YOU FROM HIM.
KISS ME.
AS IN THE FAIRY TALE, MAYBE THIS WILL BRING BACK THE HERO I KNOW IS STILL THERE BENEATH THE MONSTROUS EXTERIOR.
YOU'RE ONLY TRYING TO DELAY ME FROM MY TASK!
WELL, IT WON'T WORK! HE'LL BE DEAD WITHIN THE HOUR!
OH, GOD. HE'S GOING TO KILL AGAIN! AND I KNOW WHO HE'S SET HIS SIGHTS ON! IT MUST BE MAYOR KROL! IN THE TALE ALAN TOLD ME FROM THE END OF THE MAYA WORLD, CEELA'S MATE WAS NAMED UXMAL!

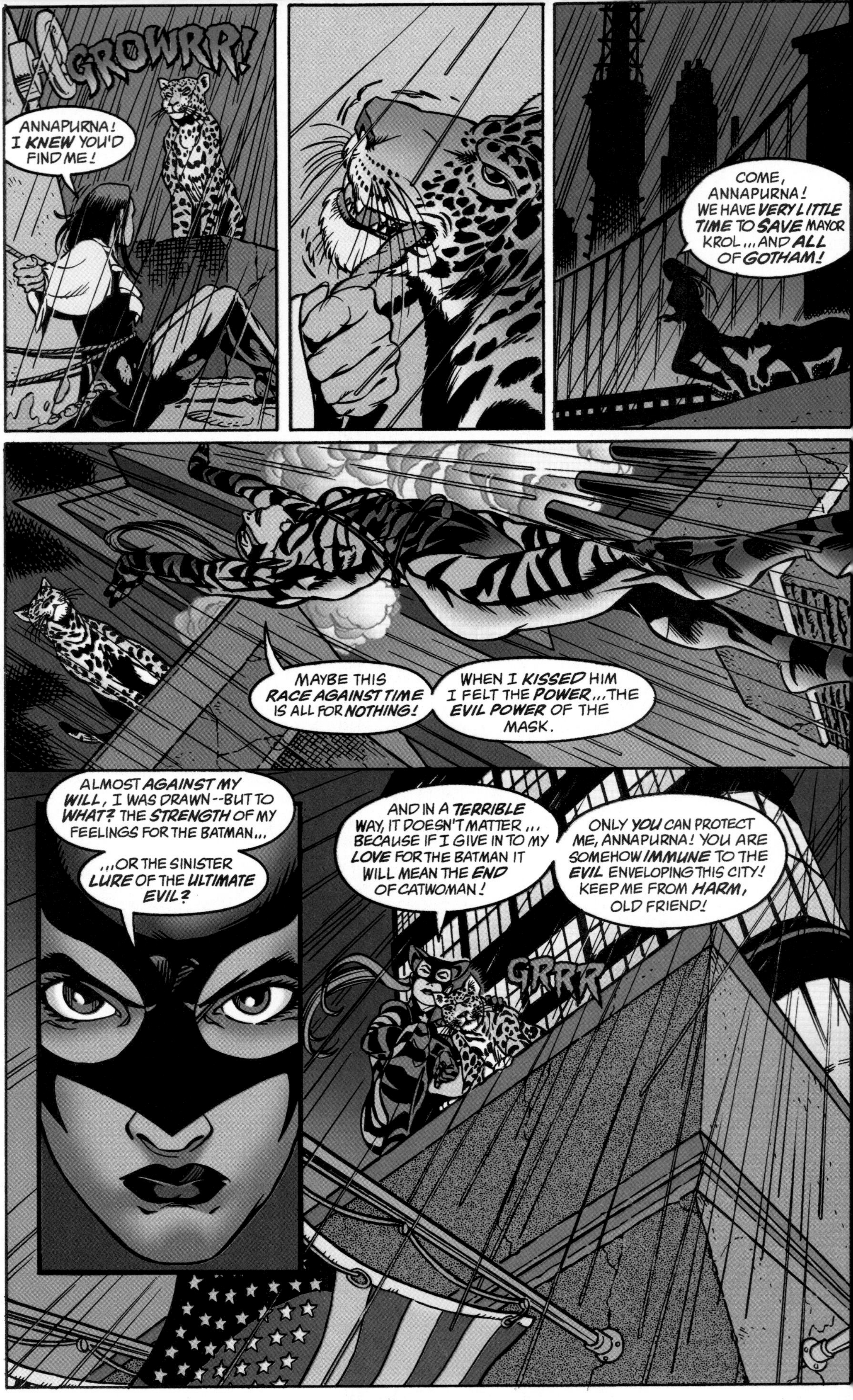
GROWRR!
ANNAPURNA! I KNEW YOU'D FIND ME!
COME, ANNAPURNA! WE HAVE VERY LITTLE TIME TO SAVE MAYOR KROL... AND ALL OF GOTHAM!
MAYBE THIS RACE AGAINST TIME IS ALL FOR NOTHING!
WHEN I KISSED HIM I FELT THE POWER... THE EVIL POWER OF THE MASK.
ALMOST AGAINST MY WILL, I WAS DRAWN--BUT TO WHAT? THE STRENGTH OF MY FEELINGS FOR THE BATMAN...
...OR THE SINISTER LURE OF THE ULTIMATE EVIL?
AND IN A TERRIBLE WAY, IT DOESN'T MATTER... BECAUSE IF I GIVE IN TO MY LOVE FOR THE BATMAN IT WILL MEAN THE END OF CATWOMAN!
ONLY YOU CAN PROTECT ME, ANNAPURNA! YOU ARE SOMEHOW IMMUNE TO THE EVIL ENVELOPING THIS CITY! KEEP ME FROM HARM, OLD FRIEND!
GRRR

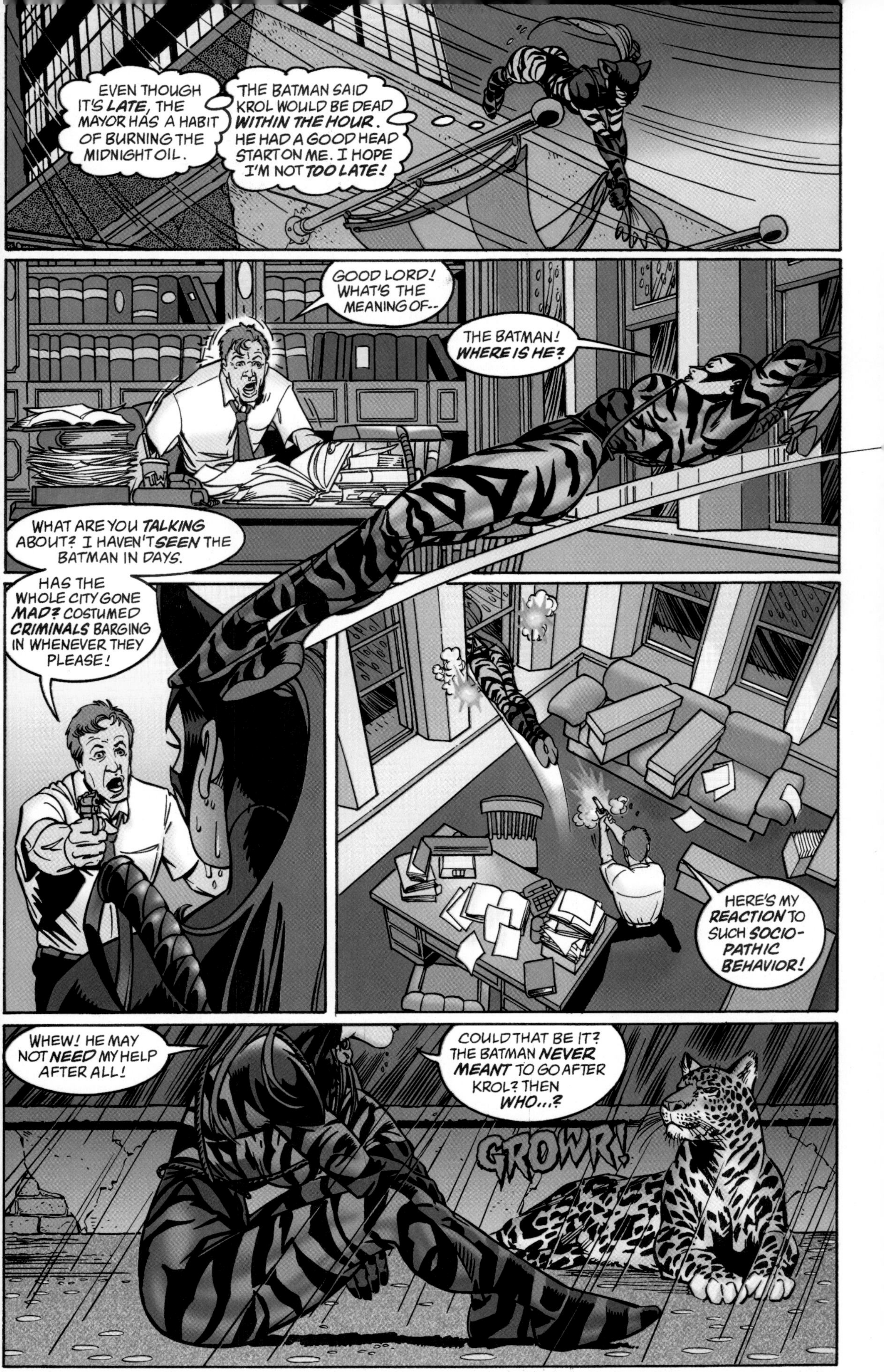
EVEN THOUGH IT'S *LATE*, THE MAYOR HAS A HABIT OF BURNING THE MIDNIGHT OIL.
THE BATMAN SAID KROL WOULD BE DEAD *WITHIN THE HOUR*. HE HAD A GOOD HEAD START ON ME. I HOPE I'M NOT *TOO LATE!*
GOOD LORD! WHAT'S THE MEANING OF--
THE BATMAN! *WHERE IS HE?*
WHAT ARE YOU *TALKING* ABOUT? I HAVEN'T *SEEN* THE BATMAN IN DAYS.
HAS THE WHOLE CITY GONE *MAD?* COSTUMED *CRIMINALS* BARGING IN WHENEVER THEY PLEASE!
HERE'S MY *REACTION* TO SUCH *SOCIO-PATHIC BEHAVIOR!*
WHEW! HE MAY NOT *NEED* MY HELP AFTER ALL!
COULD THAT BE IT? THE BATMAN *NEVER MEANT* TO GO AFTER KROL? THEN *WHO...?*
GROWR!

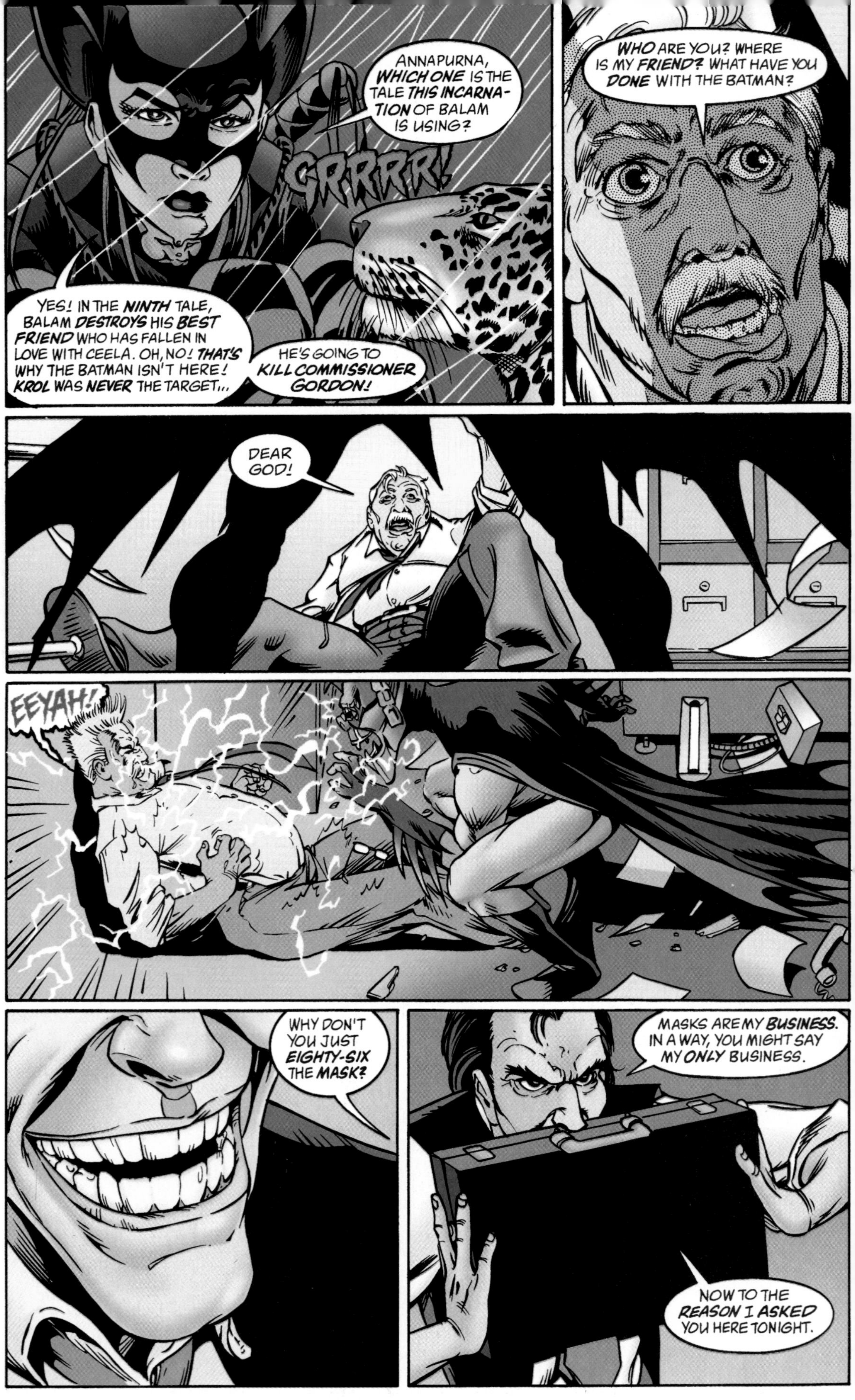
ANNAPURNA, WHICH ONE IS THE TALE THIS INCARNATION OF BALAM IS USING?
GRRRR!
YES! IN THE NINTH TALE, BALAM DESTROYS HIS BEST FRIEND WHO HAS FALLEN IN LOVE WITH CEELA. OH, NO! THAT'S WHY THE BATMAN ISN'T HERE! KROL WAS NEVER THE TARGET...
HE'S GOING TO KILL COMMISSIONER GORDON!
WHO ARE YOU? WHERE IS MY FRIEND? WHAT HAVE YOU DONE WITH THE BATMAN?
DEAR GOD!
EEYAH!
WHY DON'T YOU JUST EIGHTY-SIX THE MASK?
MASKS ARE MY BUSINESS. IN A WAY, YOU MIGHT SAY MY ONLY BUSINESS.
NOW TO THE REASON I ASKED YOU HERE TONIGHT.

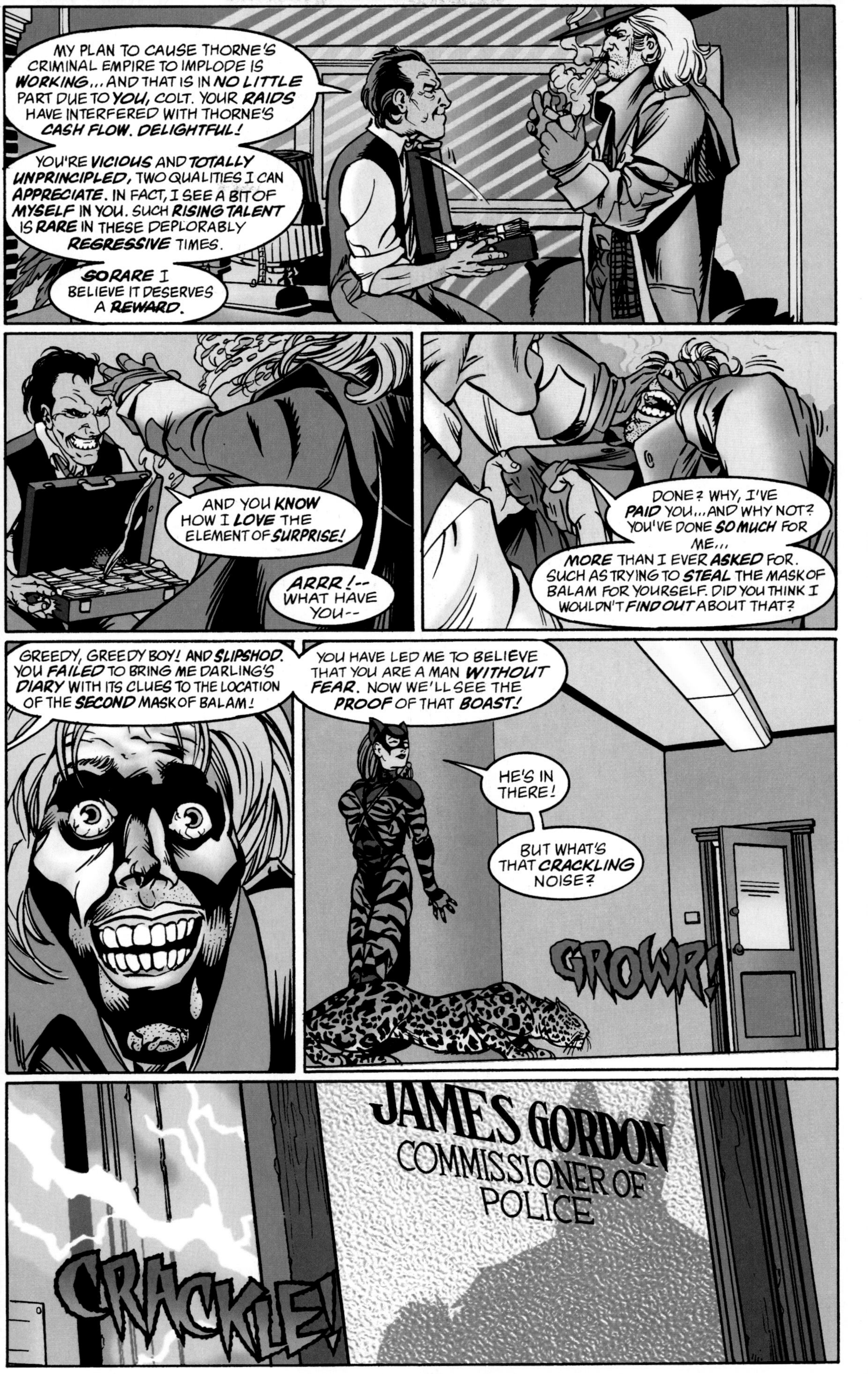
MY PLAN TO CAUSE THORNE'S CRIMINAL EMPIRE TO IMPLODE IS WORKING... AND THAT IS IN NO LITTLE PART DUE TO YOU, COLT. YOUR RAIDS HAVE INTERFERED WITH THORNE'S CASH FLOW. DELIGHTFUL!
YOU'RE VICIOUS AND TOTALLY UNPRINCIPLED, TWO QUALITIES I CAN APPRECIATE. IN FACT, I SEE A BIT OF MYSELF IN YOU. SUCH RISING TALENT IS RARE IN THESE DEPLORABLY REGRESSIVE TIMES.
SO RARE I BELIEVE IT DESERVES A REWARD.
AND YOU KNOW HOW I LOVE THE ELEMENT OF SURPRISE!
ARRR!-- WHAT HAVE YOU--
DONE? WHY, I'VE PAID YOU... AND WHY NOT? YOU'VE DONE SO MUCH FOR ME...
MORE THAN I EVER ASKED FOR. SUCH AS TRYING TO STEAL THE MASK OF BALAM FOR YOURSELF. DID YOU THINK I WOULDN'T FIND OUT ABOUT THAT?
GREEDY, GREEDY BOY! AND SLIPSHOD. YOU FAILED TO BRING ME DARLING'S DIARY WITH ITS CLUES TO THE LOCATION OF THE SECOND MASK OF BALAM!
YOU HAVE LED ME TO BELIEVE THAT YOU ARE A MAN WITHOUT FEAR. NOW WE'LL SEE THE PROOF OF THAT BOAST!
HE'S IN THERE!
BUT WHAT'S THAT CRACKLING NOISE?
GROWR!
JAMES GORDON
COMMISSIONER OF POLICE
CRACKLE!

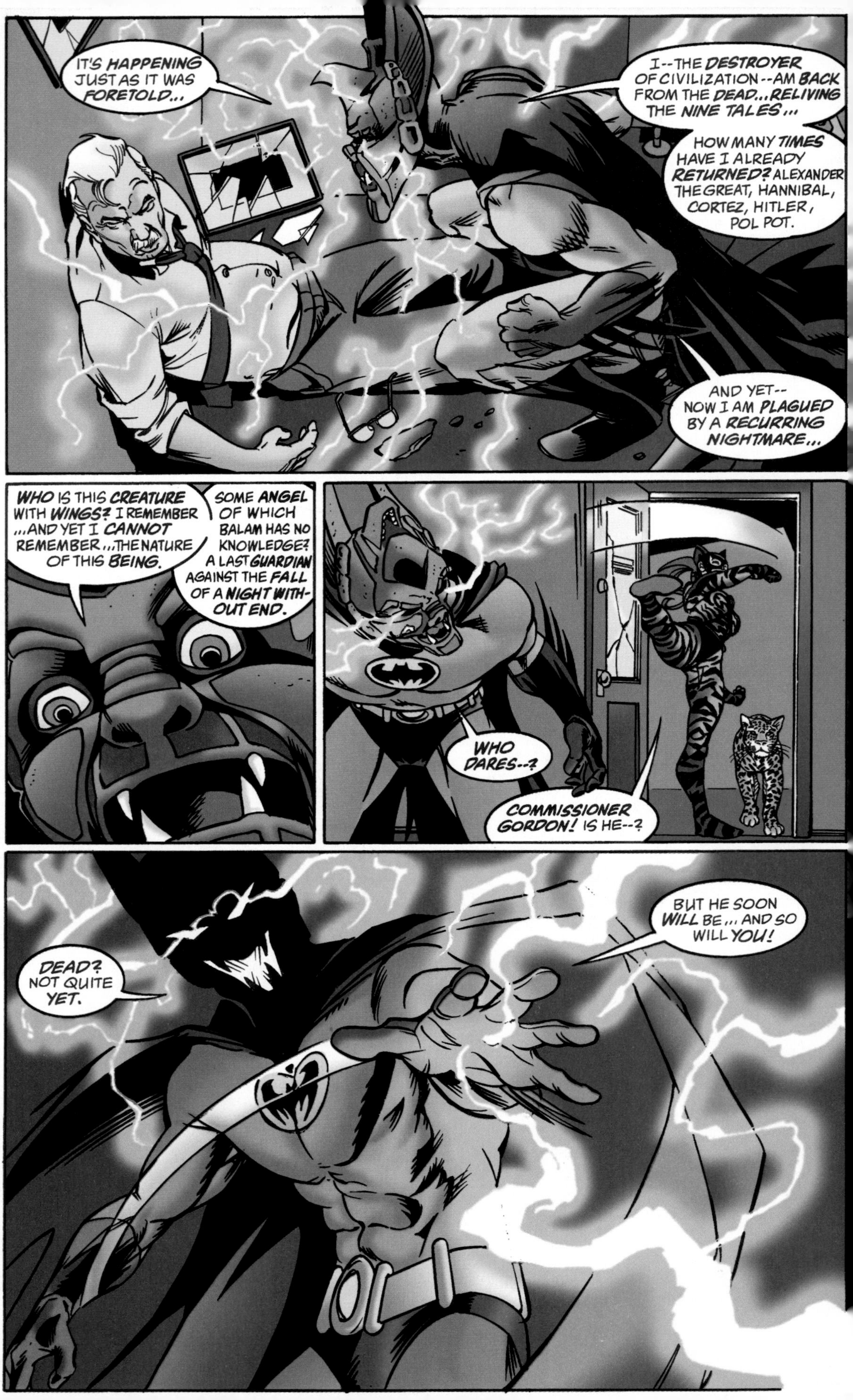
IT'S HAPPENING JUST AS IT WAS FORETOLD...
I--THE DESTROYER OF CIVILIZATION--AM BACK FROM THE DEAD...RELIVING THE NINE TALES...
HOW MANY TIMES HAVE I ALREADY RETURNED? ALEXANDER THE GREAT, HANNIBAL, CORTEZ, HITLER, POL POT.
AND YET-- NOW I AM PLAGUED BY A RECURRING NIGHTMARE...
WHO IS THIS CREATURE WITH WINGS? I REMEMBER ...AND YET I CANNOT REMEMBER...THE NATURE OF THIS BEING.
SOME ANGEL OF WHICH BALAM HAS NO KNOWLEDGE? A LAST GUARDIAN AGAINST THE FALL OF A NIGHT WITHOUT END.
WHO DARES--?
COMMISSIONER GORDON! IS HE--?
DEAD? NOT QUITE YET.
BUT HE SOON WILL BE... AND SO WILL YOU!

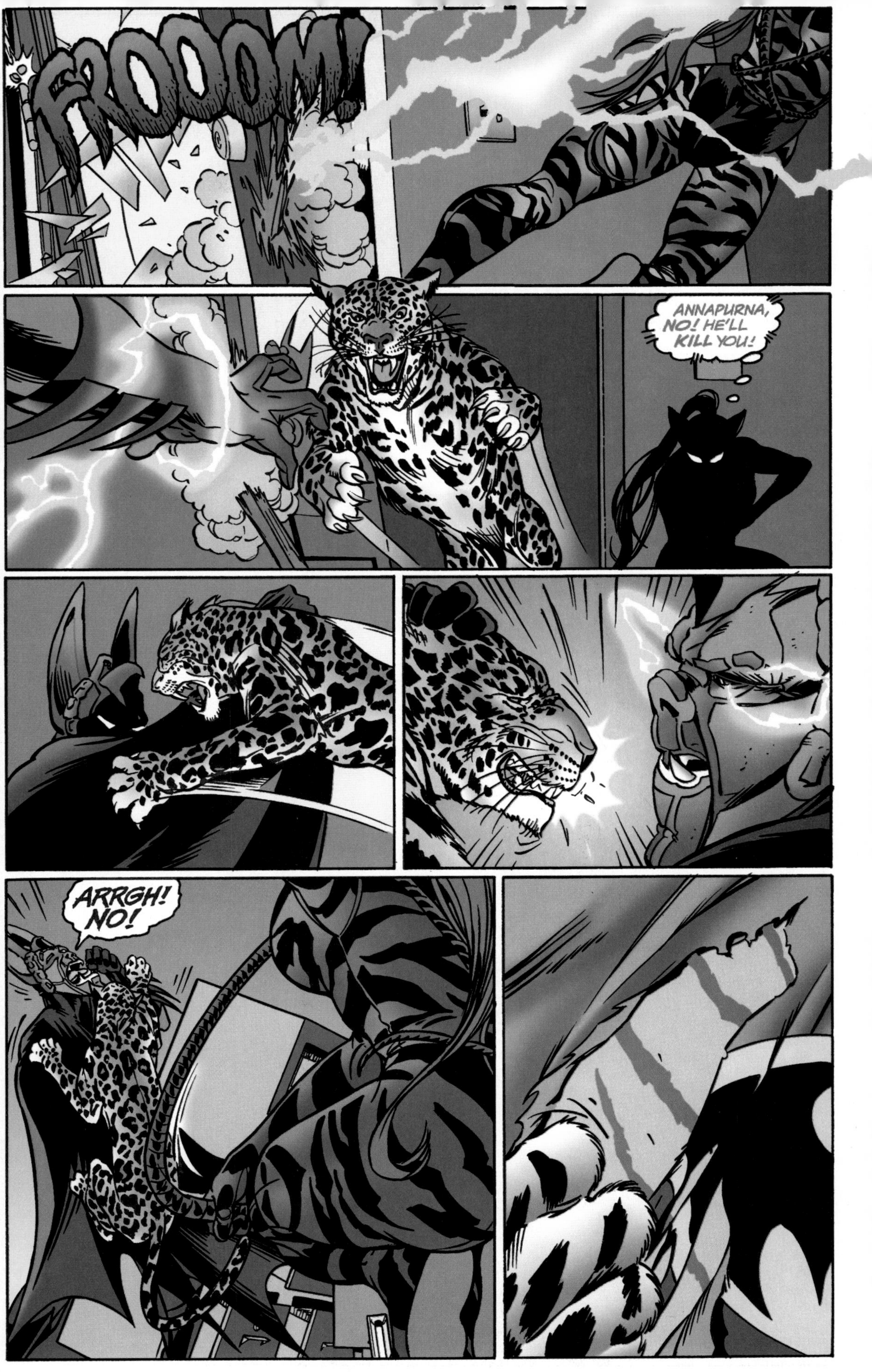
FROOOM!
ANNAPURNA, NO! HE'LL KILL YOU!
ARRGH! NO!

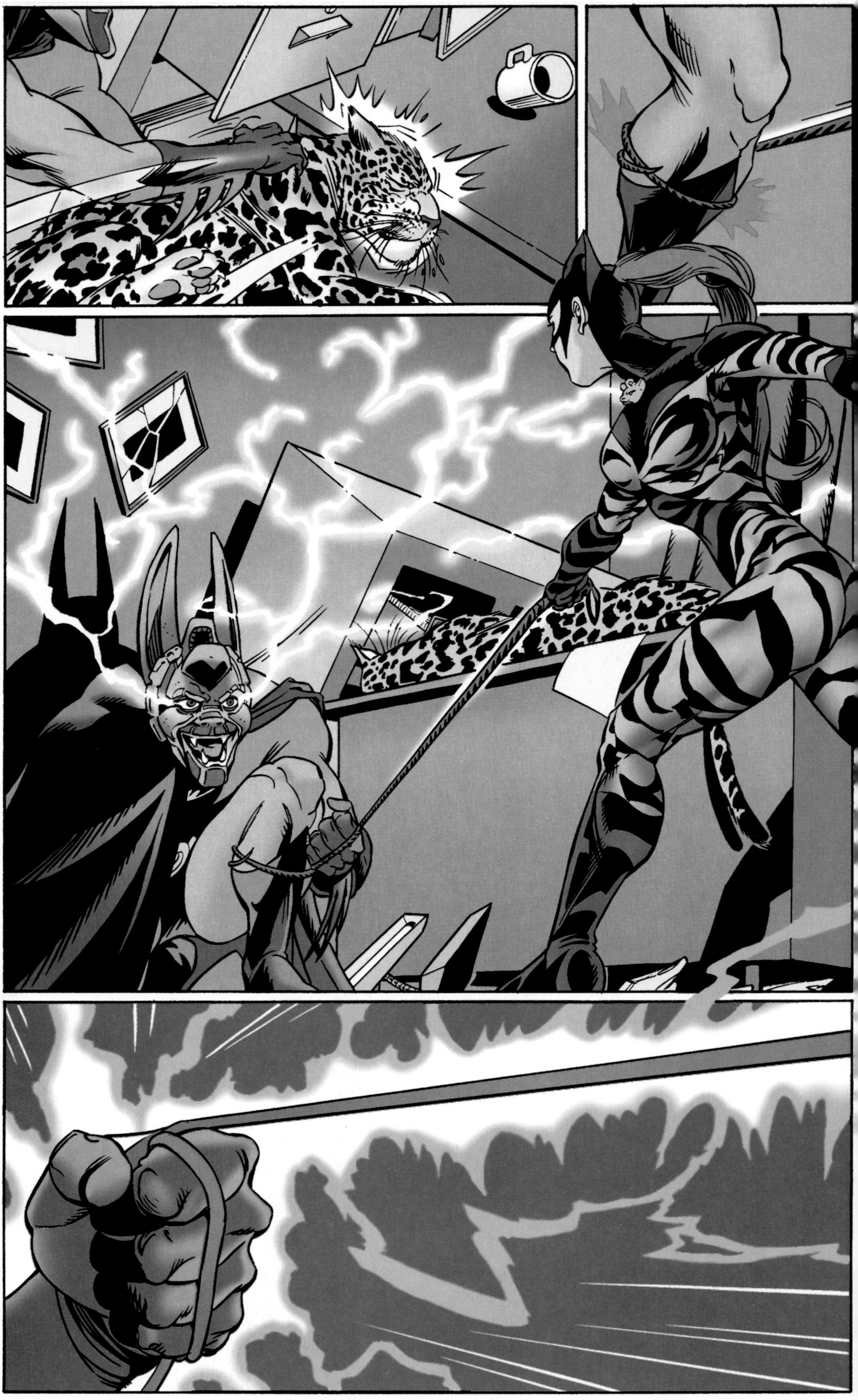

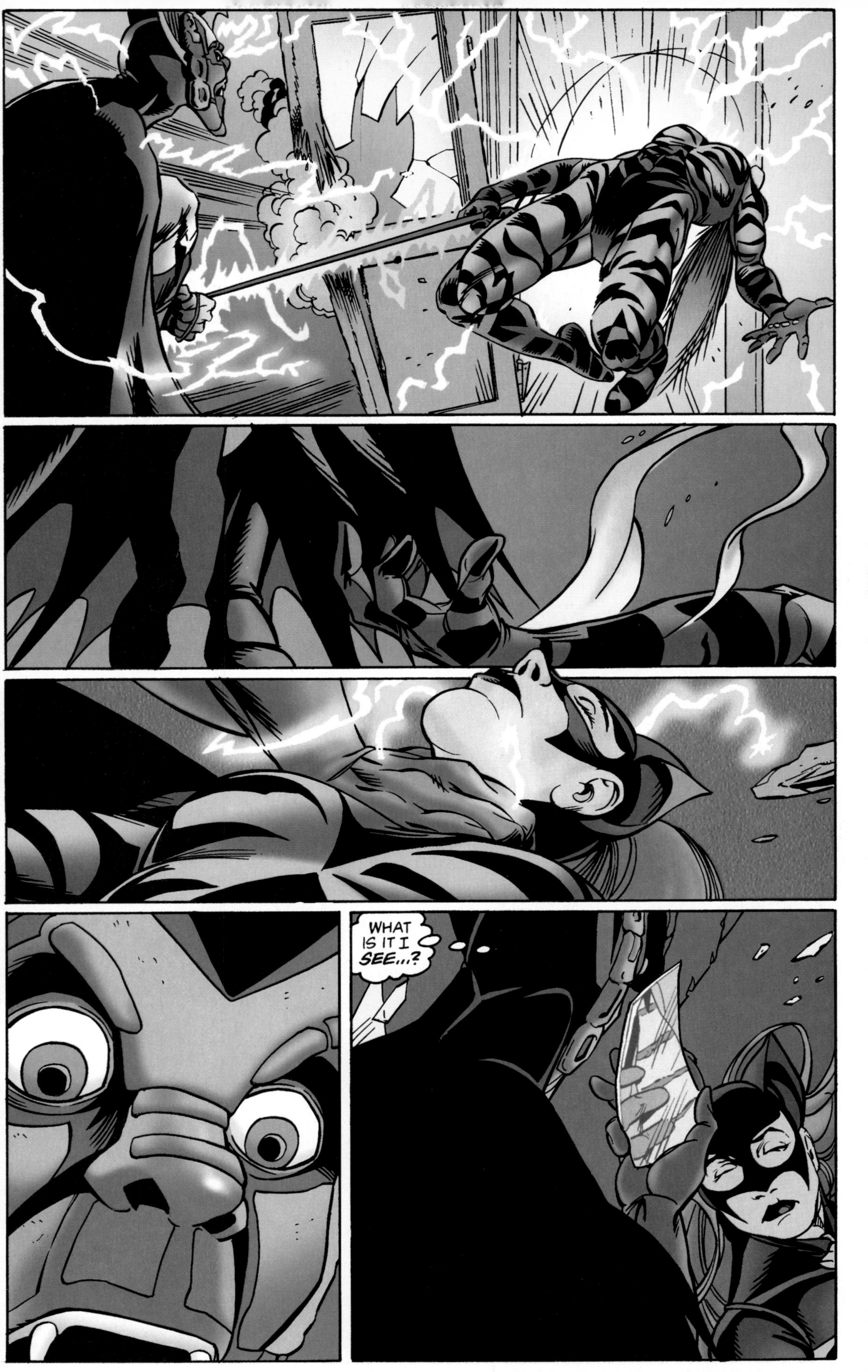
WHAT IS IT I SEE...?

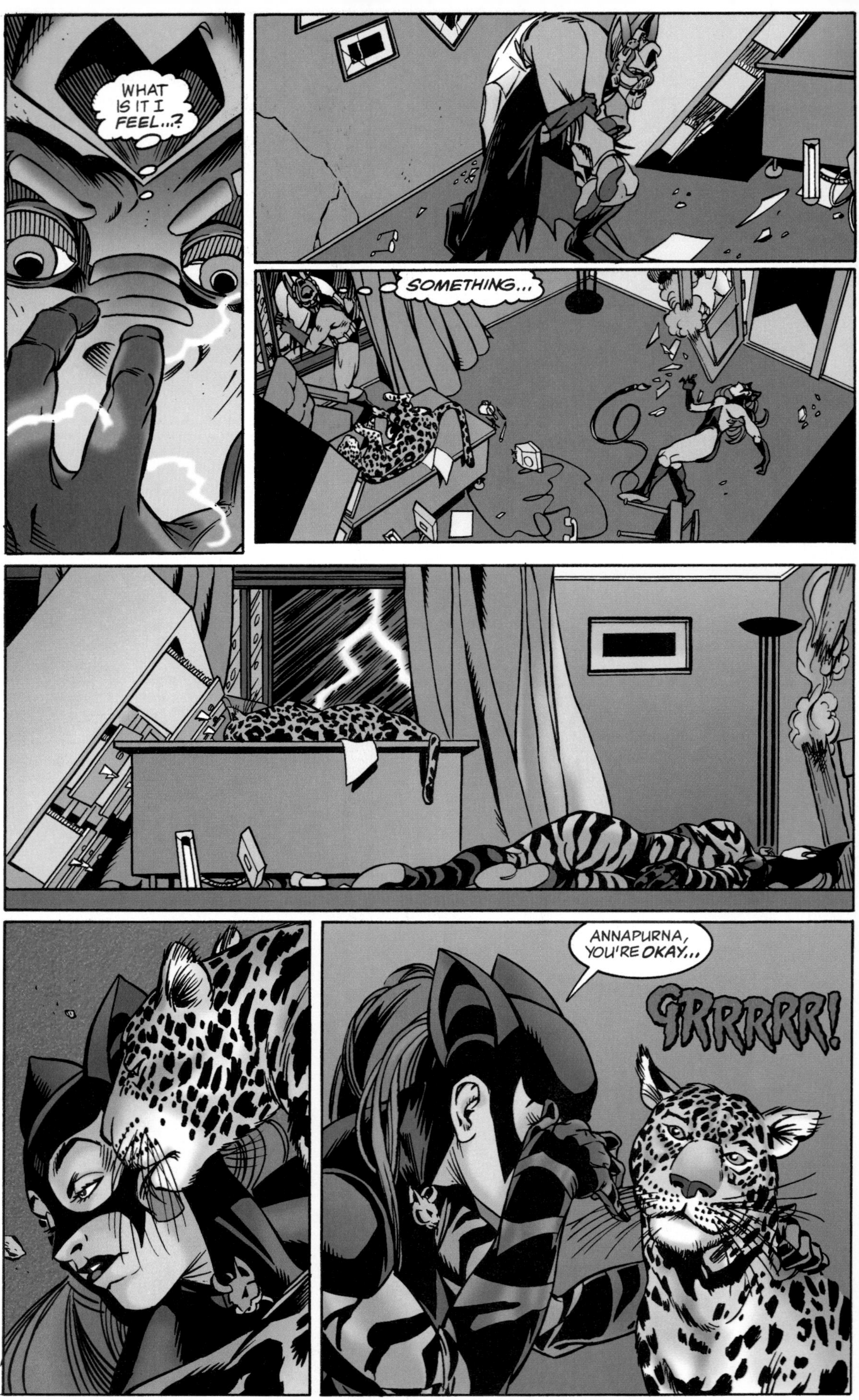
WHAT IS IT I FEEL...?
SOMETHING...
ANNAPURNA, YOU'RE OKAY...
GRRRRR!

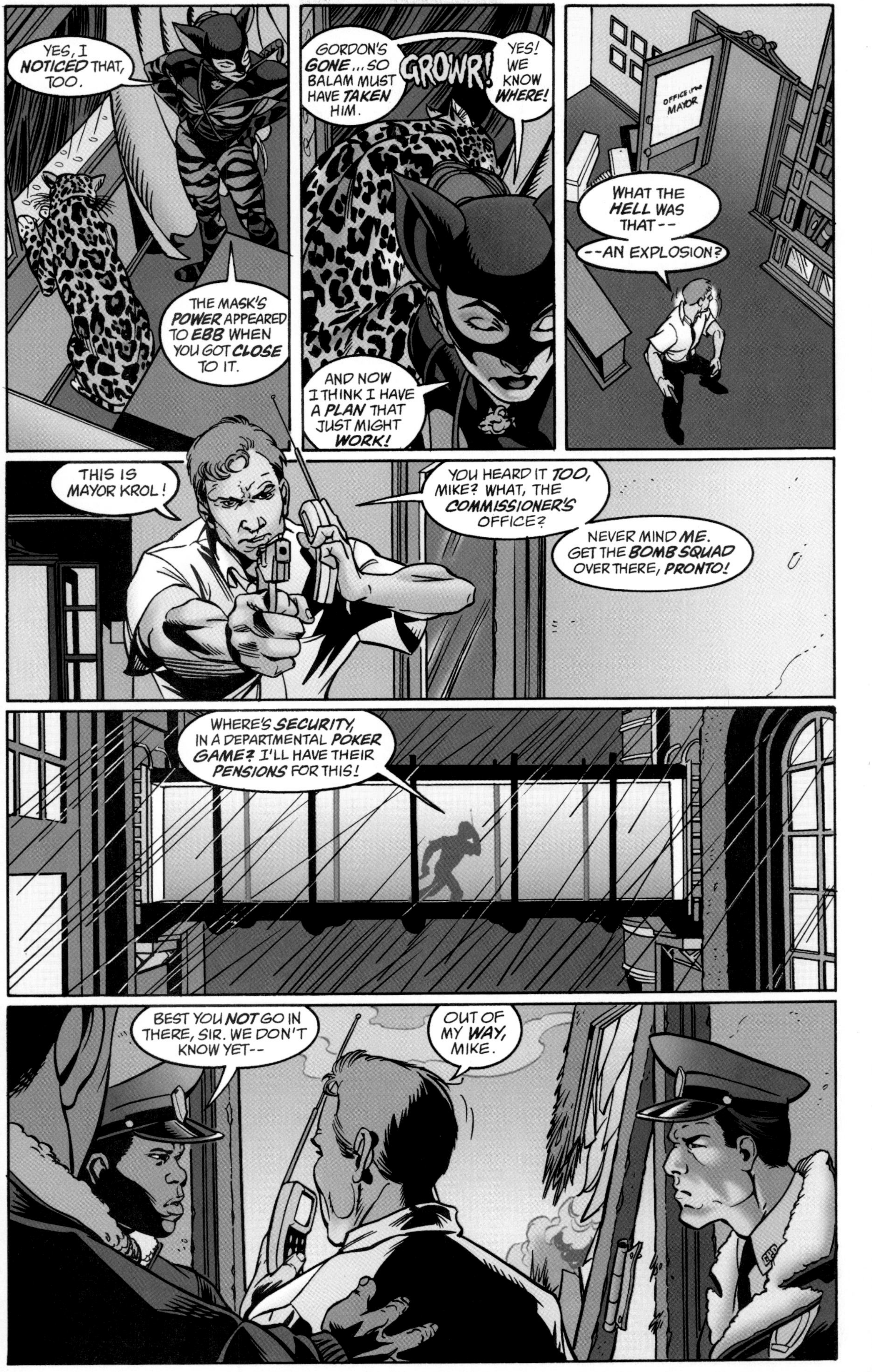
YES, I NOTICED THAT, TOO.
THE MASK'S POWER APPEARED TO EBB WHEN YOU GOT CLOSE TO IT.
GORDON'S GONE... SO BALAM MUST HAVE TAKEN HIM.
GROWR!
YES! WE KNOW WHERE!
AND NOW I THINK I HAVE A PLAN THAT JUST MIGHT WORK!
OFFICE OF THE MAYOR
WHAT THE HELL WAS THAT--
--AN EXPLOSION?
THIS IS MAYOR KROL!
YOU HEARD IT TOO, MIKE? WHAT, THE COMMISSIONER'S OFFICE?
NEVER MIND ME. GET THE BOMB SQUAD OVER THERE, PRONTO!
WHERE'S SECURITY, IN A DEPARTMENTAL POKER GAME? I'LL HAVE THEIR PENSIONS FOR THIS!
BEST YOU NOT GO IN THERE, SIR. WE DON'T KNOW YET--
OUT OF MY WAY, MIKE.

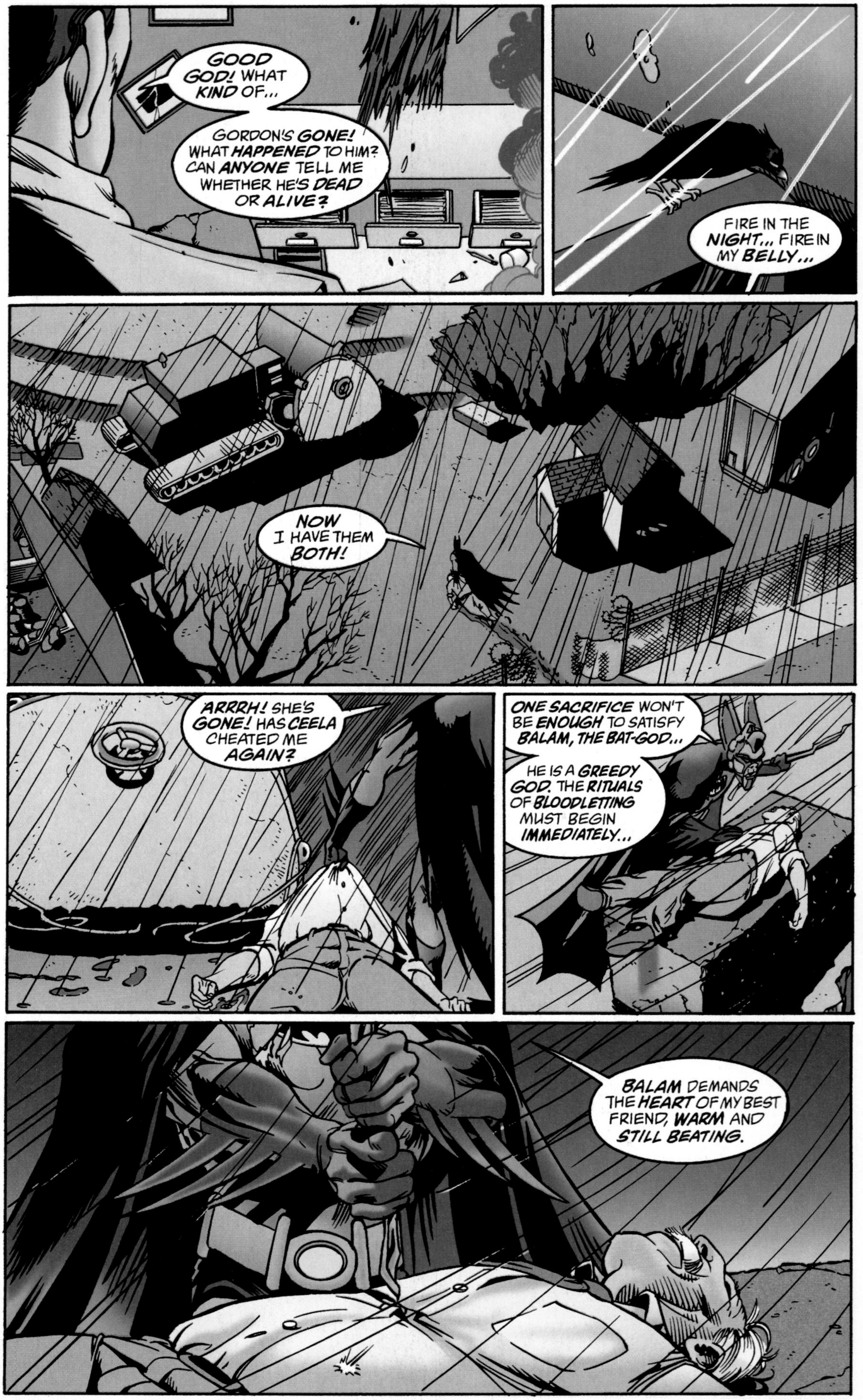
GOOD GOD! WHAT KIND OF...
GORDON'S GONE! WHAT HAPPENED TO HIM? CAN ANYONE TELL ME WHETHER HE'S DEAD OR ALIVE?
FIRE IN THE NIGHT... FIRE IN MY BELLY...
NOW I HAVE THEM BOTH!
ARRRH! SHE'S GONE! HAS CEELA CHEATED ME AGAIN?
ONE SACRIFICE WON'T BE ENOUGH TO SATISFY BALAM, THE BAT-GOD...
HE IS A GREEDY GOD. THE RITUALS OF BLOODLETTING MUST BEGIN IMMEDIATELY...
BALAM DEMANDS THE HEART OF MY BEST FRIEND, WARM AND STILL BEATING.

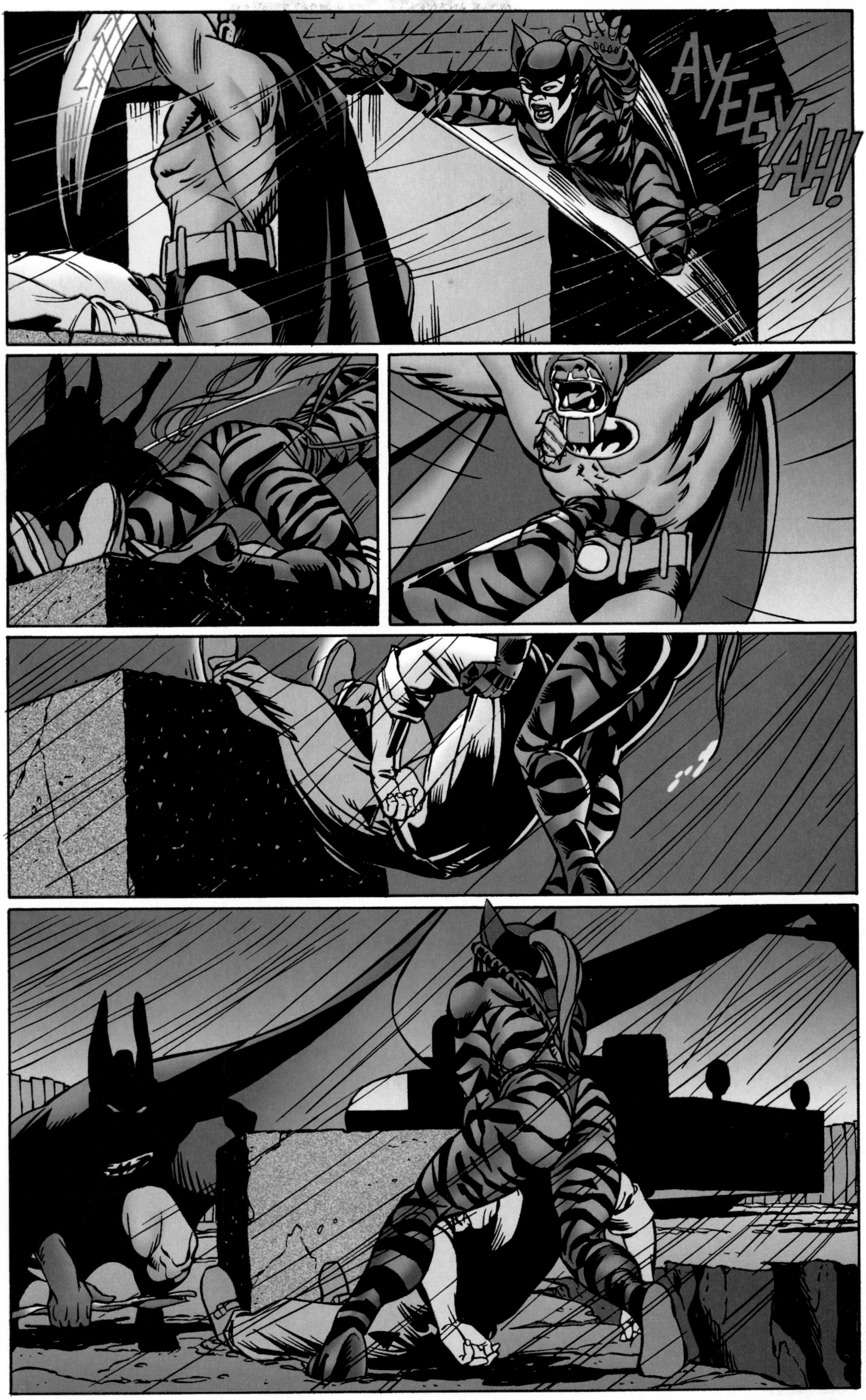
AYEEYAH!

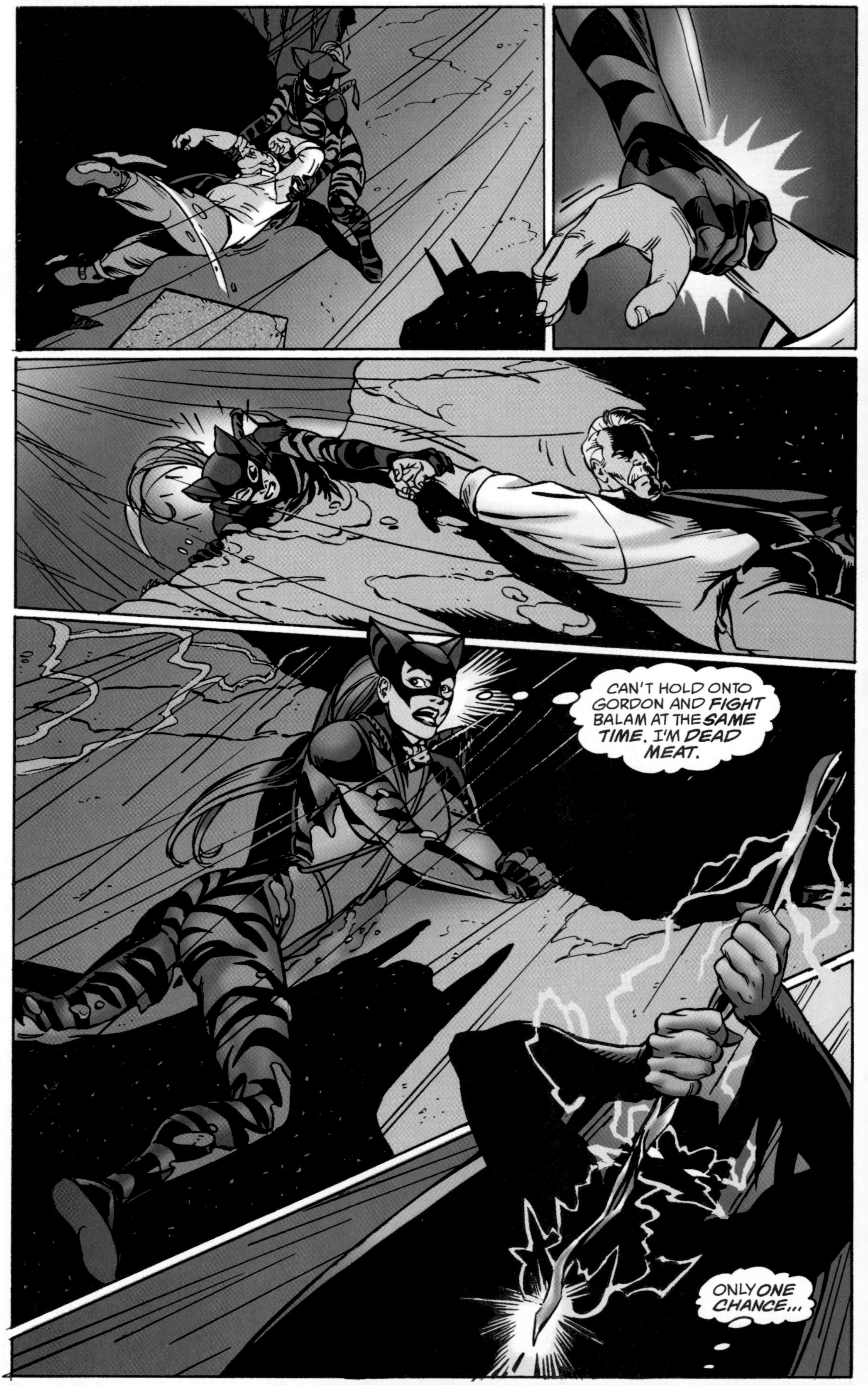

CAN'T HOLD ONTO GORDON AND FIGHT BALAM AT THE SAME TIME. I'M DEAD MEAT.
ONLY ONE CHANCE...

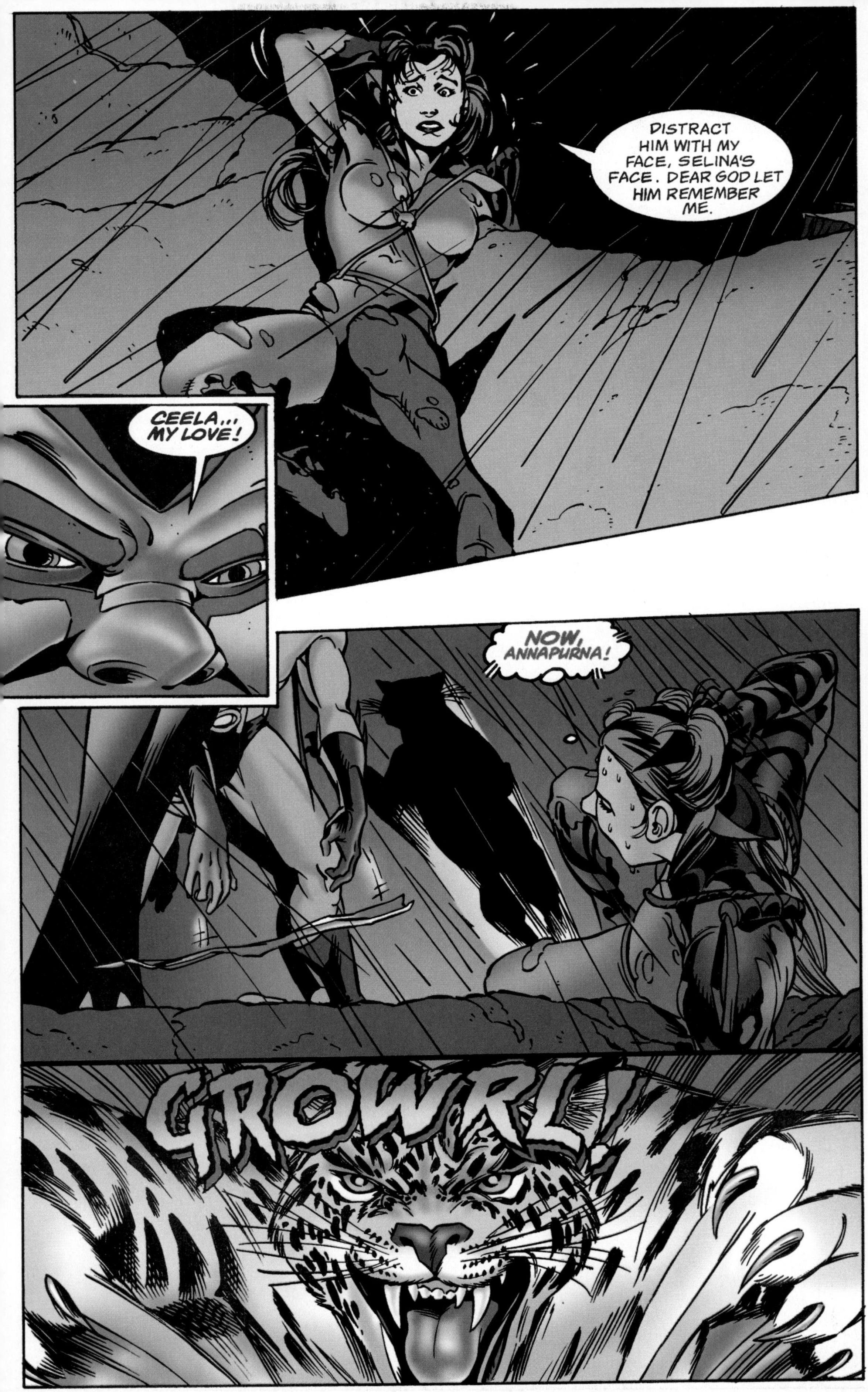
DISTRACT HIM WITH MY FACE, SELINA'S FACE. DEAR GOD LET HIM REMEMBER ME.
CEELA... MY LOVE!
NOW, ANNAPURNA!
GROWRL!

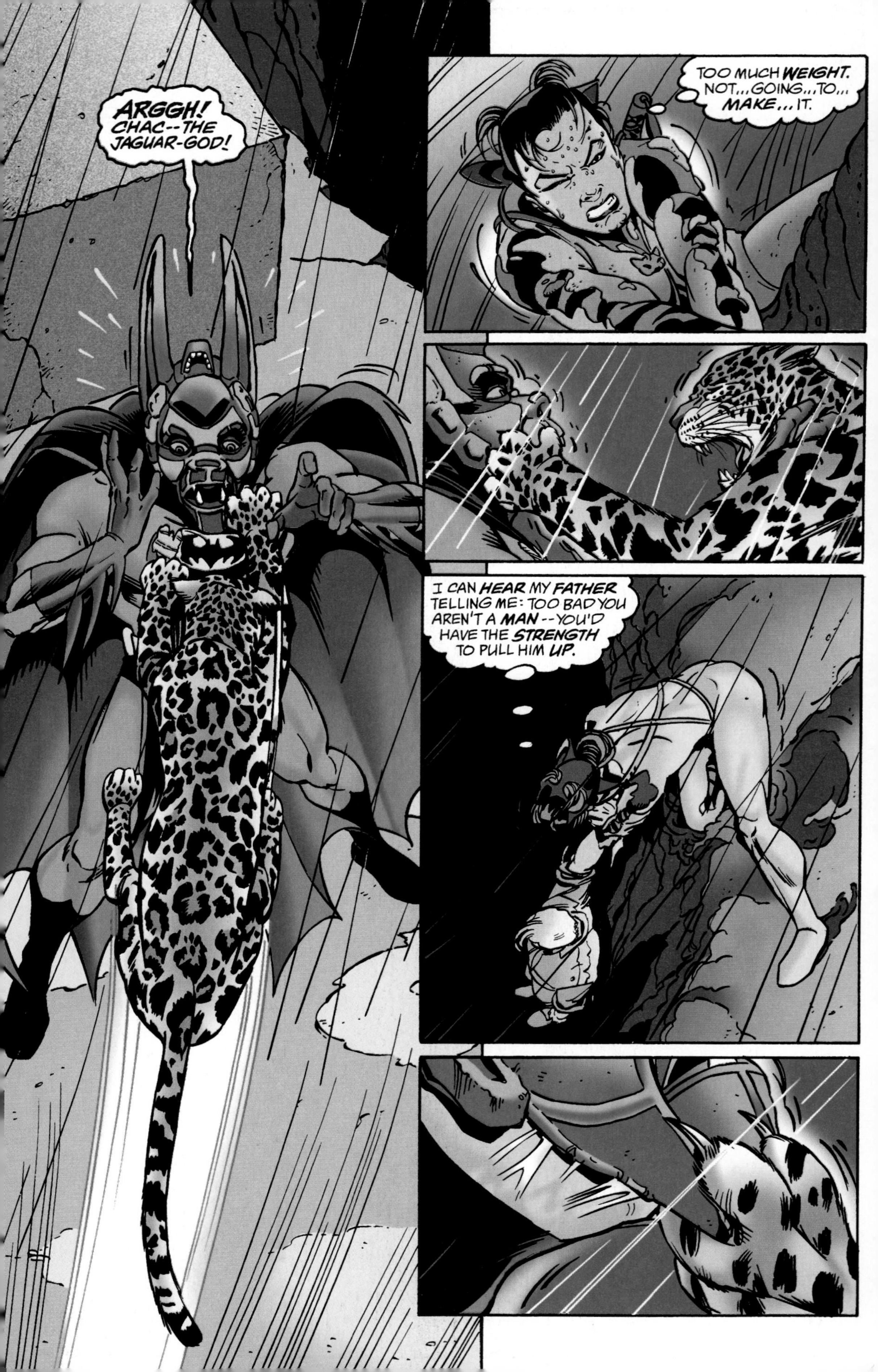

ARGGH! CHAC--THE JAGUAR-GOD!
TOO MUCH WEIGHT. NOT,,, GOING,,, TO,,, MAKE,,, IT.
I CAN HEAR MY FATHER TELLING ME: TOO BAD YOU AREN'T A MAN --YOU'D HAVE THE STRENGTH TO PULL HIM UP.

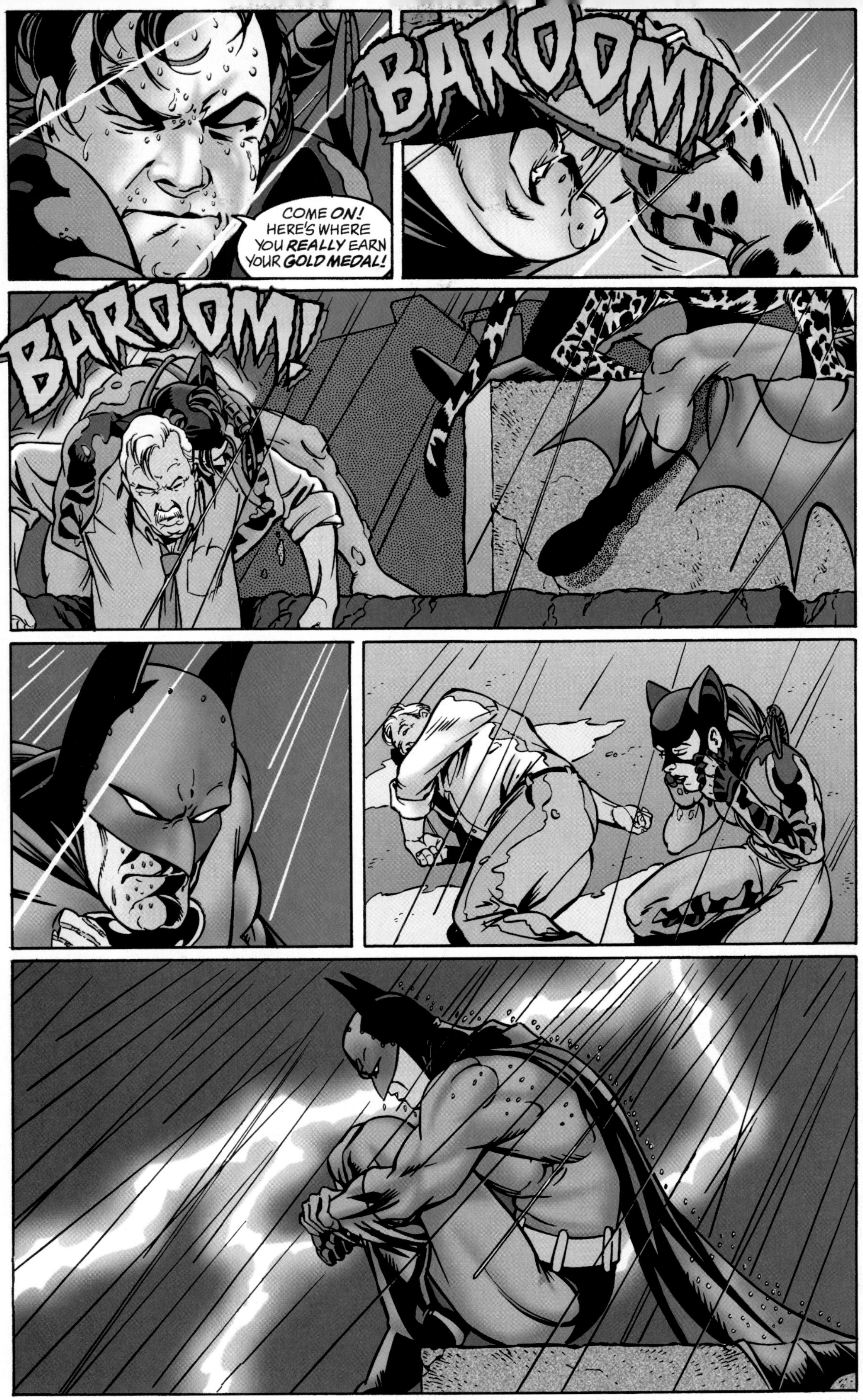
BAROOM!
COME ON! HERE'S WHERE YOU REALLY EARN YOUR GOLD MEDAL!
BAROOM!

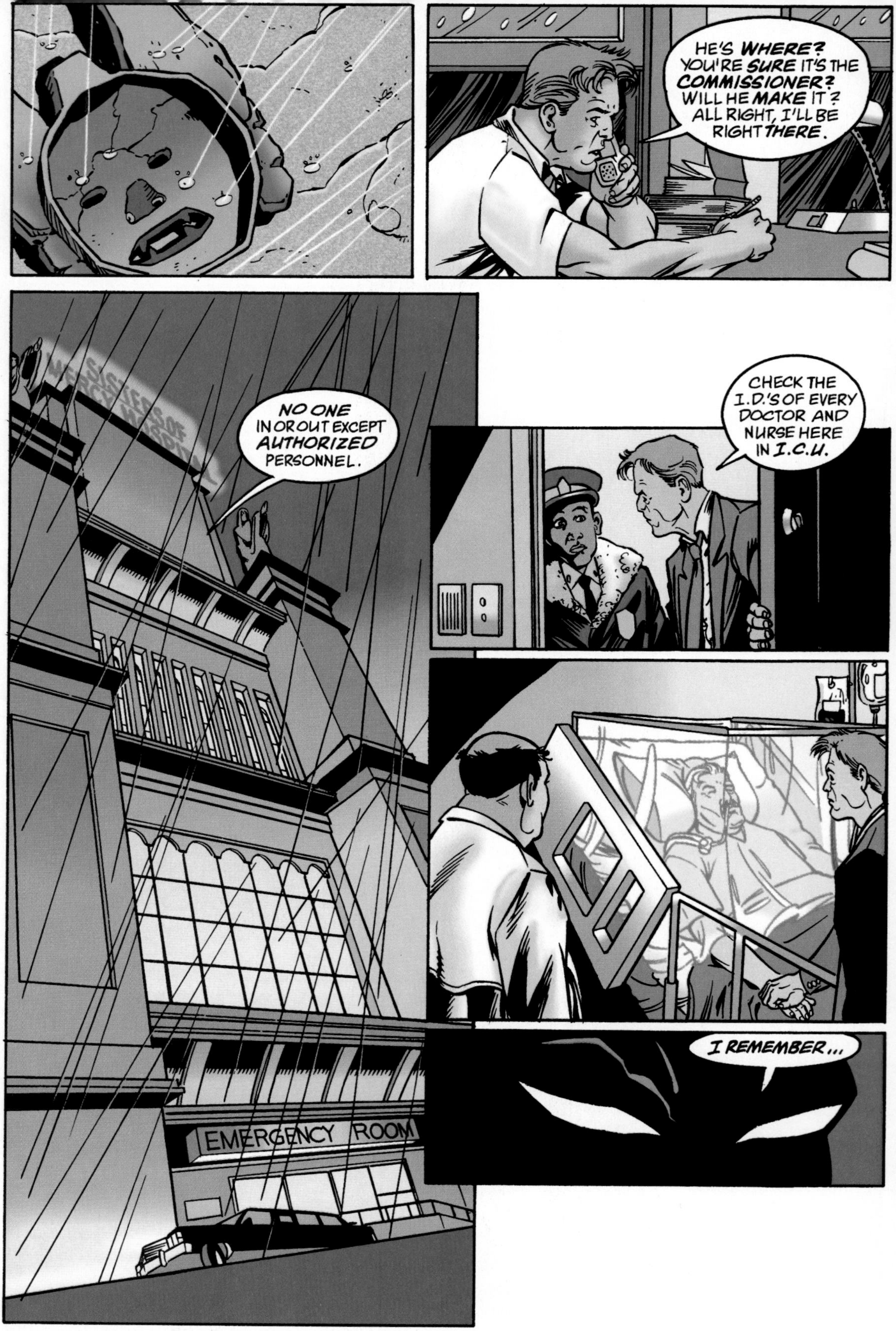
HE'S WHERE? YOU'RE SURE IT'S THE COMMISSIONER? WILL HE MAKE IT? ALL RIGHT, I'LL BE RIGHT THERE.
NO ONE IN OR OUT EXCEPT AUTHORIZED PERSONNEL.
EMERGENCY ROOM
CHECK THE I.D.'S OF EVERY DOCTOR AND NURSE HERE IN I.C.U.
I REMEMBER...

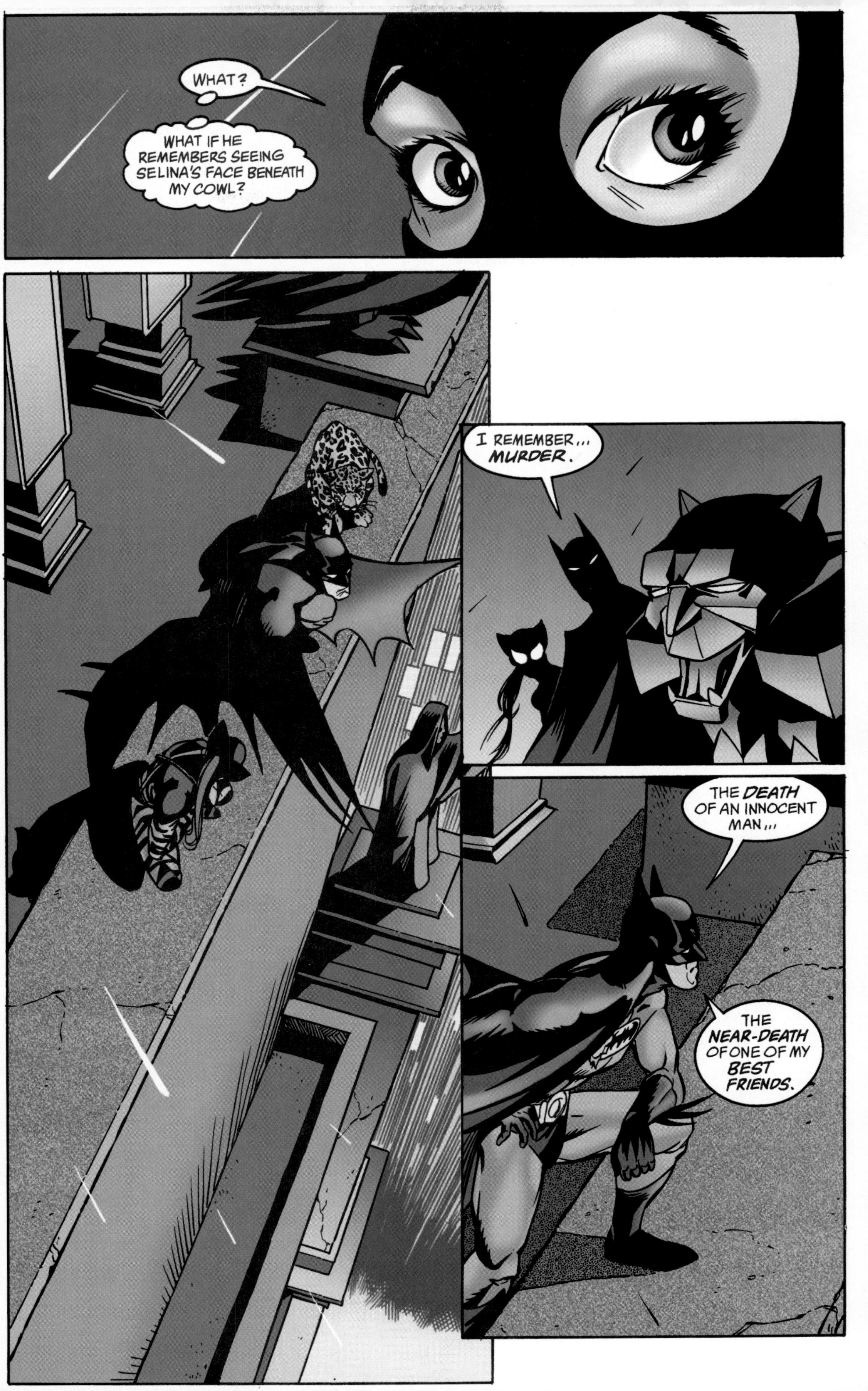
WHAT?
WHAT IF HE REMEMBERS SEEING SELINA'S FACE BENEATH MY COWL?
I REMEMBER... MURDER.
THE DEATH OF AN INNOCENT MAN...
THE NEAR-DEATH OF ONE OF MY BEST FRIENDS.

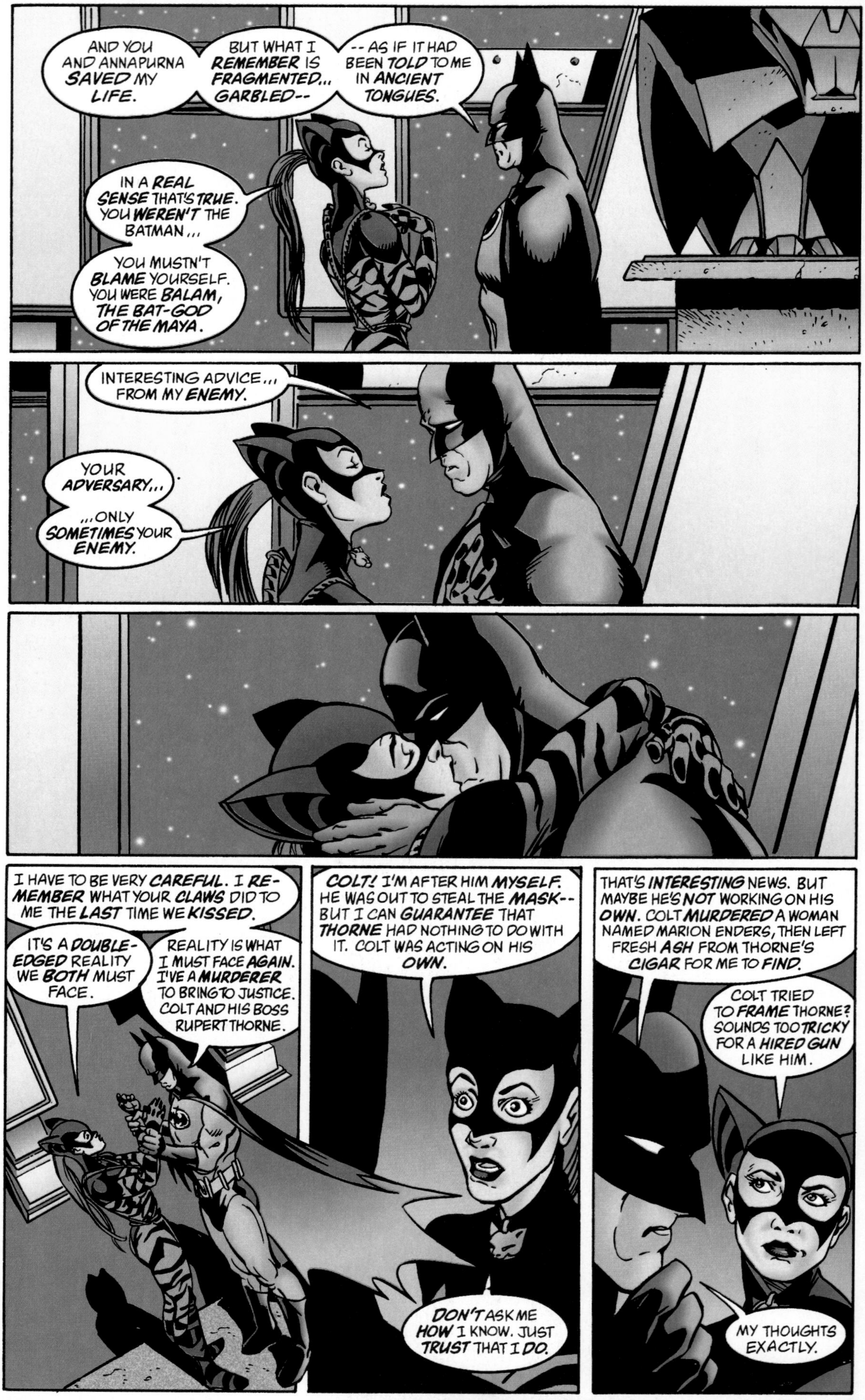
AND YOU AND ANNAPURNA SAVED MY LIFE.
BUT WHAT I REMEMBER IS FRAGMENTED... GARBLED--
--AS IF IT HAD BEEN TOLD TO ME IN ANCIENT TONGUES.
IN A REAL SENSE THAT'S TRUE. YOU WEREN'T THE BATMAN...
YOU MUSTN'T BLAME YOURSELF. YOU WERE BALAM, THE BAT-GOD OF THE MAYA.
INTERESTING ADVICE... FROM MY ENEMY.
YOUR ADVERSARY...
...ONLY SOMETIMES YOUR ENEMY.
I HAVE TO BE VERY CAREFUL. I REMEMBER WHAT YOUR CLAWS DID TO ME THE LAST TIME WE KISSED.
IT'S A DOUBLE-EDGED REALITY WE BOTH MUST FACE.
REALITY IS WHAT I MUST FACE AGAIN. I'VE A MURDERER TO BRING TO JUSTICE. COLT AND HIS BOSS RUPERT THORNE.
COLT! I'M AFTER HIM MYSELF. HE WAS OUT TO STEAL THE MASK-- BUT I CAN GUARANTEE THAT THORNE HAD NOTHING TO DO WITH IT. COLT WAS ACTING ON HIS OWN.
DON'T ASK ME HOW I KNOW. JUST TRUST THAT I DO.
THAT'S INTERESTING NEWS. BUT MAYBE HE'S NOT WORKING ON HIS OWN. COLT MURDERED A WOMAN NAMED MARION ENDERS, THEN LEFT FRESH ASH FROM THORNE'S CIGAR FOR ME TO FIND.
COLT TRIED TO FRAME THORNE? SOUNDS TOO TRICKY FOR A HIRED GUN LIKE HIM.
MY THOUGHTS EXACTLY.

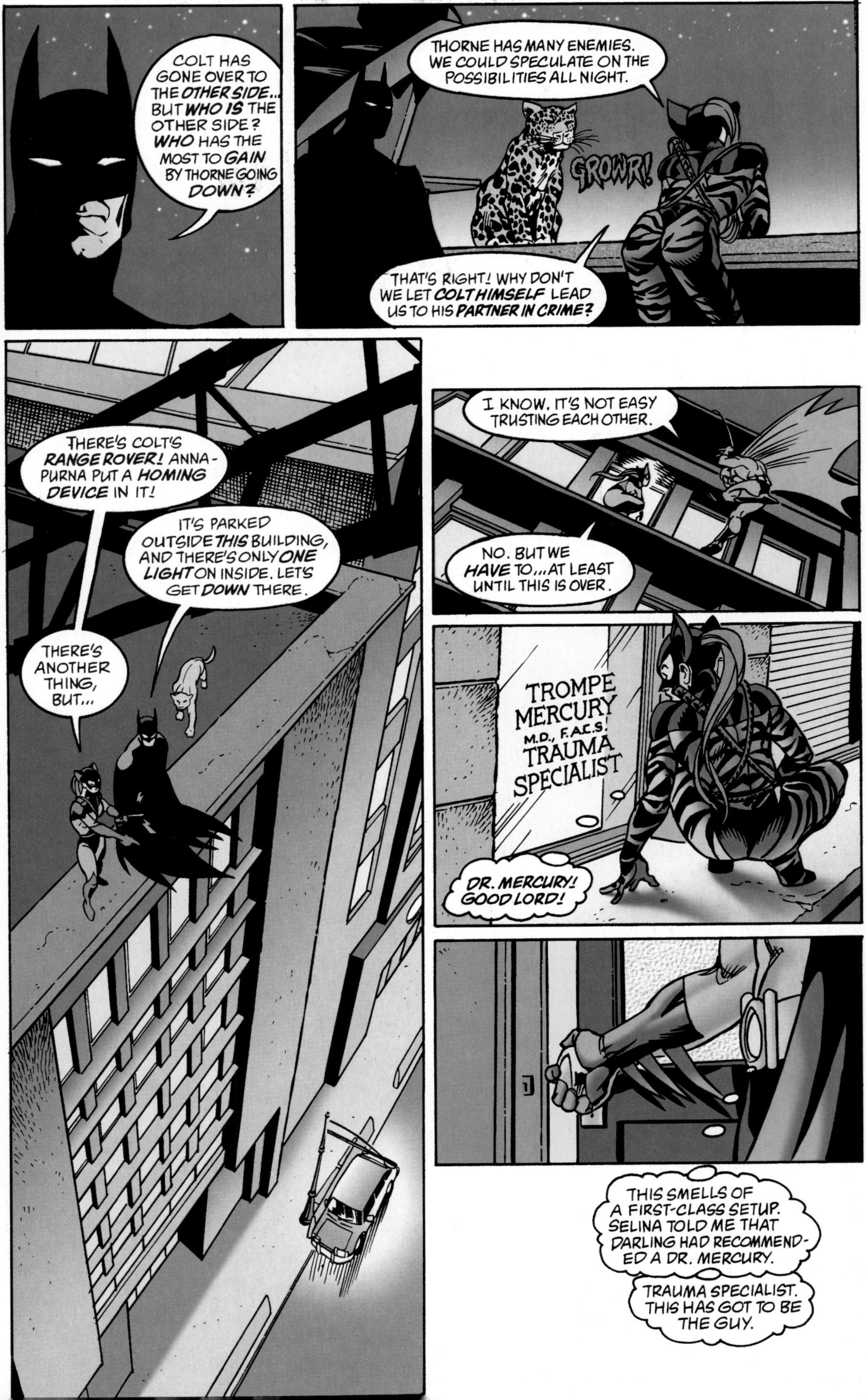

COLT HAS GONE OVER TO THE OTHER SIDE... BUT WHO IS THE OTHER SIDE? WHO HAS THE MOST TO GAIN BY THORNE GOING DOWN?
THORNE HAS MANY ENEMIES. WE COULD SPECULATE ON THE POSSIBILITIES ALL NIGHT.
GROWR!
THAT'S RIGHT! WHY DON'T WE LET COLT HIMSELF LEAD US TO HIS PARTNER IN CRIME?
THERE'S COLT'S RANGE ROVER! ANNA-PURNA PUT A HOMING DEVICE IN IT!
IT'S PARKED OUTSIDE THIS BUILDING, AND THERE'S ONLY ONE LIGHT ON INSIDE. LET'S GET DOWN THERE.
THERE'S ANOTHER THING, BUT...
I KNOW. IT'S NOT EASY TRUSTING EACH OTHER.
NO. BUT WE HAVE TO... AT LEAST UNTIL THIS IS OVER.
TROMPE MERCURY M.D., F.A.C.S. TRAUMA SPECIALIST
DR. MERCURY! GOOD LORD!
THIS SMELLS OF A FIRST-CLASS SETUP. SELINA TOLD ME THAT DARLING HAD RECOMMENDED A DR. MERCURY.
TRAUMA SPECIALIST. THIS HAS GOT TO BE THE GUY.

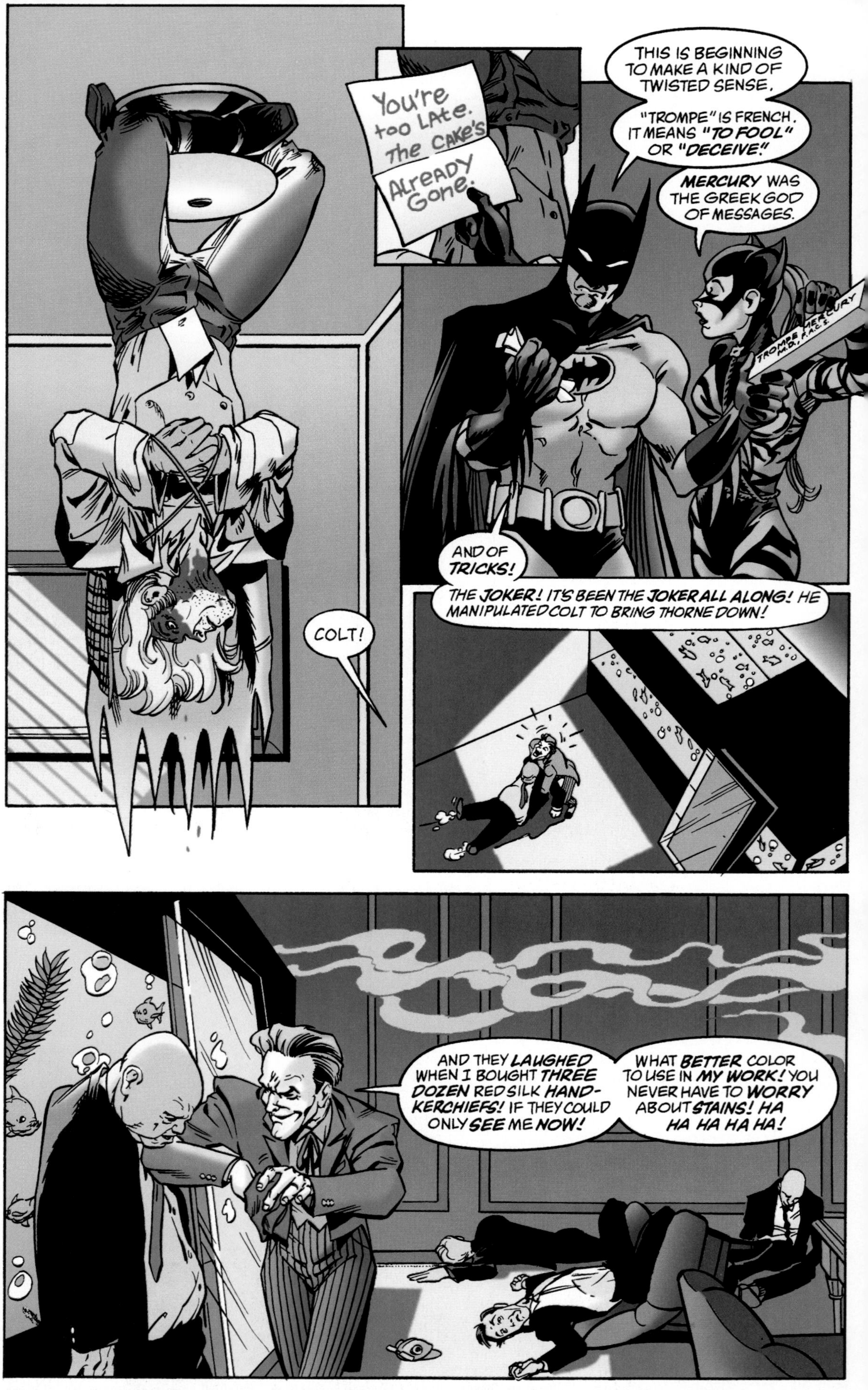
You're too LAte. The CAke's AlreADy Gone.
THIS IS BEGINNING TO MAKE A KIND OF TWISTED SENSE.
"TROMPE" IS FRENCH. IT MEANS "TO FOOL" OR "DECEIVE."
MERCURY WAS THE GREEK GOD OF MESSAGES.
TROMPE MERCURY M.D., F.A.C.S.
AND OF TRICKS!
THE JOKER! IT'S BEEN THE JOKER ALL ALONG! HE MANIPULATED COLT TO BRING THORNE DOWN!
COLT!
AND THEY LAUGHED WHEN I BOUGHT THREE DOZEN RED SILK HANDKERCHIEFS! IF THEY COULD ONLY SEE ME NOW!
WHAT BETTER COLOR TO USE IN MY WORK! YOU NEVER HAVE TO WORRY ABOUT STAINS! HA HA HA HA HA!

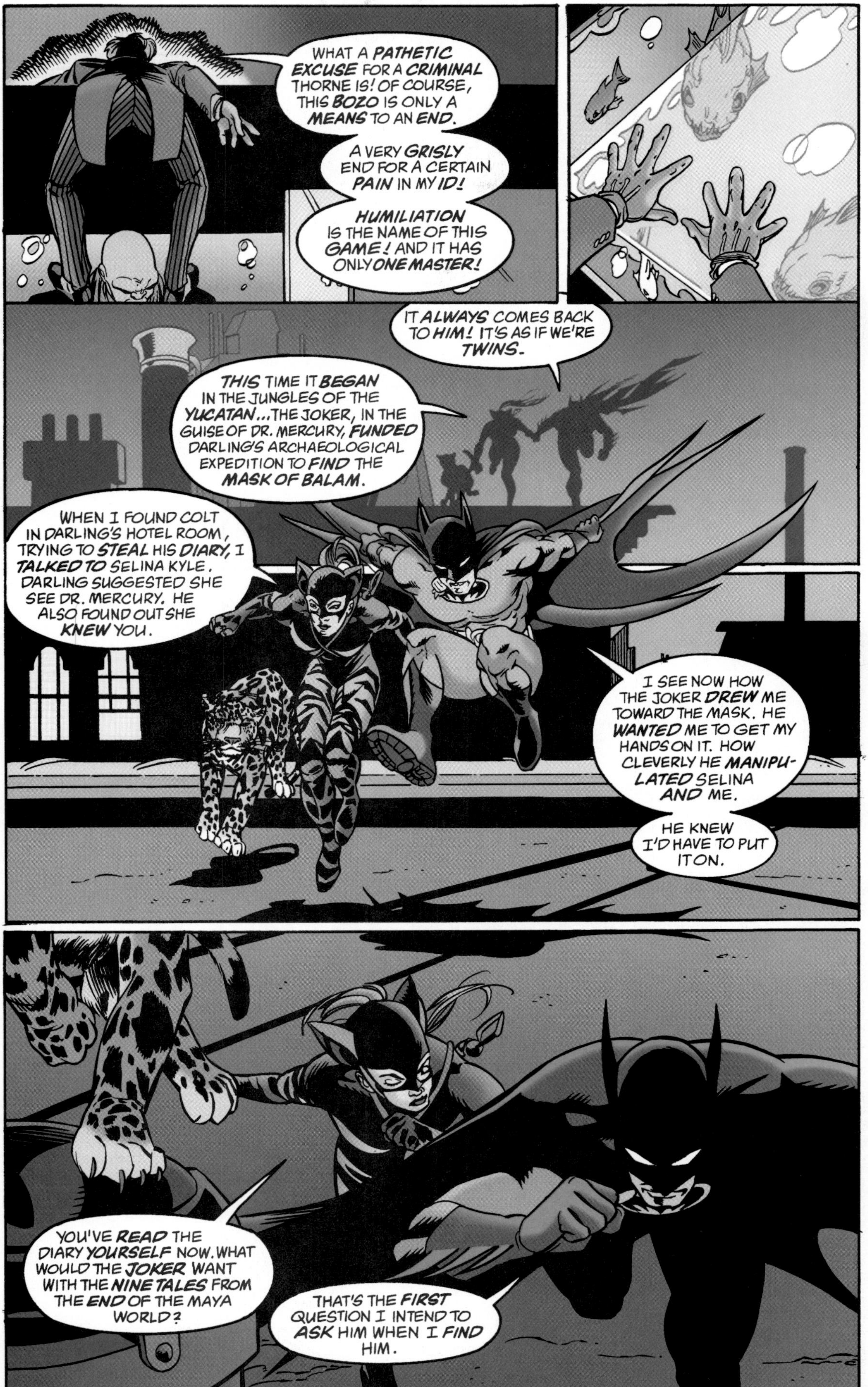
WHAT A PATHETIC EXCUSE FOR A CRIMINAL THORNE IS! OF COURSE, THIS BOZO IS ONLY A MEANS TO AN END.
A VERY GRISLY END FOR A CERTAIN PAIN IN MY ID!
HUMILIATION IS THE NAME OF THIS GAME! AND IT HAS ONLY ONE MASTER!
IT ALWAYS COMES BACK TO HIM! IT'S AS IF WE'RE TWINS.
THIS TIME IT BEGAN IN THE JUNGLES OF THE YUCATAN...THE JOKER, IN THE GUISE OF DR. MERCURY, FUNDED DARLING'S ARCHAEOLOGICAL EXPEDITION TO FIND THE MASK OF BALAM.
WHEN I FOUND COLT IN DARLING'S HOTEL ROOM, TRYING TO STEAL HIS DIARY, I TALKED TO SELINA KYLE. DARLING SUGGESTED SHE SEE DR. MERCURY. HE ALSO FOUND OUT SHE KNEW YOU.
I SEE NOW HOW THE JOKER DREW ME TOWARD THE MASK. HE WANTED ME TO GET MY HANDS ON IT. HOW CLEVERLY HE MANIPULATED SELINA AND ME.
HE KNEW I'D HAVE TO PUT IT ON.
YOU'VE READ THE DIARY YOURSELF NOW. WHAT WOULD THE JOKER WANT WITH THE NINE TALES FROM THE END OF THE MAYA WORLD?
THAT'S THE FIRST QUESTION I INTEND TO ASK HIM WHEN I FIND HIM.

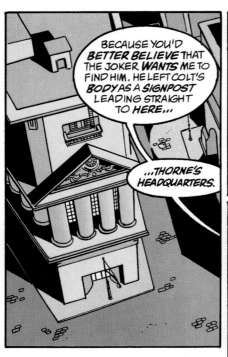

BECAUSE YOU'D *BETTER BELIEVE* THAT THE JOKER *WANTS* ME TO FIND HIM. HE LEFT COLT'S *BODY* AS A *SIGNPOST* LEADING STRAIGHT TO *HERE...*

...THORNE'S HEADQUARTERS.

I'VE BEEN *WAITING* FOR THE *RIGHT MOMENT* TO USE THIS *UNDERGROUND* ACCESS TO THORNE'S OFFICES.

YOU'RE *SURE* THE JOKER WILL *BE* HERE?

AS SURE AS I'VE *EVER* BEEN OF ANYTHING.

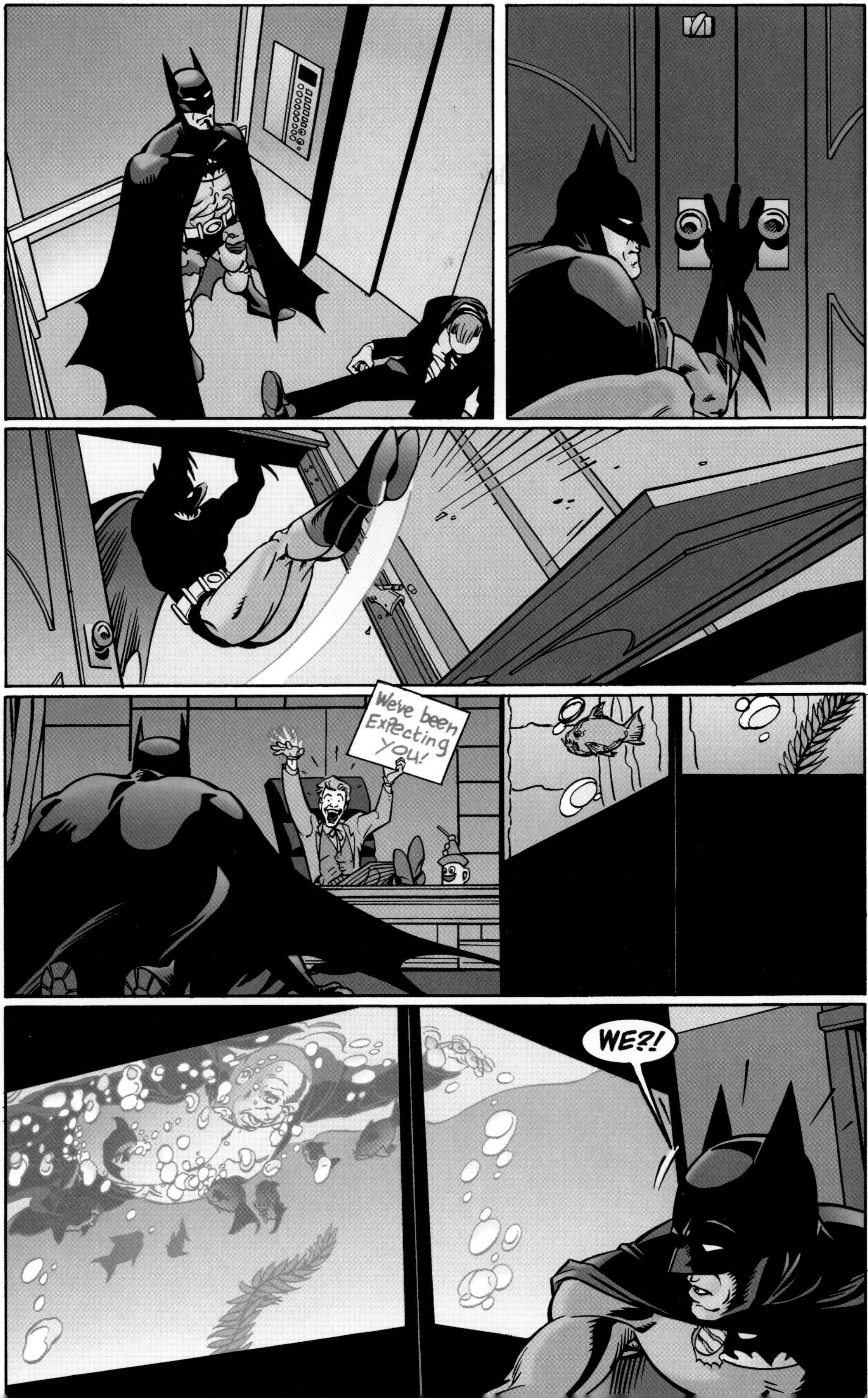
We've been Expecting YOU!
WE?!

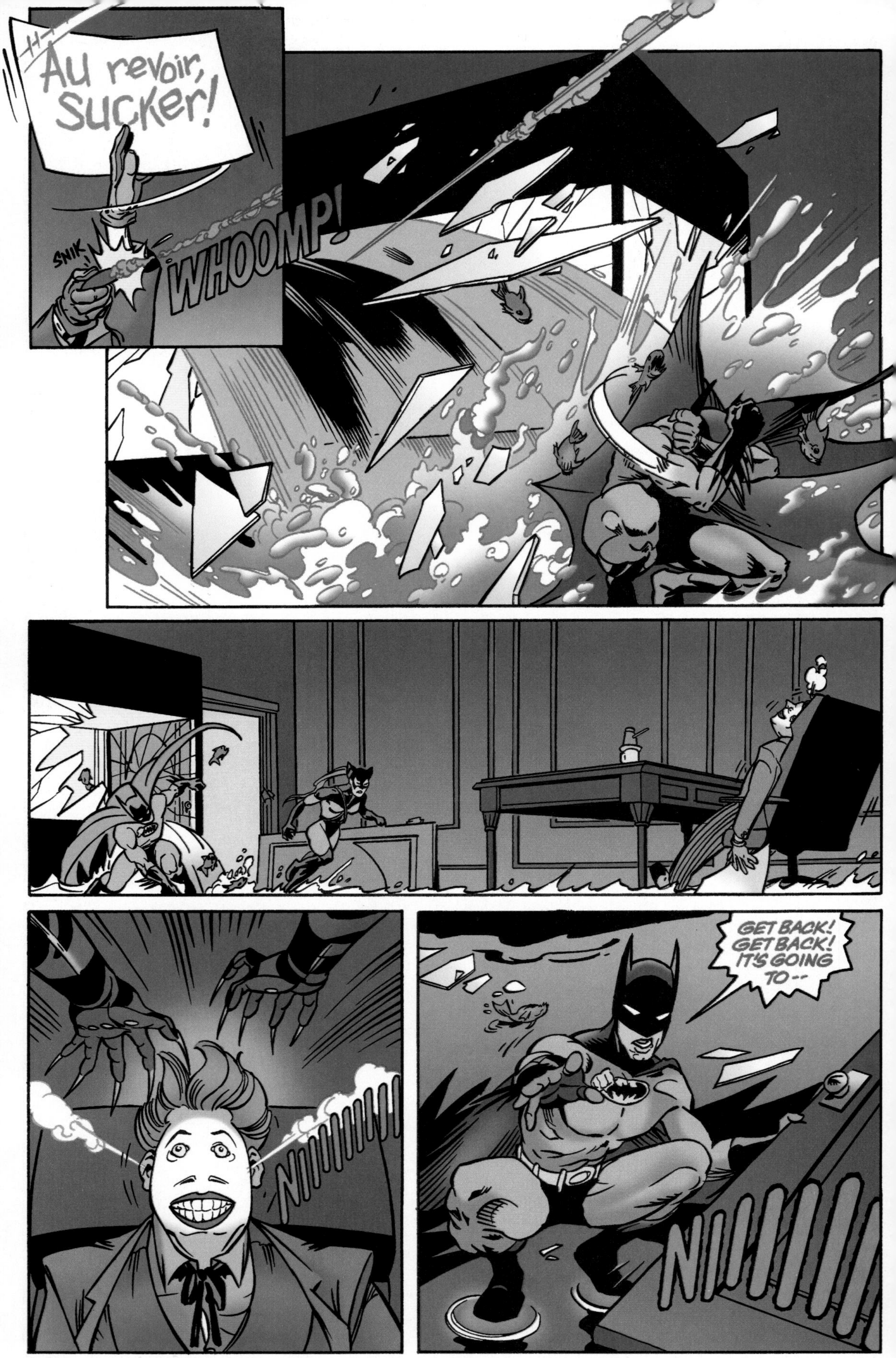

Au revoir, Sucker!
SNIK
WHOOMP!
NIIIIIIIII
GET BACK! GET BACK! IT'S GOING TO --
NIIIIIIII

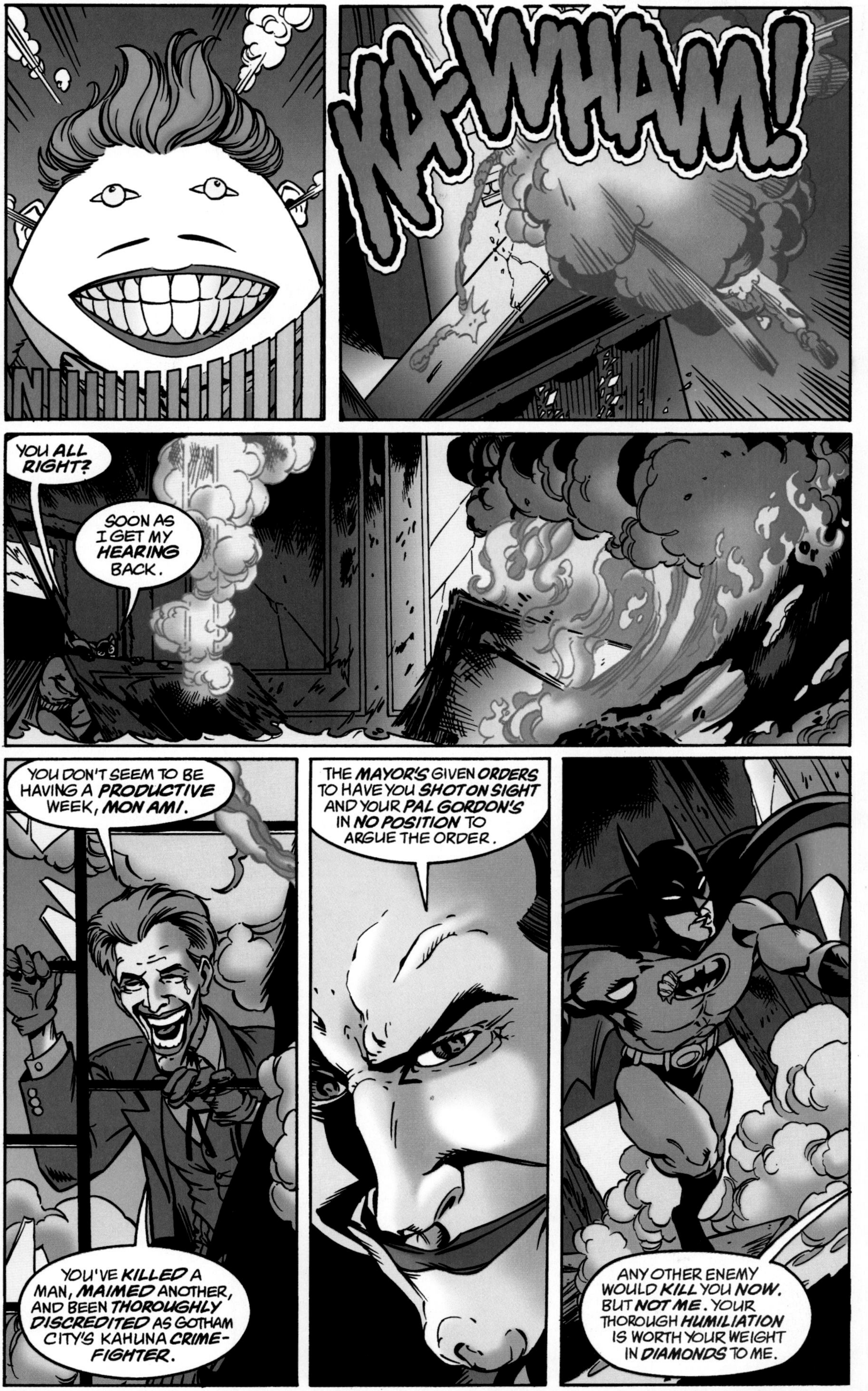
NIIIIIIIIIIII
KA-WHAM!
YOU ALL RIGHT?
SOON AS I GET MY HEARING BACK.
YOU DON'T SEEM TO BE HAVING A PRODUCTIVE WEEK, MON AMI.
YOU'VE KILLED A MAN, MAIMED ANOTHER, AND BEEN THOROUGHLY DISCREDITED AS GOTHAM CITY'S KAHUNA CRIME-FIGHTER.
THE MAYOR'S GIVEN ORDERS TO HAVE YOU SHOT ON SIGHT AND YOUR PAL GORDON'S IN NO POSITION TO ARGUE THE ORDER.
ANY OTHER ENEMY WOULD KILL YOU NOW. BUT NOT ME. YOUR THOROUGH HUMILIATION IS WORTH YOUR WEIGHT IN DIAMONDS TO ME.

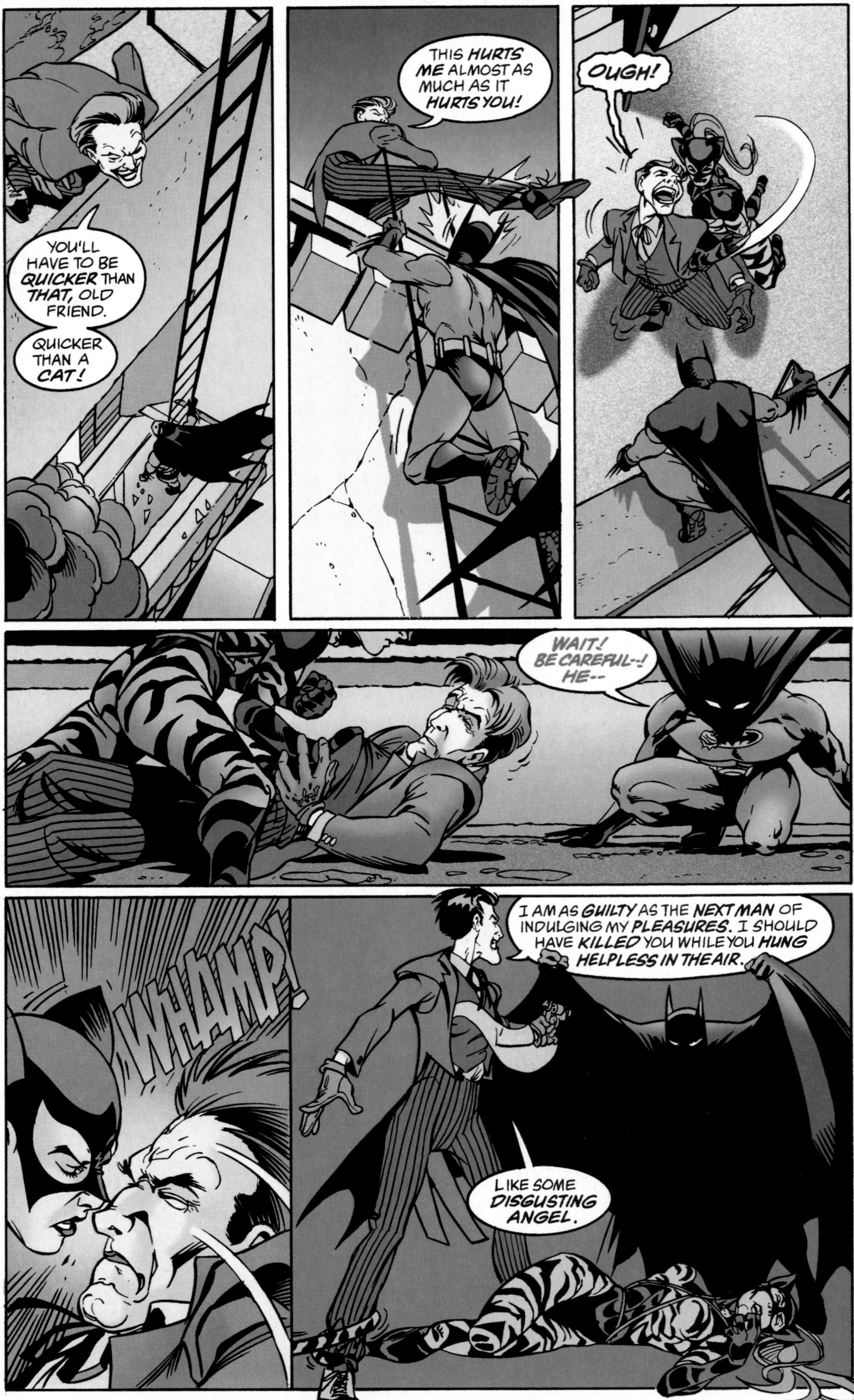
YOU'LL HAVE TO BE QUICKER THAN THAT, OLD FRIEND.
QUICKER THAN A CAT!
THIS HURTS ME ALMOST AS MUCH AS IT HURTS YOU!
OUGH!
WAIT! BE CAREFUL--! HE--
WHAMP!
I AM AS GUILTY AS THE NEXT MAN OF INDULGING MY PLEASURES. I SHOULD HAVE KILLED YOU WHILE YOU HUNG HELPLESS IN THE AIR.
LIKE SOME DISGUSTING ANGEL.

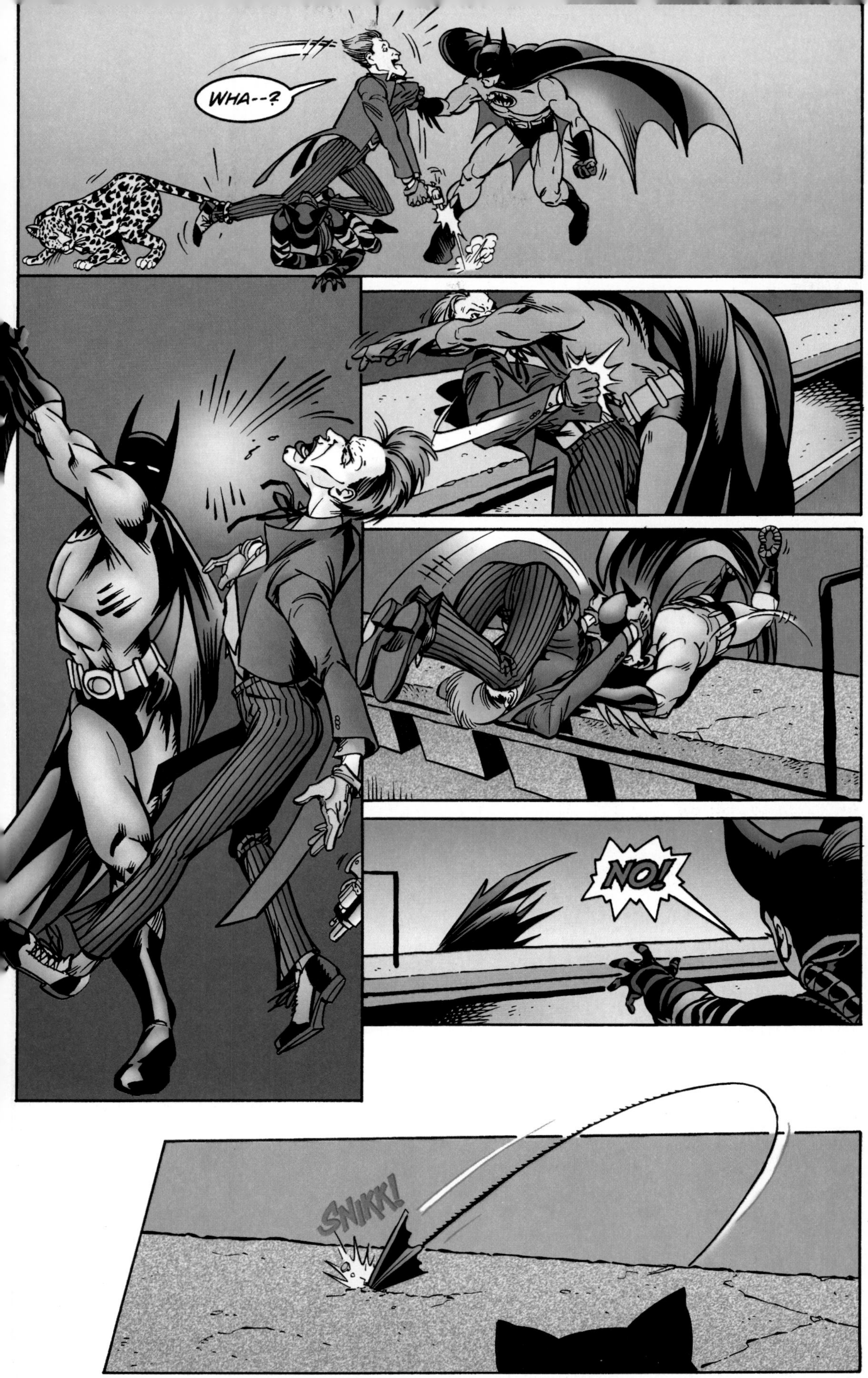
WHA--?
NO!
SNIKK!

OH, GOD! HOLD ON, BATMAN!

EYEEE!

HE'S ALL YOURS, MY DEAR! AH HA HA HA!

AGGHH!

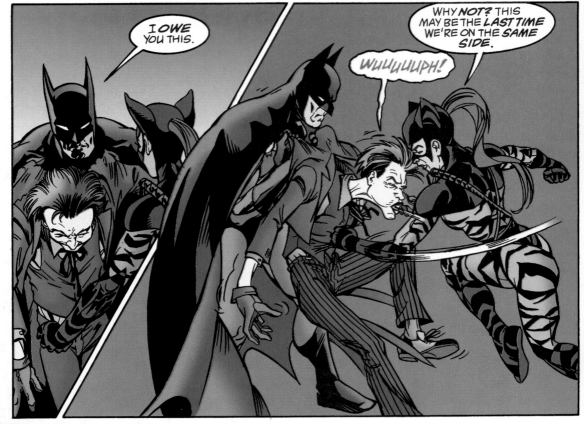

I OWE YOU THIS.

WHY NOT? THIS MAY BE THE LAST TIME WE'RE ON THE SAME SIDE.

WUUUUUPH!

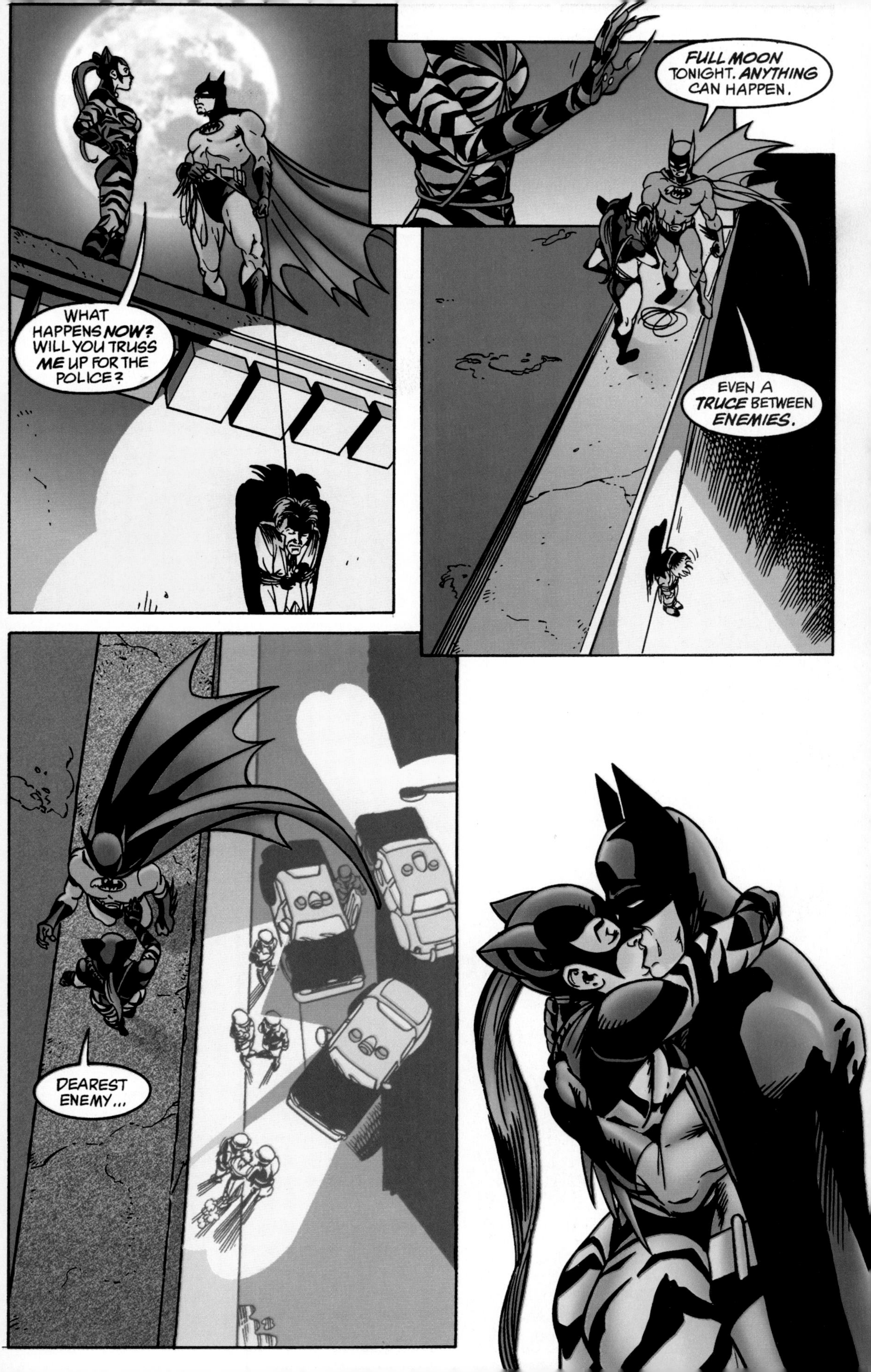
WHAT HAPPENS NOW? WILL YOU TRUSS ME UP FOR THE POLICE?
FULL MOON TONIGHT. ANYTHING CAN HAPPEN.
EVEN A TRUCE BETWEEN ENEMIES.
DEAREST ENEMY...

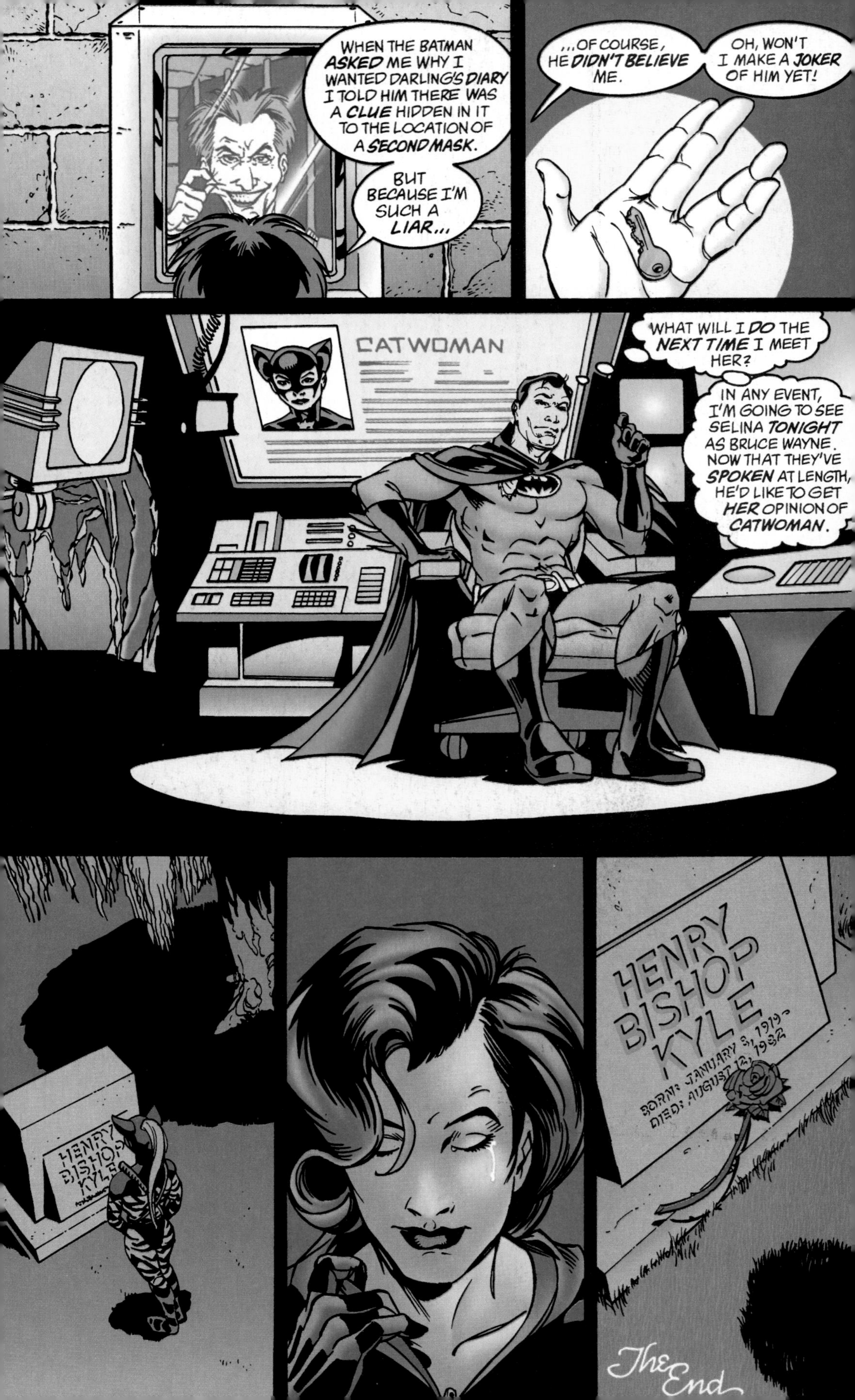
WHEN THE BATMAN ASKED ME WHY I WANTED DARLING'S DIARY I TOLD HIM THERE WAS A CLUE HIDDEN IN IT TO THE LOCATION OF A SECOND MASK.
BUT BECAUSE I'M SUCH A LIAR...
...OF COURSE, HE DIDN'T BELIEVE ME.
OH, WON'T I MAKE A JOKER OF HIM YET!
CATWOMAN
WHAT WILL I DO THE NEXT TIME I MEET HER?
IN ANY EVENT, I'M GOING TO SEE SELINA TONIGHT AS BRUCE WAYNE. NOW THAT THEY'VE SPOKEN AT LENGTH, HE'D LIKE TO GET HER OPINION OF CATWOMAN.
HENRY BISHOP KYLE
HENRY BISHOP KYLE
BORN: JANUARY 3, 1919 -
DIED: AUGUST 12, 1982
The End